This book is to be returned
the

YALE PUBLICATIONS IN THE HISTORY OF ART, 33

George L. Hersey, *editor*

The 13th-Century Church at St-Denis

CAROLINE ASTRID BRUZELIUS

YALE UNIVERSITY PRESS
New Haven and London

Designed by Margaret E.B. Joyner
and set in Bembo type
by The Composing Room of Michigan, Inc.
Printed in the United States of America by
Halliday Lithograph, West Hanover, Massachusetts.

Library of Congress Cataloging in Publication Data

Bruzelius, Caroline Astrid.
The thirteenth-century church at St-Denis.

(Yale publications in the history of art; 33)
Bibliography: p.
Includes index.
1. Eglise abbatiale de Saint-Denis.   2. Architecture,
Gothic—France—Saint-Denis.   3. Saint-Denis (France)—
Churches.   I. Title.   II. Series.
NA5551.S214B7   1985   726'.5'0944362   85-3354
ISBN 0-300-03190-4 (alk. paper)

The paper in this book meets the guidelines for
permanence and durability of the Committee on
Production Guidelines for Book Longevity
of the Council on Library Resources.

10 9 8 7 6 5 4 3 2

For MOTHER *and* BERTIE

Contents

List of Illustrations   ix
Preface   xiii

1. INTRODUCTION   I

2. THE RESTORATION   I4

3. THE NEW CHURCH
   Plan, Elevation, Sculptural Decoration, and
         Proportions   33

4. CONSTRUCTION   82

5. DATING AND CHRONOLOGY
   The Building and the Documents   I23

6. SOURCES AND INFLUENCES   I38

7. CONCLUSION   I6I

Appendix I
The Reconstruction of Troyes and St-Denis   I67
Appendix 2
Pierre de Montreuil   I73
List of Abbreviations and Short Titles   I75
Notes   I77
Selected Bibliography   2II
Index   2I7

ILLUSTRATIONS

Unless otherwise noted, all the illustrations are of St-Denis. Plates are by the author except where otherwise credited.

Plates

1. View of the interior toward the east.   2
2. The south side of the nave from the east.   5
3. Plan of the abbey church published in 1706 by Félibien (Phot. Bibl. nat. Paris).   18
4. View of the north flank of the church and the Valois Chapel prior to 1719, by Jean Marot (Phot. Bibl. nat. Paris).   20
5. View of the Turenne Chapel and the entrance to the Valois mausoleum from the south (Phot. Bibl. nat. Paris).   20
6. Plan of the northeastern bays of the north transept arm after the installation of the Turenne tomb (Phot. Bibl. nat. Paris).   21
7. *The Mass of Saint Giles,* by an unknown Flemish painter, late fifteenth century (Reproduced by courtesy of the Trustees, the National Gallery, London).   22
8. Plan of the abbey church in 1833 by François Debret (Arch. Phot. Paris/S.P.A.D.E.M.).   24
9. View of the abbey church and monastery from the south, *Monasticon Gallicanum.*   26
10. Plan of the abbey church and the monastery, eighteenth century (Phot. Bibl. nat. Paris).   27
11. View of the north flank of the abbey church by François Debret, 1830 (Arch. Phot. Paris/S.P.A.D.E.M.).   28
12. The north transept arm (Crosby).   37
13. View of the chevet from the west (Dominique Vermand).   39
14. The western bays of the north transept arm by Charles Percier, 1790s (Arch. Phot. Paris/S.P.A.D.E.M.).   40
15. View of the crossing and chevet from the west by Charles Percier, 1790s (Arch. Phot. Paris/S.P.A.D.E.M.).   40
16. View of the choir screen by Martellange (Arch. Phot. Paris/S.P.A.D.E.M.).   42
17. The upper stories of the four easternmost bays on the north side of the nave, from the west.   44
18. The south aisle from the west (Crosby).   46
19. The north wall of the chevet from the west (Crosby).   48
20. The north side of the chevet from the west.   50
21. View of the west wall of the north transept arm and north side of the nave from the southeast (Dominique Vermand).   51
22. Exterior, the east wall of the north transept arm.   53
23. Exterior, the east wall of the south transept arm.   53
24. Exterior, the chevet from the east (Arch. Phot. Paris/S.P.A.D.E.M.).   55
25. Exterior, the north transept arm (Arch. Phot. Paris/S.P.A.D.E.M.).   56
26. Exterior, buttress on the north side of the nave.   57
27. Exterior, south transept rose.   57

28. The ambulatories and hemicycle on the north side of the chevet from the west. 60
29. Triforium capitals, chevet, bay 6N–7N. 61
30. Respond and capitals on the north side of the chevet, first compound pier east of the crossing (6N). 63
31. Triforium capitals, north transept arm, north wall. 63
32. Triforium capitals, north side of the nave, bay 9N–10N. 64
33. Triforium capital, south transept arm, west wall. 64
34. Triforium capitals, south transept arm, south wall. 65
35. South side of the nave, arcade capitals of pier 11S. 65
36. Triforium capital, south side of the nave, bay 10S–11S. 66
37. Triforium capital, south side of the nave, bay 12S–13S. 67
38. Triforium capital, south side of the nave, bay 9S–10S. 67
39. South side of the nave, arcade capitals of pier 12S. 68
40. Paris, Notre-Dame, capital of the first intermediate pier from west, north side of ambulatory 69
41. Respond and capitals at 12N. 69
42. North side of the nave, arcade capitals of pier 14N. 70
43. Triforium capitals, north side of the nave, bay 13N–14N. 70
44. Triforium arcade, south side of the nave, bay 14S–15S. 71
45. Triforium capitals, north side of the nave, bay 11N–12N. 71
46. The south transept portal (Arch. Phot. Paris/S.P.A.D.E.M.). 73
47. The south transept portal, left jamb (Crosby). 74
48. The chevet arcade, 2N. 86
49. The chevet arcade, 3N. 86
50. The chevet arcade, 4S. 87
51. The chevet arcade, 5S. 87
52. View of the chevet from the southwest (Crosby). 89
53. Superimposed twelfth- and thirteenth-century plinths at 3N (Crosby). 90
54. Beaumont-sur-Oise (Oise), north side of the nave. 90
55. Ourscamp (Oise), ruins of the chevet, north side. 92
56. Bases and plinths at 6S. 96
57. The western bays on the south side of the chevet, triforium level. 100
58. The triforium in the east wall of the south transept arm. 101
59. Exterior, clerestory on the east wall of the south transept arm. 102
60. St-Germain-en-Laye, palace chapel, rose window. 108
61. St-Germain-en-Laye, clerestory tracery. 109
62. St-Germain-en-Laye, exterior. 109
63. Eastern bays on the south side of the nave. 112
64. St-Germain-des-Prés, fragments from the Virgin Chapel. 114
65. Scamozzi, plan and views of St-Denis (Arch. Phot. Paris/S.P.A.D.E.M.). 126
66. Amiens, eastern bays on the north side of the nave (Ward Archive). 141
67. Reims, the north side of the nave. 142
68. Fécamp, the north side of the nave (Arch. Phot. Paris/S.P.A.D.E.M.). 145
69. Paris, Notre-Dame, the western bays on the south side of the nave (Arch. Phot. Paris/S.P.A.D.E.M.). 146
70. Mello (Oise), exterior (Dominique Vermand). 151
71. Troyes, Cathedral of St-Pierre, the north side of the chevet. 154
72. Troyes, Cathedral of St-Pierre, triforium on the south side of the chevet. 155
73. Paris, Notre-Dame, the south tower from the west. 156
74. St-Germain-des-Prés, fragments of the portal to the Virgin Chapel. 164
75. Troyes, Cathedral of St-Pierre, triforium capitals in the chevet. 169
76. Troyes, Cathedral of St-Pierre, triforium capitals in the chevet. 169

Figures

1. Plan (Crosby).   *following page* xvi
2. Plan with destroyed thirteenth-century masonry (at ground level) indicated by
    hatched lines.   31
3. Plan prior to the inception of construction in 1231 (from Crosby).   35
4. Elevation (from Dehio, *Die Kirchliche Baukunst des Abendlandes*).   43
5. Schematic plan with designation of piers.   62
6. Base profiles, chevet hemicycle.   76
7. Base profiles, chevet.   76
8. Base profiles, chevet.   76
9. Base profiles, chevet triforium.   76
10. Base profiles, chevet triforium.   76
11. Base profiles, triforium of north transept arm and of chevet.   76
12. Base profiles, triforium of the nave.   76
13. Bases from the chapel at St-Germain-en-Laye, unrestored, from window
    responds and dado arcading.   76
14. Base profiles, triforium of south transept arm and of chevet.   78
15. Base profiles, triforium of the nave.   78
16. Base profiles, triforium of the nave.   78
17. Base profiles, triforium of the nave.   78
18. Base profiles, triforium of the nave.   78
19. Base profiles, tomb of Dagobert.   78
20. Diagonal rib in the thirteenth-century aisle vaults of the chevet.   78
21. Arcade molding in the straight bays of the chevet.   79
22. Torus molding of the hemicycle arcading in the chevet.   79
23. Plan of the church during the first stages of reconstruction, with the Carolingian
    nave intact (Warren Wilson).   83
24. The twelfth-century abaci of the hemicycle.   85
25. The twelfth-century abaci in the intermediate ambulatory columns and chapels of
    the chevet.   85
26. First phase of construction.   94
27. Abaci profiles of the first compound piers of the chevet and the northeastern
    crossing pier.   96
28. Second phase of construction.   105
29. Third phase of construction.   111
30. Fourth phase of construction.   111
31. The interruption of construction at the juncture of the south transept arm with
    the upper stories of the south side of the nave (Warren Wilson).   116
32. Fifth phase of construction.   117
33. Sixth phase of construction.   119
34. Base profiles, chevet triforium of Troyes Cathedral.   168

Preface

The abbey of St-Denis is well known to students of medieval architecture. Their attention has concentrated on the work of Abbot Suger in the twelfth century, however, and the splendid reconstruction of the church a century later has often been neglected or forgotten.

It was Sumner McKnight Crosby's suggestion that I undertake this project. In a lifelong investigation, Professor Crosby reconstructed the history of the Gallo-Roman cemetery, the Merovingian and Carolingian churches, and Suger's remarkable facade, western bays, and chevet. Crosby's careful consideration of the complex and fragmentary evidence has greatly expanded our knowledge not only of St-Denis itself, but also of the history of Carolingian and Early Gothic architecture. It was a pleasure to continue to work with Sumner Crosby after I ceased to be his student, and a sorrow that he did not live to see this study completed.

The organization of this book has been dictated by the nature of the subject itself. Since the thirteenth-century church reflects the disposition of the earlier structures at the site, these are briefly introduced in the first chapter, along with a general historical background for the rebuilding of the church beginning in 1231. Yet because much of what exists at St-Denis today is the result of nineteenth-century restoration, it is necessary to distinguish what is new from what is old. The second chapter is thus devoted to the nineteenth-century restorations.

I consider the architecture itself to be the primary "document." The design of the new church as well as the archaeological evidence of campaigns and sequence of construction as indicated by the stones themselves will therefore be considered in the third and fourth chapters, before the written sources and problems of precise dating. A discussion of the documents and the dates of the building campaigns forms the fifth chapter. This organization reflects a conviction that the interpretation of texts—which for medieval construction are frequently ambiguous and vague—hinges on the archaeological evidence. The artistic context out of which the new design emerged, the influence of that design on the architecture of its time, and the identity of the architect(s) are considered in the sixth chapter, the conclusion, and the appendices.

My work on St-Denis, inspired by Crosby, was greatly assisted by two of his friends and contemporaries, the late Louis Grodecki and Jean Bony. Grodecki's questions led to many of the thoughts and conclusions expressed here, and Jean Bony's insights and suggestions have been of immeasurable assistance.

Many colleagues have also helped. Peter Fergusson, Stephen Murray, Anne Prache, William Clark, and Harry Titus generously shared their ideas with me. Rona Goffen and John Coolidge read parts of the manuscript and made many helpful suggestions. Elizabeth A. R. Brown and Constance Berman assisted me with the historical background. I would also like to thank Alain Erlande-Brandenbourg and Fabienne Joubert at the Cluny Museum in Paris, Françoise Bercé and her colleagues at the library and archives of the Monuments Historiques, and Annie Lotte at the archives of the Musée des Monuments Français.

Other friends have made contributions as well. I would especially like to thank Louise Crane and Victoria Kent for their friendship and interest while this book was in progress. Claire Moòre Dickerson and Holly Lennihan took certain perilous measurements. Dominique Vermand has generously permitted the use of some of his photographs. I would also like to thank Mary Cash and Denise Franks, who typed the manuscript. At St-Denis itself, Madame Laurence and Bernard Mannapin welcomed me and treated me with utmost kindness.

I was fortunate to be able to devote two virtually uninterrupted years to this study, thanks to a grant from the National Endowment for the Humanities in 1979–80 for research in Paris and a grant from the Mellon Foundation in 1980–81 for research at Harvard University. I would also like to thank the Research Council of Duke University, which supported the last stages of my work in Paris, and the Samuel H. Kress Foundation for supporting the costs of drawings and plans, several of which were splendidly executed by Warren Wilson. The Department of Art and Art History at Duke University, where I now teach, has consistently been most encouraging and benevolent.

In no respect am I more fortunate than in the help of my family. My sister Ellen held the other end of the tape measure many times and made life in Paris much more agreeable through her presence. My mother and my late stepfather, Eugene Albertus Pharr, read and edited the manuscript; it is to them that this book is dedicated.

Finally, I should like to thank Robert Wallace, who helped me with the interpretation of a Latin passage at the beginning of this project and married me at the end of it. His patience and his careful reading of the text were of the greatest assistance.

The Thirteenth-Century Church at St-Denis

1 ❖

Introduction

Among the great churches and abbeys of France, St-Denis was unique.[1] Dedicated to the cult of the relics of Saint Denis, first bishop of Paris and the "Apostle of the Gauls,"[2] it was also the burial place of the kings of France and one of the oldest monastic communities in that country. No other church or abbey had a comparable constellation of attributes and continuity of tradition. The cult of Saint Denis dates to the third century; the monastic community was probably formed sometime in the fifth; and the burial of kings began in the seventh century. As early as the sixth or seventh century, copies of royal documents were kept at St-Denis, copies that later served as the basis for a series of chronicles of the history of France. Beginning with the reign of Philip I (1060–1108), the king of France owed fealty to the abbey as its vassal for the county of the Vexin and took from the abbey the great battle flag, the Oriflamme, when he rode to war. The name of St-Denis was shouted in the ancient war cry "Monjoie St-Denis": victory, survival, and the invocation of the saint became one. Such was the fame of this sanctuary just north of Paris.[3]

The succession of churches at St-Denis embodies, in stone, the history of that abbey. This book is about the last of these churches, begun by Abbot Eudes Clément du Mez in 1231 in the early years of the reign of Louis IX, almost one thousand years after the martyrdom of Saint Denis (plate 1). The design of the thirteenth-century church was conceived to unite and to provide a magnificent setting for the accumulation of traditions. Just as Abbot Suger in the twelfth century had preserved the earlier Carolingian crypt and its ninth-century extension,[4] so his own western bays and facade, his crypt, and the lower story of his chevet were in turn retained in the thirteenth-century rebuilding. At St-Denis, the churches themselves were venerated and the old stones treated as relics.[5]

Given this veneration of the old, it may seem paradoxical that St-Denis is best known today as the site of revolutionary achievements in architecture. Yet the special genius of Abbot Suger in using the texts of Dionysius the Pseudo-Areopagite[6] as an inspiration for his new program transformed the architecture

Plate 1. View of the interior toward the east.

of his time and created the style now known as Gothic. This receptivity to new ideas—this genius for building—was equally present in the design for the new church begun by Abbot Eudes Clément in 1231.

The history of the succession of churches at the site is fairly well documented.[7] Saint Denis was martyred and buried in the village of Catulliacum, which later was called by his name.[8] Although the tomb itself was probably identified by some sort of marker or monument, the first church was not erected until the late fifth or early sixth century. This fact is known from the life of Saint Geneviève, one of whose worthy deeds was persuading her fellow citizens to build a church over the grave of the martyr.[9] There is evidence that by that time a community of monks had been established, perhaps including lay members.[10] In the seventh century, the first church was extended, remodeled, and lavishly decorated by King Dagobert (c. 612–c. 639). Subsequently, the extent of Dagobert's patronage was gradually expanded into a legend that he had built a completely new church; thus Dagobert came to be considered the "founder" of the abbey.[11] By the eleventh century, a second legend, in which Christ miraculously consecrated "Dagobert's" church, established a tradition that weighed heavily on abbots Suger and Eudes in their reconstructions of the church in the twelfth and thirteenth centuries.[12]

The second church was built by Abbot Fulrad and consecrated in 775.[13] Portions of its apse are still visible in the crypt, and the extensive excavations undertaken by Crosby have permitted the reconstruction of the entire plan. This church is now known to be one of the major monuments of the Carolingian *renovatio*.[14] The disposition of the nave and transepts as well as the presence of an annular crypt indicates that the Carolingian basilica was built according to "Roman custom."[15] In the ninth century, Abbot Hilduin extended the church by adding a larger crypt to the east, designed to provide more space for the growing numbers of relics and also to relieve the congestion of the many pilgrims who came to venerate the relics in the tight, narrow spaces of the eighth-century crypt.[16]

During these early centuries, the cult of Saint Denis and the importance of the abbey were actively promoted by its monks.[17] Their efforts reached a peak about 835, when Abbot Hilduin wrote the *Historia sancti Dionysii*, which established the official biography of the saint.[18] At the request of Louis the Pious, who had recently acquired a manuscript of the writings of Dionysius the Areopagite, Hilduin composed a life of the saint in which three separate individuals were conflated into a composite personality.[19] The French saint was identified both with Dionysius the Areopagite, mentioned by Luke as an Athenian converted by Paul (Acts 17:34), and with the late fifth- or early sixth-century mystic now known as Dionysius the Pseudo-Areopagite.[20] The mystical treatises of the Pseudo-Areopagite were attributed to Saint Denis of Paris and thus associated with the abbey of St-Denis.[21]

The legend of the miraculous consecration by Christ added to the re-
nown of the abbey and endowed the church with extraordinary sanctity. Hence,
when Abbot Suger decided to rebuild it in the 1130s, the sacredness of the old
structure was a major consideration. In his writings Suger refers to his own
veneration for the old stones and alludes to the miraculous consecration of the
abbey church.[22] In light of this, his strategy in the reconstruction was remarkably shrewd. Leaving the old Carolingian nave largely intact, Suger extended it
to the west by several bays to build a magnificent new facade that, with its twin
towers, rose window, sculptured portals, and crenellations, made reference to
many of the historical associations of the abbey.[23] On the east end Suger enclosed the foundations of the earlier crypts—parts of these preserved structures
can still be seen—in a new chevet. He thereby gave a demonstration of the
dazzling new Gothic style and created a monumental shrine for the relics prior to
commencing the reconstruction of the sacred old Carolingian nave.[24] As Suger
indicates in his writings, certain aspects of the design of the new church reflected
the mystical theories of light, radiance, and harmony of the Pseudo-Dionysius.
The walls of the chevet thus became a frame for a series of windows that
illuminated the radiating chapels and ambulatories with spiritual allegories in
stained glass.[25] Hence the philosophy of the saint was expressed in the building
believed to contain his tomb.

Undoubtedly these ideas also informed the conception of the thirteenth-
century church, begun by Abbot Eudes Clément in 1231 and consecrated by his
successor, Mathieu de Vendôme, in 1281.[26] In the new church, the wall is
reduced to a thin membrane of masonry penetrated everywhere by windows,
perhaps the first statement of the style we have come to call Rayonnant Gothic
(plate 1). By whatever label, the thirteenth-century church represents a vision of
Gothic space and structure that departs from that of the great Ile-de-France
cathedrals begun in the preceding decades. At St-Denis a number of new ideas
are introduced and old ideas are given new life: the ubiquitous High Gothic
cantonnated pier, for example, is abandoned, and the Romanesque compound
pier is revived, with the grouping of shafts around a diamond-shaped core
reflecting every aspect of the ribs and moldings in the aisles, arcade, and main
vaults above. The uninterrupted shafts rise to the springing of every arch to
accent the vertical and visually to transfer the weight of the wall and vaults to the
base of the pier (plate 2). Here for the first time in a major Gothic monument the
back wall of the triforium passage is glazed, so that light now penetrates the wall
on three levels of the elevation: arcade, triforium, and clerestory. The church has
become, as Dom Germain Millet wrote in 1644, a "lantern of glass,"[27] for
everywhere the architectural structure is set off by the luminous membrane of
the wall (plates 1 and 2).

No visitor to St-Denis can remain indifferent to its spaciousness. The
slender, widely spaced nave piers, the double aisles of the transepts, and the low
pitch of the main vaults all open up the central space and swell it outward into the
lateral volumes of the aisles (fig. 1). How different this is from the tight, concen-

Plate 2. The south side of the nave from the east.

trated verticality of Amiens, begun only a decade before, where one's attention is funneled upward to the startling height of the vaults. At St-Denis, the lateral, or horizontal, view, the perspectives from the nave across the aisles and diagonally into the transept arms are as important as the inevitable verticality of a Gothic church. The new church is in harmony with the earlier structure built by Abbot Suger but also creates a magnificent setting for the tombs of the kings and the monumental shrine of one of the great saints of France. The design is nowhere more striking than in the view of the apse from the nave, where the walls of the chevet spread outward as though to embrace the nave and the visitor within it (plate 1). The simplified, elongated lancets of the clerestory of the chevet, combined with its narrower proportions, make this the intense and concentrated culmination of the broad and balanced design found elsewhere in the church.

Prior to the detailed analysis of the new basilica, several preliminary issues must be addressed. To what extent were the kings of France, and particularly Louis IX in the thirteenth century, involved in the fate, fortune, and finances of the abbey? Why was the work of Abbot Suger on the rebuilding of the church suspended for almost a century, and what was the impetus for the construction of the new church beginning in 1231? These questions serve as the foundation for the discussion of the structure and construction of the new building in the chapters that follow.

ST-DENIS AND ITS ABBOTS, 1151–1229

At St-Denis construction of the church thrived under certain abbots and faltered under others.[28] Not surprisingly, perhaps, the abbots most distinguished for their parts in history were often those responsible for the new buildings. If the building projects were undertaken only after consultation with the rest of the monastic community, and sometimes with the king, it was nonetheless the abbot who marshaled the resources, orchestrated the program, and commanded the architect. Furthermore, the abbots often specified many features of the design (at least one suspects this of Suger). Chief among their intentions must have been the desire to enhance the prestige of the abbey, to provide a fitting shrine for the relics and liturgical space for the mass, and, increasingly, to erect a suitable mausoleum for the kings of France.

In their building programs the abbots were not free to do entirely as they wished, however. As noted above, the traditions and legends connected with the site meant that the stones themselves were imbued with sanctity. Furthermore, as Suger remarked in his life of Louis VI, both law and custom forbade the moving of a king's body after burial. The writings of Abbot Suger and the more fragmentary documentation for the thirteenth-century church suggest that the miraculous consecration in particular presented an impediment to remodeling, and Suger of course planned his reconstruction around the old church, even though he intended in the end to replace it.

The years between the death of Suger in 1151 and the accession of Eudes Clément in 1228 form something of a lacuna in the internal history of the abbey. At the death of Suger, the fortunes of St-Denis, so ably and energetically directed during his twenty-nine-year abbacy, went into a decline. One reason for this may have been that in the year before his death, the abbot had tried to initiate a new crusade, an enterprise which met with little enthusiasm on the part of his contemporaries. Large sums from the coffers and regular income of St-Denis were sent to Jerusalem, thus almost certainly diverting money intended at least in part for the fabric of his new church. Indeed, there are indications that Suger himself anticipated the possibility of not being able to complete the reconstruction. Thus, for example, he wrote in *De Administratione*:

> if in our own time or under our successors, work on the nave of the church could only be done intermittently, whenever the towers would afford the opportunity, the nave would not be completed according to plan without much delay, or, in case of any unlucky development, never. For no difficulty would embarrass those [then] in power but that the link between the old and the new work should suffer long postponement. However, since it has already been started with the extension of the side-aisles, it will be completed either through us or through those whom the Lord shall elect, He, Himself, helping.[29]

It would seem, however, that the Lord did not elect any of Suger's immediate successors to complete the church.[30] The next abbot was Eudes de Deuil, a monk whose close ties to Suger and to the royal family qualified him well for the prominent position of abbot of St-Denis.[31] Nonetheless, Eudes' early years as Suger's successor were full of dissension and controversy. The new abbot was accused of bad management of the abbey's affairs and of ingratitude to his predecessor by causing difficulties for Suger's family and friends. These charges extended even to holding the abbot responsible for the murder of one of Suger's nephews, though the exact circumstances of the crime and the nature of the charge have never been clear. In spite of all this, Eudes remained in office until 1162. The later years of his tenure passed somewhat more peacefully, although there continued to be bad feeling among the different factions of the monastic community. Even so, Eudes was able to acquire a considerable amount of property for the monastery, he was an effective mediator with the contentious local nobility, and he was generous in gifts of property to the nearby Cistercian foundations of Ourscamp and Châalis.[32]

Although construction on the church was interrupted by Suger's death, there are certain indications that some work was accomplished during the abbacy of Abbot Eudes or his successor. The most conspicuous evidence for this is the north transept arm portal, known as the Valois Portal, usually dated in the 1160s or early 1170s.[33] However, whether it was actually installed in the twelfth century or simply carved and left in the workshop until its insertion in the thirteenth-century transept remains unclear.

Eudes de Deuil was succeeded by Eudes de Taverny, whose four years in office (until about 1169) have been described by Félibien as "rien de fort remarquable."[34] Aside from the consolidation of various properties, perhaps the most noteworthy event during these years was the acquisition from Cologne of relics of Saint Ursula and some of her companions. The next abbacy, under Yves II, also lasted four years. He was replaced in 1173 by Guillaume, a doctor and man of learning. Under Guillaume new powers were conferred on the chapter, notably the institution of a new and separate seal for the abbot when he functioned in a private capacity, so that the abbot's personal business and that of the monastery became distinct. The old seal was now used for all official acts, which were read to and approved by the chapter. Abbots were henceforth restricted in the amount of money that they could borrow without the permission of the chapter; they were allowed to grant positions only for the duration of an abbacy or for as long as the abbot and the chapter decided was proper, rather than for life; and they were not permitted to alienate, sell, or enfeoff any property belonging to the abbey. These measures were clearly designed not only to counteract abuses that had occurred during previous abbacies—abuses that resulted in the dispersal and loss of some of the monastery's important properties and sources of income—but also to curtail the authority and independence of the abbot.

But if these reforms limited the authority of the abbot, in other respects his prestige was greatly increased. During Guillaume's abbacy, the abbot of St-Denis was granted the privilege of wearing the mitre, the ring, and the sandals of a bishop. This placed the abbot in a position equal to that of bishops, a situation that seems to have strained ecclesiastical protocol when the latter were included in certain royal funerary processions at the abbey.

Further reforms in the early 1180s consisted in the confirmation of the properties, privileges, and exemptions of the abbey, as well as in the reaffirmation of the Benedictine rule regarding the election of abbots and other internal matters, confirmed by a papal bull of Lucian III in 1183.

Abbot Guillaume's zeal in attending to the temporal affairs of the monastery is attested in the documents; nonetheless, the monk Rigord recorded that strict observance of the monastic rule suffered during his administration, and the abbot was obliged to resign by Philip Augustus in 1186. Hughes Foucault, a well-known preacher, was elected in his place.

The decades after 1186 were characterized by a series of short abbacies. The most important event, and perhaps the most serious threat to the prestige of the abbey, was the claim of the canons of Notre-Dame in Paris on the cranium of Saint Denis.[35] The abbey of St-Denis promptly responded by opening the tomb of the saint and exposing his relics. To discourage the claims of Notre-Dame, the skull of Saint Denis was not returned to the marble tomb but remained on the altar for a full year, after which it was placed in its own separate reliquary.[36] In 1216 Pope Innocent III addressed a letter to the abbey in which he described the several legends associated with Saint Denis but avoided taking a position on the various claims made to the possession of his remains. In order to resolve any further doubts, however, he sent to the abbey the recently discovered relics of Saint Dionysius the Areopagite, brought from Greece. St-Denis thus became the repository of the relics of both Saint Denis of Paris and Saint Dionysius, though no real effort seems to have been made to distinguish the separate identities of the two. The pope also declared forty days of indulgence for those who visited the new relics, which were placed in the same tomb in the chevet that contained the relics of Saint Denis of Paris and his two companions.

ST-DENIS AND THE KINGS OF FRANCE

The thirteenth-century rebuilding of the abbey church was undertaken during the early years of the reign of Louis IX. The young king seems to have had a special veneration for Saint Denis, as will be seen, but in this he was also following an ancient royal tradition. Since Clothair in the early seventh century, Saint Denis had been considered the "particular patron" and "singular protector" of the realm.[37] The history of the abbey and its succession of churches was thus closely allied to the history of the kings of France. Dagobert had particular affection for the abbey and its patron saint, a compliment returned by the monks of St-Denis, who considered the king their principal patron and even the founder of the monastery. With the advent of the Carolingian dynasty St-Denis seems to have been especially favored, and the abbots consistently assumed the position of advisor and counselor to the king.[38] In 754, Pepin the Short was crowned king of France in the abbey church by Pope Stephen II, an event orchestrated by Abbot Fulrad. The abbot, who had been instrumental in paving the way for this momentous installation of a new ruling dynasty, served Pepin as a trusted advisor and was also responsible for the construction of a new church at St-Denis. When Fulrad's church was consecrated in 775, Charlemagne attended the ceremonies.

In the ninth century, Abbot Hilduin, who had erected an extension to the crypt, became involved in an insurrection led by Prince Lothair against his father, Louis the Pious. Although temporarily exiled, Hilduin was soon restored to favor, and he returned to St-Denis to concentrate on internal matters; it was at this point, at the request of Louis the Pious, that he translated the works of Dionysius the Areopagite and composed the *Historia sancti Dionysii.*

In the second half of the ninth century, the ties between the abbey and the crown were reinforced when Charles the Bald assumed the title of lay abbot of St-Denis. The title was held by most of his successors and not relinquished until 968, when Hugh Capet gave it up as part of his reform of the monastery.[39]

At the end of the eleventh century, the Norman county of the Vexin, given to St-Denis at an early date, became part of the royal domain. Thus the king became count of Vexin—and thereby the vassal of the monastery.[40] This, in effect, established the primacy of St-Denis over the throne of France. The king's fealty was confirmed in a royal act of homage, the yearly presentation of a gift of four coins at the altar of the abbey church, as well as in the ceremonies connected with the taking of the Oriflamme prior to going to war.[41]

But ties between the crown and the abbey were perhaps strongest under Abbot Suger, who served as the counselor and friend to two kings, Louis VI and Louis VII.[42] Suger shrewdly involved Louis VII in the rebuilding of the church, inviting the king to attend the ceremonies of the laying of the first stone and to participate in raising of revenues for the completion of the work.[43] Suger in every way emphasized the importance of St-Denis as the "protector of the realm," a role stated explicitly in his writings, given tangible form in the design for his new west facade, and confirmed by his regency while Louis VII was on crusade.

The role of the abbey of St-Denis as defender of the kingdom was interpreted literally in the use of the monastery's treasury to store the regalia. This tradition, which seems to date back to Merovingian times, was not without significant interruptions, but after 1260, when Louis IX returned the royal insignia to the abbey, the regalia remained at St-Denis.[44]

The strongest link between the royalty and the monastery, however, was the use of St-Denis as the traditional burial place of kings.[45] The burial of royalty, which probably goes back to the sixth century, received further impetus with the burial of Dagobert in 639.[46] His tomb was placed underneath an arcosoleum to the right of the main altar, a location preserved in the thirteenth-century reconstruction of the church and tomb. Dagobert's son Clovis II was also interred at St-Denis, although his grandson Childeric renewed still older tradition and was buried instead at the abbey of St-Vincent in Paris.

The Carolingian kings sporadically continued the tradition of royal burial at St-Denis. Charles Martel was interred there in 741, and Pepin the Short at his own request was buried face downward outside the west doors of the church. Although Charlemagne at one time expressed his intention to be buried at St-Denis, his remains were finally interred in his palace chapel at Aachen.[47] The later Carolingian kings varied in their choice of burial place.

The tradition of burial at St-Denis was continued with the Capetian kings of France. That the saint seems to have played an increasingly important role in the protection of the person of the king in death as well as in life was later made explicit by Suger in his biography of Louis VI: "In that place he awaits the resurrection of the dead at the last day. At St-Denis he is closer in spirit to the army of the saints because his body is buried close to the holy martyrs. . . . And so on the last day he will benefit from their advocacy."[48]

Although two Capetian kings of the twelfth century chose to be buried elsewhere,[49] Louis IX reaffirmed the role of St-Denis as the royal necropolis in the thirteenth century. Thenceforward the abbey was considered the official necropolis of kings.

The kings of France were also great patrons of the abbey. We have already seen how Dagobert expanded and decorated the earliest church, and many of his successors were also generous. Charles the Bald lavishly decorated the main altar with a golden antependium, candlesticks, and silver lamps and donated relics of Saint Stephen, Saint Vincent, and Saint James to the monastery.[50] In the obituaries of the abbey, Philip Augustus is considered equal to Charles the Bald and second only to Dagobert as a patron of St-Denis:[51] he gave the abbey a piece of the True Cross, some hair from the head of Christ, one of the thorns from the Crown of Thorns, and a rib and tooth of Saint Philip.[52] At his death in 1223, Philip Augustus bequeathed to the abbey his jewels and a golden crown, all to be sold in order to buy land for the maintenance of twenty additional monks. These jewels were bought back by Louis VIII for 12,000 *livres parisis*.[53] Louis IX followed the example of his progenitors and was a model of patronage and devotion to the abbey of St-Denis.

EUDES CLÉMENT AND LOUIS IX: THE BACKGROUND FOR THE NEW CHURCH

As "protector of the realm" and patron of kings, St-Denis stood in a special relationship to the monarchy. That tie was rarely so strong as during the early years of the reign of Louis IX (1226–70), which coincided with the abbacy of Eudes Clément (1228–45). The contacts between these two men bear particular examination here, as it is they who establish the context for the rebuilding of the church.

Abbot Eudes came from one of the great families of France.[54] His grandfather, Robert Clément du Mez, had been a minister of state and regent under Philip Augustus; his father had fought in the battle of Bouvines with the same king; and his brother Jean was a marshal of France after 1225. A man of great energy, Eudes began his administration by reforming the collegiate church of St-Paul, a dependency of the abbey, and by consolidating the properties of St-Denis.[55] He began planning to reconstruct the old basilica within the first year or two of his abbacy. The historian Guillaume de Nangis has stated that the rebuilding proceeded only after the abbot consulted with Louis IX and his mother, Blanche de Castille, as the legendary consecration had prevented its reconstruction at an earlier date.[56] In a document of 1241, Abbot Eudes (like Suger before him) mentioned that the old church had been on the verge of ruin and that its reconstruction was unavoidable.[57] According to the *Chronicon Sancti Dionysii ad cyclos paschales,* work was begun in the chevet in 1231; plans for the rebuilding must therefore have been started at least a year before, probably at the very beginning of Eudes' abbacy.[58]

By the time of Eudes' election, Louis IX had been king for three years. As he was a minor, the regency was held by his mother, Blanche de Castille, who, in spite of the double disadvantage of being both a woman and a foreigner, guided her son and the kingdom through repeated threats to the crown until the majority of Louis.[59] Blanche succeeded in defending her son's right to the throne in a series of military campaigns against rebellious barons, including the king's uncle, Philip Hurepel. These struggles lasted from 1227 to 1231, the first four years of Louis's reign.

The decision to rebuild the basilica was made midway through this difficult period. Given the attested involvement of the young king and his mother in the plans for the reconstruction, the personal devotion Louis seems to have had for Saint Denis, and the king's friendship with Abbot Eudes, it is likely that the rebuilding of St-Denis formed part of a larger scheme to reinforce the authority and security of the throne.[60] In the new church the role of the abbey as the burial place of kings was made explicit as never before. The series of newly carved tombs of the king's ancestors, installed in the transept in the 1260s, was an affirmation of the tradition of royal burial and may have been envisioned from the start as part of the new program as conceived in 1230–31. The patronage of Louis IX and Blanche de Castille renewed a tradition that dated back to Dagobert himself, and the arrangement of the royal tombs was designed to reinforce the legitimacy of the Capetian line.[61]

Although he was a great patron of many monastic establishments, Louis consistently demonstrated his devotion to Saint Denis and the abbey of St-Denis.[62] There seems to have been a chapel dedicated to Saint Denis next to the king's bedroom in the royal palace in Paris, and Saint Denis was one of the three saints especially invoked by Louis at his death outside the walls of Carthage.[63] Every year on the feast of Saint Denis, Louis came to the abbey of St-Denis and, kneeling with bared head before the high altar, faithfully performed the act of homage by offering four besants of gold to the holy martyr in return for the saint's protection of the king's person and his realm.[64] When Louis returned from his first crusade in 1254, he made a collective offering of twenty-eight besants, four for each of the seven years he had been absent.

The precise nature of Louis's involvement in the rebuilding of the church of St-Denis is impossible to determine, however. Although Guillaume de Nangis stated that the rebuilding was undertaken *in consilio* with the king and his mother and though the church was decorated with painted and relief decoration of fleur-de-lys and the arms of Castile,[65] no documents survive giving explicit evidence of financial contributions. But the absence of documents should not be interpreted as the absence of patronage,[66] and in any case, at an abbey as wealthy as St-Denis, donations from the throne for the reconstruction might not have been imperative. There is every reason to think that Blanche de Castille and Louix IX were involved in the plans for the rebuilding and that the abbey had both personal and official significance for them. Furthermore, the striking similarities in the design and details of St-Denis and the contemporary chapel built by the king at St-Germain-en-Laye in the mid 1230s indicate very close ties indeed: most probably both throne and abbey employed the same architect.[67]

These issues and personalities will be considered again in later chapters in relation to certain aspects of the function, design, and dating of the new church. But
at St-Denis reconstructions, refurbishings, redecorations, and restorations have
modified many parts of the original structure. It is necessary, therefore, to
discuss these transformations, to separate what is new from what is old, before
turning to the thirteenth-century church itself.

2 ◆

The Restoration

ST-DENIS WAS THE FIRST LARGE-SCALE MEDIEVAL MONUMENT TO BE RESTORED IN nineteenth-century France. It may also possess the unfortunate distinction of having been under restoration longer than any other church, with each new architect in charge making significant changes to the work of his predecessors. Just as the mutilation of the church in the French Revolution was in large part the result of its close ties to royalty, so too the various stages of its restoration were subject to the uncertainties of political fortune. Each regime left its mark upon the monument. Begun under Napoleon in 1806, the first decade of work was designed to transform the Gothic structure into a classicized imperial mausoleum.[1] With the involvement of Eugène Viollet-le-Duc after 1847, efforts were made to return the church to its original disposition, but by this time money was short and much of the original fabric had been destroyed.[2] Continuation of the restoration after 1860 depended on the interest and patronage of Napoleon III; his involvement was encouraged by the creation of an imperial mausoleum inside the foundations of the Carolingian apse.[3] But as with his work at Notre-Dame in Paris, Viollet-le-Duc was at times more faithful to his own vision of Gothic than to the monument itself or to historical accuracy.[4]

There is perhaps no more telling and sadly comical insight into the vicissitudes of the restoration than the history of the painted interior decoration in the first three or four decades of the nineteenth century. In 1793 much of the original decoration of fleur-de-lys and castles was removed with antiroyalist fervor. After 1806, Napoleon's architects designed a new decoration for the eastern parts of the church that consisted in the initial *N*, bees, and the eagle; the rest of the interior was whitewashed.[5] These elements were hastily removed in 1814 when Napoleon fell from power and replaced with the monogram *L* and the fleur-de-lys for Louis XVIII.[6] Upon Napoleon's return shortly thereafter, this decoration was painted over once again with the emperor's monogram, eagles, and bees.[7] After Waterloo, the royal symbols were restored for Louis XVIII,[8] but remained in place only until 1831, when the political upheavals at the end of Charles X's reign led to an edict forbidding the use of the fleur-de-lys in any public monument.[9] Subsequently the chapels and columns of the chevet were decorated with innocuous floral and geometric ornament and the vaults with stars.[10] Nonetheless, in 1853 some of the Napoleonic motifs reappeared. One can imagine the vast expense that all this redecorating must have entailed.

The endless restoration and the restorations of the restorations did permit the monument to be preserved, however, and spared it the fate that befell Cluny, Royaumont, Cambrai, Arras, Valenciennes, and many other large-scale medieval churches in the decades following the French Revolution.[11] Though much of what was done at St-Denis has been the object of scorn and ridicule,[12] the early phases of this work were undertaken considerably before the beginning of the Gothic Revival in France and before any commitment or policy was developed to further the serious and archaeologically correct restoration of medieval monuments.[13] It is inappropriate to judge the early architects of St-Denis, emerging as they did from the strictly neoclassical training of the École des Beaux-Arts, by the same standards we apply to the work of Viollet-le-Duc, César Daly, and J.-B. A. Lassus, who represent a second generation that was more sensitive to the nuances and problems of architectural restoration.[14] The Gothic Revival in France began only slowly, inspired in part by the publication of Victor Hugo's *Notre-Dame de Paris* in 1831 and confirmed by the formation of the Société française d'archéologie in 1834 and publication of Didron's *Annales archéologiques* beginning in 1839.[15] Whereas the architects who worked on St-Denis under Napoleon were born in the 1760s and 1770s, the critics who were so scornful of the work of these men—and who laid the foundations of the Gothic Revival in France—were all born forty years later, in the beginning of the nineteenth century.[16]

In short, the restoration of St-Denis was begun long before that of other medieval churches in France; it was the laboratory for the earliest work on medieval restoration in that country. The all-too-evident mistakes made were a lesson to several succeeding generations of French architects who occupied themselves with Gothic monuments.[17] In the broader perspective of the revival as a whole, the restoration of St-Denis up to 1847 may seem wanting, but in the early nineteenth century, when so many other churches of major importance were being torn down, it was surprising and gratifying that a Gothic monument should survive at all. Furthermore, the often intense arguments and discussions on the philosophy of restoration that began only in the 1840s still await resolution today.[18]

Changes to the fabric of the thirteenth-century church began not long after its consecration in 1281. In the early fourteenth century, six chapels were added between the buttresses on the north side of the nave.[19] The wall between the responds along the north side of the church was entirely destroyed to permit the light from the chapel windows to penetrate into the northern aisle.[20]

Also in the early fourteenth century, a chapel dedicated to Saint Louis was added to the eastern side of the south transept arm.[21] This chapel, now austere, was once decorated with wall paintings and hangings, none of which has survived.[22] By the seventeenth century, it had been converted into a sacristy, an arrangement that perhaps suggests the need for more than one such structure—possibly even that the Saint Louis Chapel occupied a location that had formerly been a sacristy.[23] Later in the fourteenth century, the chapel of St. John the Baptist, in the innermost aisle of the east side of the south transept arm, was extended to the south by a chapel inserted between the buttresses (plate 3).[24]

The final major addition to the church before the nineteenth century was the Valois Chapel, attached to the exterior of the north transept arm. It was begun in 1559 (plate 4), abandoned, incomplete, in 1587,[25] and left in that state until 1719, when the danger of its imminent collapse led to its destruction.[26] A doorway was pierced in the north wall in the first bay east of the north transept terminal, in the chapel dedicated to Notre-Dame-la-Blanche (plates 5 and 6), in order to provide access to the chapel. The doorway, decorated with classical ornament consistent with the style of the monument to which it gave access, survived long after the destruction of the chapel itself; in a guidebook of 1815, it is described as a blocked-up opening. It was restored to an approximation of its original disposition by François Debret between 1815 and 1822.[27]

In a redecoration of the interior for the coronation of Marie de Medici in 1610, the location of the altar and steps leading from the transept to the chevet was changed. The primary document for the organization of the eastern parts of the church prior to this is a painting of the *Mass of Saint Giles,* now in the National Gallery in London, that is set in front of the main altar of the abbey church (plate 7).[28]

The chapel flanking that of Notre-Dame-la-Blanche to the east has traditionally been dedicated to Saint Eustache.[29] After the death of the Vicomte de Turenne in 1675, it was transformed into a monument in his honor (plates 5 and 6).[30] The thirteenth-century responds were cut back and covered with a marble and plaster revetment, a dome was inserted in place of the rib-vault, and a splendid tomb by Lebrun was placed against the north wall, concealing and probably destroying the second window on the eastern side of the north transept arm (plate 6). The tomb of Turenne was moved to the Invalides in 1796, and the chapel was restored to its earlier disposition by Legrand in 1806 and 1807.[31] The responds and walls in this chapel are thus completely nineteenth-century work. This part of the church suffered further indignities when a new chapel was added in the 1820s by François Debret east of the Turenne Chapel and used as a vestiary for the choirboys (plate 8).[32] This structure, described by the Baron de Guilhermy as "fort insignificant," was removed after 1850 by Viollet-le-Duc.[33]

The relationship between the abbey church and the conventual buildings, so crucial for an understanding of the sequence of construction in the thirteenth century, has also been transformed (plate 9). Beginning in 1700, the old conventual complex of the twelfth and thirteenth centuries was destroyed and replaced by a magnificently austere ensemble designed by Robert de Cotte and Christophe (plate 10).[34] For lack of funds, the reconstruction progressed slowly, and the new monastery was finished only in 1786, less than a decade before the French Revolution destroyed the last vestiges of monastic life at the abbey and wrought havoc upon the church and its decoration.[35] The rebuildings of the conventual buildings erased the earlier structures, so that there is little concrete information as to the location, disposition, and date of the buildings that adjoined the church, with the slight exception of the treasury, the plan of which was published by Félibien in 1706, a century prior to its destruction in the early nineteenth century (plate 3).[36]

The remaining transformations and depredations are largely the story of the nineteenth-century restoration.[37] Some of this work, such as the restoration of the west facade and crypt, has been outlined before in detail and need not be repeated here. But the restoration also touched almost every part of the thirteenth-century church, and an understanding of what is old and what is new is fundamental to a study of the new edifice as it was conceived and constructed. To that end, the discussion here will focus on the way in which the restoration affected the Rayonnant church rather than its predecessors.[38]

The last services at St-Denis were celebrated on September 14, 1792, and the church was subsequently converted to parish use. In 1793, revolutionary mobs dug up and pillaged the royal tombs and mutilated the sculpture on the portals.[39] The church was subsequently disaffected and mass was celebrated in the Hôtel-Dieu. In November 1793, St-Denis was transformed into a Temple of Reason and used for services until April 1794. But when the lead was removed from the roofs in 1794–96 to be used for war supplies, the church became unusable for any sort of service, and the tombs and what was left of the glass were removed by Alexandre Lenoir between 1796 and 1799 to the Musée des Monuments Français.[40] Because the building was now without any purpose, proposals were put forward for its future destruction, but it was saved by the Commission temporaire des arts, which blocked its sale.[41] For a short period it was used as a storehouse for wheat and cereals, but the dampness that penetrated through the exposed and unprotected vaults soon made storage impossible. According to the Baron de Guilhermy, a troop of itinerant actors received permission to put on shows in the church, while the conventual buildings were converted in 1795 to a military hospital.[42] In 1800 a proposition to convert the entire church into a covered market by dismantling the vaults and the clerestory and roofing over the nave at the level of the triforium was narrowly avoided.[43] Because he already had in his Musée des Monuments Français all that he desired, Alexandre Lenoir, often considered an enlightened soul, viewed the proposal to convert the basilica into a market as "plein de sagacité," fulfilling at once "le but des arts et celui de l'utilité pratique."[44]

A description of grass growing on the altars and birds flying freely through the open windows paints a vivid picture of the condition of the monument at the turn of the century.[45] But unlike its ruined counterparts in the

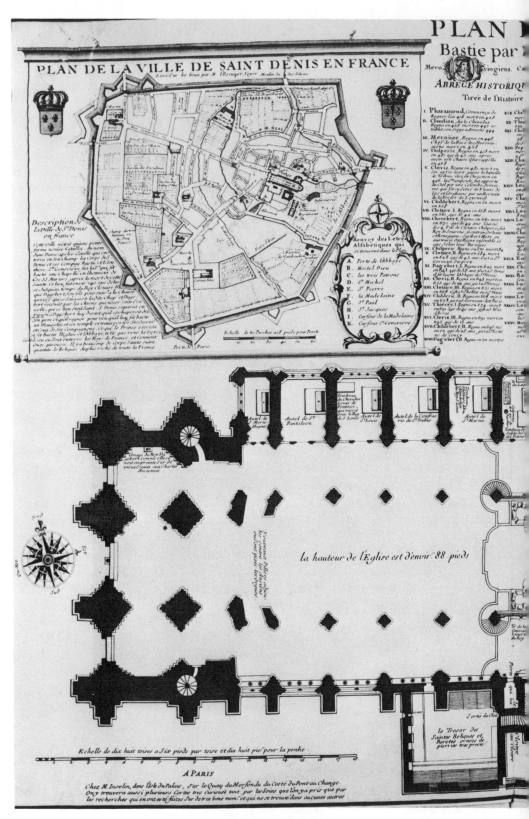

Plate 3. Plan of the abbey church published in 1706 by Félibien.

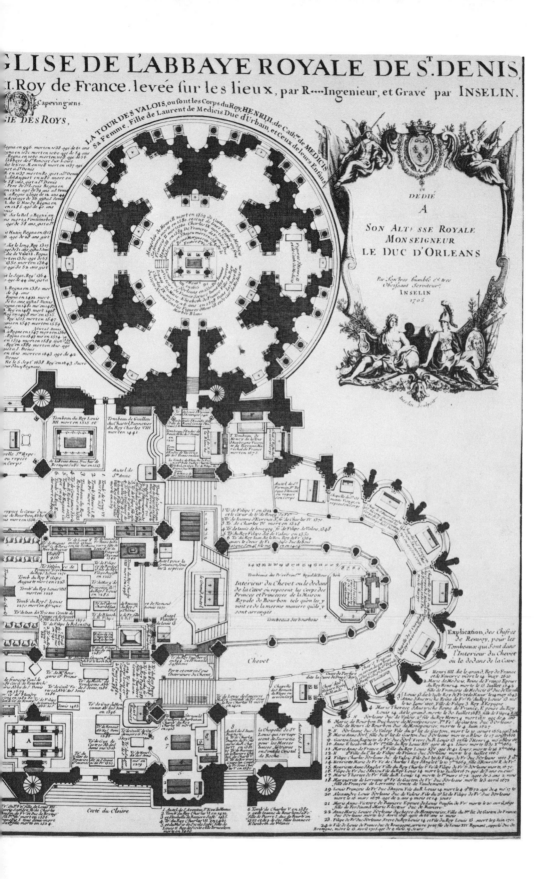

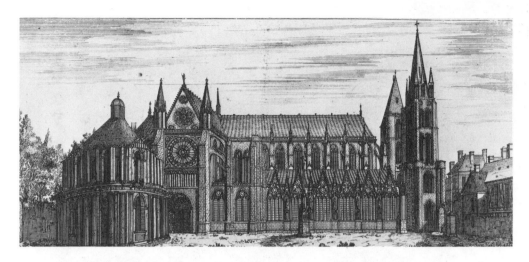

Plate 4. View of the north flank of the church and the Valois Chapel prior to 1719, by Jean Marot.

Plate 5. View of the Turenne Chapel and the entrance to the Valois mausoleum from the south.

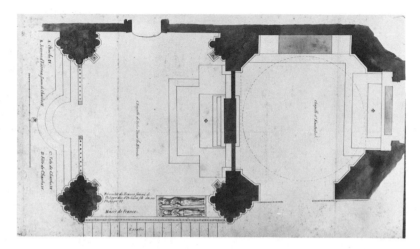

Plate 6. Plan of the northeastern bays of the north transept arm after the
installation of the Turenne tomb.

country, such as the abbeys of Royaumont and Ourscamp, where the growth of
vines and trees soon transformed ragged ruins to picturesque and poetic effect,
the urban ruins of St-Denis, with mold creeping down the walls and great,
gaping holes in the pavement where the royal tombs had been unearthed, must
have been a dismal sight indeed.

Restoration was begun in 1806 by Napoleon, whose vision of his role in
history easily accommodated his own burial in the necropolis of the kings of
France and the transformation of the ancient church from a royal to an imperial
burial place.[46] The initial work on the restoration was entrusted to Jacques
Legrand. First he rebuilt the roof over the nave; this was done at a lower level
than the front gable, a procedure he defended as increasing the beauty of the
monument.[47] The vaults were restored and the pavement was replaced with a
harsh pattern of black and white marble.[48] Lean-to roofs were constructed over
the aisles in such a way that they blocked the glazed triforium, dramatically
changing the character of the interior.[49] Then the entire interior was scraped and
whitewashed. This phase of the restoration, accomplished with limited means,
was designed to provide a suitably lugubrious mausoleum for the emperor. The
restoration of the church as a respectable religious institution also aided
Napoleon in his revival of the Catholic faith in France. To that end, a chapter was
founded that consisted of canons chosen from bishops over sixty years old.[50]

Legrand died in 1807; after a brief interruption, his work was continued
by Jacques Cellerier beginning in 1808.[51] The restoration now changed somewhat: its purpose was no longer to consolidate the old structure but to transform
the interior. A long chapel to be used as a parish church was planned to flank the
south aisle (plate 8). This chapel, the construction of which was projected as
early as 1809, was begun in the summer of 1812 and completed only in 1832.[52] Its

Plate 7. *The Mass of Saint Giles,* by an unknown Flemish painter, late fifteenth century.

erection entailed destruction of the entire south wall of the nave, excepting the responds, as well as the old treasury tucked between the south transept arm and the south flank of the nave (see the plan published by Félibien, plate 3). The wall buttresses on the exterior were largely destroyed, and the responds along the south wall on the interior were incorporated into the new structure as extended intermediate piers in what became essentially a double aisle on the south side of the church (plate 8).

One of the most momentous events in the early nineteenth-century restorations occurred in 1811, when Napoleon visited the site and found the restoration unsatisfactory, comparing the quality of the work on the basilica to that of barbarian tribes.[53] Although his precise meaning has never been elucidated, the net effect was that the restoration became much more thorough. Cellerier, somewhat discredited, continued to direct the work at the site.[54] Enormous sums were appropriated. It was decreed that the floor level of the nave be raised by approximately two meters in order to diminish the differences in level between the crossing and the chevet. This entailed destruction of the plinths and bases in the piers throughout the nave and transept as well as the dado arcading in the walls of the aisles.[55] At the same time new plans were made for grand staircases from the transept to the crypt, to be situated in the outermost bays to the north and south on the east side of the transept. The change in level between the transept and the chevet was moved to the west, in line with the eastern crossing piers, so that the two eastern aisles of the transept were now on the same level as the chevet (plate 8). Another series of steps was placed in the third bay west of the crossing, marking a change in level almost halfway down the nave. Innumerable dedications of chapels were transferred and the chapels themselves transformed; the new arrangement of the chapels and tombs bore little resemblance to the original disposition.[56]

In 1813, François Debret, an architect who had trained under Charles Percier at the École des Beaux-Arts, took over the direction of the restoration.[57] Owing to political uncertainties and a lack of funds, little was done to the structure of the church itself during the first few years of his tenure, but in the 1820s, movement detected in the fliers and buttresses along the south flank of the nave, the result of the chipping away of the supports below for the construction of the parish church along the south flank, was the point of departure for a whole new phase of drastic reworking of the upper walls and the fliers, carried out with increasingly large subventions.[58] At first this work consisted in the reinforcement of the buttresses along the nave. As funds were augmented, work began on the replacement of the masonry and tracery in the clerestory of all the upper parts of the structure, much of which was cracking and threatening to collapse because of the mining of the supports along the south flank of the nave.[59] Work on the reconstruction of these parts of the building progressed by and large counterclockwise around the church, beginning with the south flank of the nave, where the damage was most visible, and working its way around the chevet to the north side of the nave. Much of this was done with considerable attention to

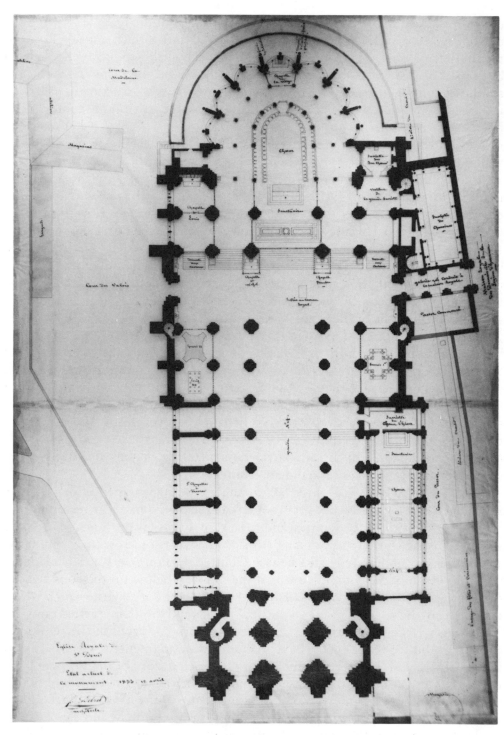

Plate 8. Plan of the abbey church in 1833 by François Debret.

detail, and Debret left records of his work, specifying where old stone was replaced, recut, or left untouched in place.[60] The triforium windows were restored by the substitution of terrace roofs for the lean-to roofs erected in 1806–07 by Legrand that had blocked the windows in the back wall. This was not altogether a blessing, however, as Debret devised a system of flat, cement terrace roofs that were supported by brick arches hidden above the aisle vaults (plate 11).[61] During this period a chapel was added east of the chapel of Saint Eustache to be used as a vestry, and a small chapel that served as its foundation was also added to the crypt (plate 8).[62]

Gradually, Debret's work became more comprehensive, and appropriations for the restoration increasingly generous during the later 1820s, 1830s, and early 1840s. The transept roses were entirely restored in 1839–41; the roof over the main vaults was rebuilt with an elaborate iron framework in 1843–44; and beginning about 1827, the program of new stained glass designed by Debret was installed in the nave, transept, and upper stories of the chevet.[63] The westernmost nave windows were blocked in 1838 when the new organ was installed between them, and this also obscured the continuity of the nave to the upper chapel of Suger's westwork and the rose window in the facade.[64] The most disastrous part of the restoration, the redecoration of the west facade and the reconstruction of the northwest tower, took place in the 1840s. The cracks that appeared in the fabric of the rebuilt tower and the facade below immediately upon its reconstruction led to a public outcry against Debret and finally to his removal from office in 1846.[65]

The restoration of St-Denis during the thirties and forties was a rallying point for a small but dedicated group committed to the preservation and responsible restoration of medieval monuments in France. As early as 1833, L. Vitet, inspector for the Commission des Monuments Historiques, had suggested in vain that Debret abandon or limit his redecoration of the interior of St-Denis.[66] In 1841, the commission as a whole attacked Debret's work, but he was vigorously defended by his colleagues at the École des Beaux-Arts and the Académie des Inscriptions et Belles Lettres.[67] Much of the early outcry against Debret concerned the decoration of the interior; the revelations of his catastrophic work on the west facade and the debacle of the northwest tower were yet to come. But complaint was also raised over the fact that the church had been transformed into a "museum" of medieval sculpture. Beginning with the restoration of the monarchy with Louis XVIII in 1816, the royal tombs began gradually to be moved back to the abbey. In his enthusiasm, Debret arranged for the removal to St-Denis not only of the tombs that had formerly been there, but also of virtually every other piece of medieval sculpture that formed part of the Musée des Monuments Français.[68] The chapel along the south flank of the nave, transformed into a winter chapel by the erection of walls separating it from the church and by the addition of central heating, was decorated with the surviving apostles from the Ste-Chapelle. The crypt and choir chapels became congested and cluttered with figures from all periods of medieval sculpture, reidentified as various

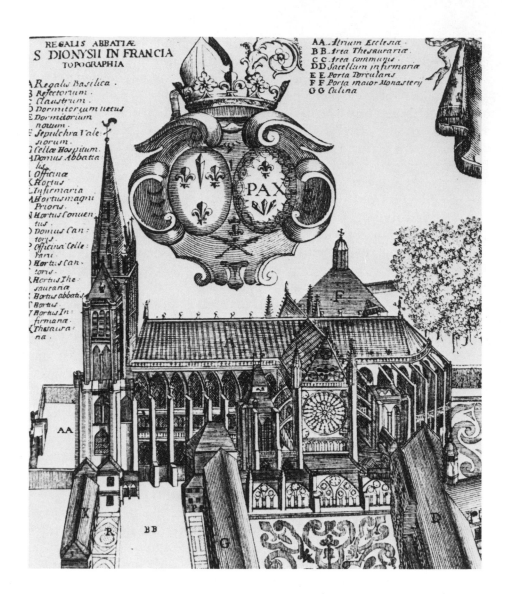

Plate 9. View of the abbey church and monastery from the south, *Monasticon Gallicanum*.

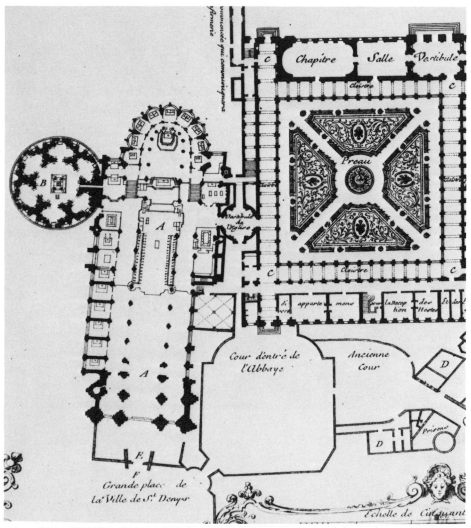

Plate 10. Plan of the abbey church and the monastery, eighteenth century.

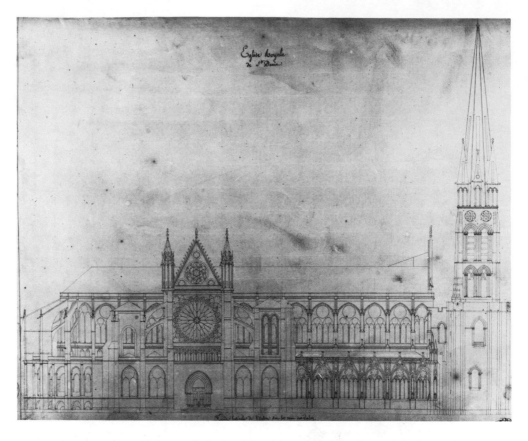

Plate 11. View of the north flank of the abbey church by François Debret, 1830.

"missing" royal personages to form a complete "set" of the kings and queens of France.[69] The Baron de Guilhermy, who for all his outrage still possessed a sense of humor, described the decoration of the interior:

> Les savants, les architectes, ou autres, qui furent chargés du classe-
> ment des tombeaux et des statues rapportés à Saint-Denis, semblent
> avoir été préoccupés d'une fantaisie matrimoniale des plus étranges.
> Après avoir fait le compte de leurs personnages, il arrêtèrent que chaque
> roi de marbre aurait droit à une épouse de même matière qui partagerait
> avec lui les ennuis de la tombe. La position personelle de chacune des
> princesses représentées par les statues qu'il s'agissait de replacer, leurs
> engagements antérieurs, leurs affections légitimes, ne mirent point
> obstacle à la classification projetée. Les princes de second ordre furent
> condamnés à céder aux rois leurs épouses, bon gré mal gré, sauf réclama-
> tion dans le cas ou, tout partage terminé, il s'en trouverait quelqu'une en
> surnombre. De cette arbitraire mesure, il résulta de singuliers incestes de

pierre, et des adultères de marbre de la pire espèce. C'était un scandale à faire rougir les piliers vénérables de la crypte.[70]

The completion of the work on the west facade and the reconstruction of the northwest tower, which soon had to be taken down again to save the facade, provided the long-sought opportunity to remove Debret from his position. In 1846, Didron declared that St-Denis no longer held any esthetic interest and that he would rather see the church destroyed than so dishonored.[71] The Baron de Guilhermy once again summarized the situation neatly: the church had been "nivelé, régularisé, gratté, embelli, agrandi, et raccommodé . . . ," and Debret's unfortunate windows were "les plus laides, les plus difformes, les plus misérables, qui aient été faites dans notre pays."[72] Viollet-le-Duc, who succeeded Debret, also catalogued the indignities to which the church had been subjected: "piliers sapés, le sol relevé sans nécessité, les cryptes gratées, les sculptures retaillées, les pavements recoupés, tout le bâs-côté sud détruit, et partout l'édifice retouché, arrangé, remis à neuf sans avoir égard aux traces anciennes et surtout à la stabilité."[73] He also speaks of the decoration of the interior: "d'affreux vitraux posés dans les baies, les débris du Musée des Monuments Français arrangés en manière de magasin de bric-à-brac, d'admirables tombeaux sciés, dédoublés, recomposés, des monuments faits avec des fragments de toutes les époques."[74]

It should be remembered, however, that this point of view was a new one. In 1811, Napoleon seems to have been dissatisfied because the restoration had not been thorough enough; the plans to raise the level of the nave and transept, add the parish chapel along the south flank, and redecorate the interior to give the monument the proper "caractère funèbre" were the suggestion of his architect, Pierre Fontaine. A. Gilbert, in his description and guide to St-Denis published in 1815, refers to the new floor level as creating "une belle unité, maintenant si judicieusement rétablie."[75] And on the additions to the fabric of the thirteenth-century church, Gilbert adds:

> L'extérieur et l'intérieur ont été restaurés avec le plus grand soin. On voit avec satisfaction que les architectes qui se sont succédés dans la conduite des travaux ont scrupuleusement suivi le système d'unité dans les constructions qu'on y a ajoutées, comme dans la restauration des ornements que l'injure du temps ou le vandalisme révolutionnaire avoient détruits.[76]

In another guidebook, Flamand-Grétry was fulsome in his praise: the church was "plus imposante que jamais," and François Debret "un des plus habiles architectes de Paris."[77] Gilbert also sang the praises of Debret, who had "autant de goût que d'intelligence et de célébrité."[78] Though a few isolated individuals may have been critical of the restoration from the start, the early stages of the work were for the most part generally applauded as having saved the monument from destruction. If Gilbert had a few residual doubts (he deplored the loss of the original proportions of the interior in the creation of that "belle unité"), and if Flamand–Grétry was singularly obtuse in his understanding of architecture (he attributes the west facade to Charlemagne), Debret's work was firmly supported by his professional associates in the École des Beaux-Arts.[79]

Serious interest in archaeologically correct restoration began to appear in the 1830s with the involvement of Montalembert, the Baron de Guilhermy, Mérimée, Vitet, and Didron. Indeed, the founding of the *Annales archéologiques* in 1839 was to a large extent prompted by the restoration inflicted upon the abbey church of St-Denis, which figures prominently in the introductory essay of the first issue.[80] The purpose of the founders was to provide a source of scholarship and information on medieval art and architecture so that comparable misfortunes could be avoided in the future. One of the regular features of the *Annales* was a section entitled "Actes de vandalisme," in which monuments that were being destroyed either by neglect or excessive restoration were brought to public attention. In the November 1844 issue a long article on the restoration of St-Denis pointed out the garbled Latin inscriptions and the additional figures carved on the facade (in imitation of Notre-Dame-la-Grande in Poitiers) as well as the absurdity of the interior decoration, though its author (Didron) scrupulously avoided mentioning the name of the architect in charge.[81]

Debret was entrenched in his position, however, and only the dramatic cracks that appeared in the west facade after the reconstruction of the northwest tower led to his dismissal. In order to avoid the imminent collapse of both tower and facade, the order was given in February 1846 to destroy both the *flèche* and the tower.[82] The appropriation of funds for this work was discussed by the Chamber of Deputies, the enormous expense of the restorations came to the attention of the public, and Debret was (gently, it seems) removed to a higher position in the Conseil des bâtiments civils, where he was able to survey and control the work of his successor at St-Denis and effectively prevent any major changes or modifications until his death in 1850.[83]

The situation at St-Denis was so serious that Félix Duban, who had directed the restoration of the Ste-Chapelle and the Château of Blois, refused the commission. Almost a year later, after extensive study, Eugène Viollet-le-Duc, who had worked with Lassus on the restoration of Notre-Dame, took responsibility for the rescue of the abbey church.

Debret had been in charge of the restoration of St-Denis for over thirty years. Viollet-le-Duc nearly equaled him, directing the work from 1847 until his death in 1879. But once the restoration was in more responsible hands, funds for continuation of the work were lacking.[84] Between 1850 and 1858, the major work undertaken consisted in the removal of Debret's decoration of the chevet, the restoration of the proper inscriptions on the tombs, and the repair of what survived of the twelfth-century glass in the chevet.[85]

With the accession of Napoleon III, the abbey church once again became an imperial necropolis. Viollet-le-Duc at last received funds for the restoration

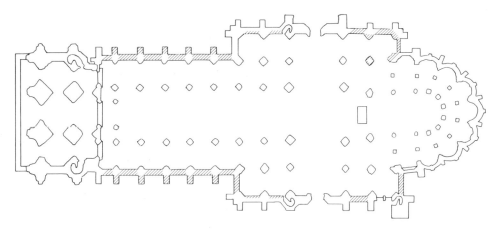

Figure 2. Plan with destroyed thirteenth-century masonry (at ground level)
indicated by hatched lines.

and urgent repair of those parts of the structure that had been severely de-
stabilized by the raising of the floor level and the construction of the winter
chapel. To ensure the commitment of funds to the work at St-Denis, an imperial
mausoleum was created underneath the main altar, in the interior of the foundations of the Carolingian apse. During the 1860s, most of Viollet-le-Duc's proposals for the restoration of various parts of the building were approved, with
the fortunate exception of his plan to rebuild the facade.[86] The pavement was
returned to its original level, with the bases and plinths of the piers reconstructed, and the dado arcading was gradually restored throughout the building.[87] The
staircases to the chevet and crypt were returned to the disposition established in
1610 for the coronation of Marie de Medici. At the same time, the aisle walls and
windows were restored along both sides of the nave; the winter chapel, which
had threatened the stability of the structure, was demolished; and the vaults,
flyers, and buttresses, threatened by Cellerier and Debret's undercutting of the
lower supports, were reinforced and reconstructed (fig. 2). The doorway along
the south aisle, which gives access to the abandoned field on the south side of the
church, is entirely a creation of Viollet-le-Duc; no doorway of this type existed
in the original thirteenth-century structure (plate 3).[88]

The Franco-Prussian War and the formation of the commune of 1871
interrupted the restoration. During the invasion of 1871 the building suffered
some damage, but on the whole the precautionary measures taken by Viollet-le-
Duc and his assistant and successor, Denis Darcy, prevented serious damage to
the interior and what survived of the old glass.[89] On the death of Viollet-le-Duc
in 1879, Darcy took over and continued his predecessor's work, consolidating
the buttresses, restoring the crenellations of the west facade, and most important, discovering and disengaging the south transept portal, which had been
mutilated and concealed by the structures attached to the church in the eighteenth century.

The last century of work at St-Denis has been somewhat less controversial and dramatic. Although repairs have been made to various parts of the church at frequent intervals, none of these has involved major reconstruction. A Musée Lapidaire was installed in the orangerie to the northeast of the church in 1935; a number of fragments of sculpture are presently kept there in a certain state of disorder.

In 1942 Jules Formigé was appointed architect in charge of the restoration.[90] His plan for a modern "crypte royale" inside the old Carolingian apse was quashed by the protests of art historians, archaeologists, and serious amateurs, and the remainder of his work consisted largely in the restoration of the buttresses and the rearrangement of the crypt and the chevet.[91] In 1957–58 the main flight of stairs behind the altar rising from the crossing to the chevet was rebuilt; Viollet-le-Duc had restored it to an arrangement similar to that in Félibien's plan (plate 3), which reflects the disposition after the changes of 1610 made for Marie de Medici. During the same years, the nineteenth-century decoration was removed from the chevet, and the whitewash that covered most of the central vessel was scraped off; it still covers the western aisles.

The stone used in much of the nineteenth-century restoration was of poor quality, and much of it has had to be replaced. Restoration is being carried out at present on the transept and along the flanks of the nave, all parts of the church that had been reconstructed in the nineteenth century. This type of work will probably have to continue indefinitely because of the dense pollution of the area and the ravages of earlier work.

3 ❖

The New Church

PLAN, ELEVATION, SCULPTURAL DECORATION, AND PROPORTIONS

F EW VISITORS TO THE ABBEY REMAIN UNMOVED BY THE GRACE AND SPLENDOR OF the interior of St-Denis (plate 1). Though the building has been ravaged by the restorations discussed in the preceding chapter, and though the nineteenth-century glass in the clerestory dominates the interior with lurid intensity, the elevation nonetheless radiates a balance, harmony, and clarity of conception that led Erwin Panofsky to see this structure as the architectural expression of scholastic thought.[1] While Panofsky's theory has by no means been universally accepted, it seems undeniable that the new church was the result of an inspired and profound rationalism. This is visible in the plan, in the elevation, and in the relationship between the two. Although there were various modifications in design during the fifty years of construction, it is almost certain that the plan and elevation of the entire church were conceived prior to the reworking of the chevet, as the discussion of measurements below will indicate. Throughout the new building the principles of harmony and concordance took precedence over both a natural inclination to complete the church with a more modern and up-to-date design and the desires of the succeeding architects to leave the imprint of their personal style on the building.[2] The program begun in 1231 was already largely *dépassé* by 1245–55, not to speak of the years between 1259 and circa 1275, when the church was finally completed. Yet the temptation to modernize was subjugated to the principles of internal unity and homogeneity, so that the changes in design are modest indeed and reveal themselves only gradually to the eye of the observer.

THE PLAN

The plan of St-Denis as it stands today is a composite of three major building programs and numerous later additions.[3] The thirteenth-century reconstruction includes the upper stories of the chevet and extends to Suger's western bays of the nave. Given the impossibility of adding to the length of the church without destroying Suger's structures to the east and west, it is perhaps not surprising that it expands in width—not along the length of the nave, as Suger had intended with his projected plan of double aisles on either side of the nave, but in the swelling of the transept into a great centralized space in the middle of the church.[4] In the most general sense, the Gothic plan is usually characterized by an enlargement of the chevet with additional bays and double aisles, but at St-Denis, Suger's small-scale chevet is retained and the expansion takes place in the transept instead (fig. 1).[5] I know of no other example of the use of four aisles in the transept; this particular feature can be explained only in terms of the use of the transept for royal burials.[6] The special function of the building is thus reflected in a unique approach to the plan, and it is no coincidence that it is the area in which the tombs are placed that underwent a radical transformation from the standard High Gothic disposition.

Sixteenth-century descriptions of the church speak of its three parts, and it seems clear that this was how the plan was conceived from the start: a shrine for the saint in a special, high, enclosed space; a magnificent and monumental royal burial area just beneath the shrine; and finally, liturgical accommodations for the monastic community who kept these other two traditions alive and flourishing.[7] The loss of the original screens establishing these divisions and separations gives a false impression of the space as it was initially conceived.[8] While one of the dominant characteristics of the design of the Gothic church is its unity of plan and elevation, this unity was made up of a multiplicity of parts that applied to the spatial divisions within the church as well as to the structure itself. Indeed, a medieval church "makes sense" only if those original divisions, each with its particular purpose, are kept in mind.

We know little about the appearance of St-Denis between the death of Abbot Suger and the beginning of the reconstruction in 1231. The surviving evidence suggests that the completed chevet was still joined to the Carolingian nave (fig. 3).[9] While some work had been done on the twelfth-century nave, and elements intended for this structure were reused in the foundations of the thirteenth-century church, the construction of this part of the building does not seem to have progressed very far.[10]

As Crosby has pointed out, Suger's twelfth-century transept was to be nonprojecting.[11] Thus in the rebuilding by Suger, the relationship between the Carolingian church and the conventual buildings would have remained the same, as his transept did not extend beyond its Carolingian predecessor.[12] As discovered by Crosby in his excavations, the twelfth-century transept would have continued the alignment of the double aisles and straight walls of Suger's chevet, and indeed the surviving twelfth-century masonry of the transept incorporated some of the Carolingian walls.[13]

The plan of the thirteenth-century church with its greatly expanded transept is therefore a radical departure from Suger's intended structure, even though it incorporates at its eastern and western extremities significant parts of his work (fig. 1). Instead of the relatively narrow spaces of the twelfth-century

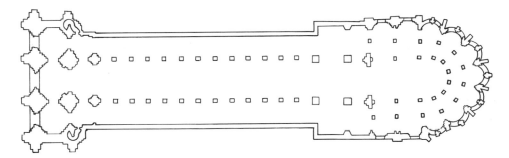

Figure 3. Plan prior to the inception of construction in 1231.

building, the new plan was conceived as creating a completely different type of interior space. As the new dimensions of the transept called for the destruction and rebuilding of the adjoining buildings on the northeastern side of the cloister, Abbot Eudes' rebuilding probably also envisioned from the outset the reconstruction of a large part of the monastery.

Suger's west facade and two western bays precede a thirteenth-century nave eight bays long.[14] The westernmost of the new bays is considerably narrower than those to the east and is presently partially concealed by the organ loft added in the 1820s.[15] This is a bay of adjustment between the thirteenth-century church and the older western bays, similar in its abbreviated form to the corresponding western bay in the nave of Chartres, for example.[16]

The nave culminates in a transept of magnificent proportions; it is two bays deep, and the double aisles on either side create a great expansion within the central part of the church (fig. 1). The doubling of the aisles in the transept leads to a fluidity of space around the crossing; the eastern end of the nave tends to become absorbed into the central part of the church, as the nave and transept have two bays of the arcade in common. This arrangement occurs also on the eastern side of the transept, though here the change in levels between the eastern and western aisles creates a sharper differentiation of space, as do the obliquely planted walls of the chevet east of the crossing piers.[17] The shared territory of nave and transept unifies these two parts of the plan, while the chevet, raised by its placement over the crypt, remains a separate and distinct entity.

The significance of the transept lies not only in the prominence of its double aisles, but also in the way in which its corners are emphasized by the heavier intermediate piers between the double aisles on all four sides (fig. 1). These supports, which have the same diameter as the crossing piers, carry the greater weight of the four towers planted above the outer corners of the transept arms. On the exterior, of course, the towers create the dramatic massing of the transept facades, from which they are separated by one bay of the aisle (plate 11). They also serve to support the fliers for the main vaults of the transept, the west bays of the chevet, and the east bays of the nave.[18] Their further importance in marking the symbolic aspect of the transept as a necropolis will be discussed in a later chapter.[19]

These detached towers are unique to St-Denis, for the normal arrangement in churches with transept towers, such as Laon, Chartres, and Reims, had been to attach the towers to the transept terminal wall, creating a massive facade often equal in importance to that at the west. The transept facades at St-Denis, however, are split into their component parts; and the towers detached from the mass of the terminal wall emphasize on the exterior the expansion of the transept which is so striking in the interior (plate 11). The upper half of the surface of the transept terminal walls consists almost exclusively of the huge rose window, voiding the wall, as it were, both inside and out (plates 12 and 25). The transept thereby acquires a personality distinct from that of the twelfth-century facade, with its more massive and monumental character.[20] At the same time, the detachment of the towers from the central block allows light to flow unimpeded into the interior through the windows of the clerestory and triforium in the transept.[21]

The location of the thirteenth-century crossing corresponds to that of its Carolingian predecessor; in fact, the latter is contained within the former, according to Crosby's reconstruction of the Carolingian plan.[22] This means that the traditional position of the main altar east of the crossing and monks' choir in the eastern bays of the nave remained much the same, even after Abbot Eudes' rebuilding of the church. Suger's twelfth-century apse and radiating chapels had provided a new sanctuary for the relics of Saint Denis, as well as for those of other saints acquired over the centuries, in a new chevet outside the fabric of the Carolingian church and its ninth-century extension. But the location of the main altar in Suger's church retained its position above the *confessio* of the Carolingian church in which the relics had been kept, and this location was in turn preserved when the church was rebuilt beginning in 1231.[23]

Suger's plan seems to have made no provision for accommodating the type of royal necropolis that seems intrinsic to the design of the thirteenth-century church. Indeed, in Suger's day and throughout the remainder of the twelfth century, some of the royal tombs were apparently not even marked.[24] Abbot Suger's main object was the creation of a plan that allowed for the dramatic setting of the relics in a structure that on the one hand provided enough space for the throngs of pilgrims (hence, in part, the double aisles in the nave), and on the other remained in concordance and harmony with the old church.[25] In the more complex design of the thirteenth century, the concept of royal burial was adopted as another of the main functions of the abbey church, and the transept was expanded to the north, south, east, and west to make room for the tombs. The inflation of this part of the church to a scale and complexity unprecedented in medieval architecture was thus a recognition in the very design of the plan of the established tradition of royal burial.[26] It has been recorded that by the mid–twelfth century, the crossing and transept were so crowded with royal tombs that it was difficult if not impossible to find space for the new arrivals;[27] the expansion of the transept was a logical solution to this problem.

Plate 12. The north transept arm.

The larger transept may also have reflected the necessity of making adequate provision in the plan for the increasingly large tomb structures that became popular in the second half of the twelfth and the early thirteenth centuries. In Suger's time, tombs had usually been flat plaques that were flush with the floor and could be walked upon and therefore did not disrupt the flow of traffic through the church.[28] By the late twelfth century, in a period of growing interest in lineage and genealogy, tombs were generally raised on bases and the figures carved in higher relief (plate 21).[29] Since the burial of kings was one of the most highly prized privileges of St-Denis, it is natural to assume that this became an important factor in the new plan.

The relationship between the plan of the Carolingian church and its thirteenth-century successor has important implications for the progress of the reconstruction, as will be demonstrated in the following chapter. At the same time, it reflects the importance of continuity of site for certain functions within the church, as suggested above. This applied equally to the more general use of certain spaces. The monks' choir, for example, in the first three bays of the nave west of the crossing in the present church, occupied the same place as its Carolingian predecessor. Indeed, the Carolingian nave, which fits neatly within the thirteenth-century piers, probably continued to be used while the new church was being constructed as an envelope around it, and may have been demolished only at a fairly late date, when the new choir was complete (fig. 31).[30] In short, though the side walls of the thirteenth-century church were expanded around the older central core, this enlargement of the church had little effect on the original locations of the old sacred spaces.

What was the original arrangement of the east end of the thirteenth-century church at St-Denis? A reconstruction can be only hypothetical, as the eastern parts of the church have been through innumerable changes and restorations since the early seventeenth century (plate 13). But a painting of *The Mass of Saint Giles* set in the eastern parts of the church, confirmed by various descriptions of this area prior to 1610, permits some observations on the organization of the interior (plate 7).[31] To this evidence can be added a few drawings by the neoclassical architect Charles Percier—made after the church had been abandoned in 1792—which confirm some details provided by the other documents (plates 14 and 15).

The painting by the Master of Saint Giles shows the main altar placed to the east of the eastern crossing piers, in a location slightly west of where the main altar is today. Behind the altar and the reliquary for the bones of Saint Louis can be seen a wall between the first pair of piers east of the crossing. This wall was pierced in the center by a doorway leading down into the crypt, its only entrance until the disposition was changed, perhaps in 1610.[32] By about 1500, the wall was topped by a wooden screen.[33] A staircase on the south side of the altar can be seen rising to the upper level of the chevet, access to the latter being cut off by a door and a wooden porch. As a description of 1517 speaks of the relics as being placed in an area accessible by "geminis schalis, quas ex utroque cornu habet,

Plate 13. View of the chevet from the west.

Plate 14. The western bays of the north transept arm by Charles Percier, 1790s.

Plate 15. View of the crossing and chevet from the west by Charles Percier, 1790s.

ascenditur XVIII gradibus,"[34] a corresponding door and porch must have existed on the north side. Two other staircases rose from the transept proper to the
ambulatory around the chevet. It seems highly probable that from the start the
entire area of the apse was separated from the ambulatory by wooden screens
placed between the cylindrical piers of the chevet, as is indicated in Félibien's
plan (plate 3), an arrangement still visible today in some Flemish paintings, such
as the *Exhumation of Saint Hubert* by a follower of Roger van der Weyden.[35]

Whatever the exact details of this disposition, one can be quite certain
that the entire east end of the church was kept distinct and separate from the
transept. Even after the eastern part of the crossing was rearranged in 1610 for
the coronation of Marie de Medici, the chevet remained closed off by a high
wall, still visible in the 1790s in a drawing by Percier (plate 15).

The separation of the chevet from the rest of the church emphasizes the
fact that the hemicycle was seen as a raised sanctuary for the relics of the saint, not
unlike the Trinity Chapel of Canterbury, begun after 1178. At Canterbury,
William the Englishman built a much taller and more spacious extension to the
Romanesque crypt, which dramatically raised the floor level of the Trinity
Chapel, thus placing the shrine of Thomas Becket in full view.[36] In both churches, the effect of the raised chevet is to create an elevated, enclosed, and intimate
setting for the relics of the saint that differs markedly from the more spacious and
ample volumes of the transept and nave.[37]

At St-Denis a further division existed in the first three bays of the nave, in
the form of a choir screen that closed off the monks' choir from the aisles and the
western bays (plate 3). This structure was preserved until the eighteenth century.[38] The accounts of the *Grande commanderie* provide some indications of the
work done on the stalls in 1286 and 1287, and a drawing of the interior by
Martellange in 1641 provides the only surviving view of the screen itself (plate
16).[39] Only a small number of fragments of this structure survive, and the stalls
themselves, carved with great care and expense in the thirteenth century, were
demolished in the eighteenth.[40]

The plan of St-Denis is unusual in its incorporation of significant parts of
an earlier structure into a new program. There are, as a result, considerable
changes in scale between the twelfth-century ambulatory and the new thirteenth-century church. As at Canterbury, however, the architect of the new
church was remarkably successful in integrating the new church with the old,
and the changes in level between the transept and the chevet help in the transition
as well as in the creation of a dramatic focus for religious veneration.

The decision to preserve earlier parts of the church meant that the plan of
St-Denis differs in character from the previous generation of High Gothic cathedrals. Whereas there is an expansion of the chevet in most Gothic buildings, with
an increasing number of bays between the crossing and the apse, often flanked by
double aisles, the effect at St-Denis is otherwise. Here the spatial volumes become smaller and more intimate as they move from the crossing eastward. In the

Plate 16. View of the choir screen by Martellange.

interior the consequence is to heighten the intensity in the easternmost parts of
the church by condensing the volumes.

THE ELEVATION

The elevation of the thirteenth-century church of St-Denis is, generally
speaking, the product of a concern for luminosity, wall texture, lightness of
structure, and the relation of each part to the whole (plate 1). Luminosity is
achieved by the reduction of the flat surface of the wall to an absolute minimum
and the substitution of glass for masonry wherever possible. The unification of
the elevation is brought about by the repetition of forms from one level to the
next and by the continuation of vertical elements through more than one story
(fig. 4 and plate 2). This concern for internal unity leads to a design of the pier as a

grouping of shafts which reflects every aspect of the vaults above. The pier thus forms part of a skeletal framework of shafts, ribs, and arches, between which are stretched the diaphanous web of the clerestory and triforium. But the skeletal character of the elevation does not imply flatness, for at St-Denis the multiplication of forms and the repetition of decorative elements from one level to the next results in a bundling of shafts in the arcade and triforium that creates a richly textured surface.[41] The uninterrupted responds rising from the pier contain the wall of each bay, while the linkage of the triforium and clerestory brings these two upper stories together as a unit within the bay (fig. 4 and plate 17). The linkage and grouping of elements are further enhanced by the continuous emphasis on breadth and depth within the elevation. The aisles are circumnavigated by a wall-passage that sets the aisle windows back in a deeper plane of the outer

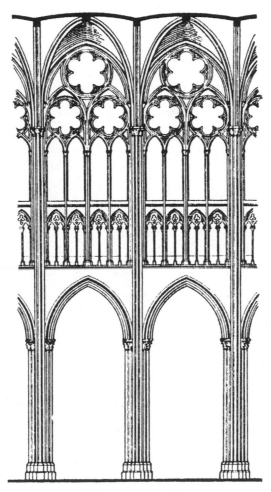

Figure 4. Elevation.

Plate 17. The upper stories of the four easternmost bays on the north side of the nave, from the west.

wall (plate 18). Widely spaced and slender arcade openings enable the lateral volumes of the aisles to define the spatial volumes of the nave, while setting back the triforium and clerestory leads to a slight expansion in width and depth as the eye moves upward (plate 17). This taste for breadth and amplitude is also evident in the large rosettes and short lancets in the clerestory and the broadly pitched vaults. The interpretation of space and the treatment of detail are, as a result, quite different from those in contemporary monuments as Reims, Amiens, and Beauvais. Everything in the design of the elevation of St-Denis bespeaks a rethinking of the standard features of Gothic design and a synthetic approach toward outdated or regional elements, here revived and brought together to create a new vision of architectural space.

The three-story elevation consists of an arcade, triforium, and clerestory, with the arcade equaling somewhat less than half the total height. The compound piers support the shafts under the diagonal and transverse ribs of the main vaults, while the shafts supporting the wall-rib rise only from the base of the triforium, setting back these two stories in a wall plane behind that of the arcade.

The design of the rebuilt thirteenth-century elevation is composed of two parts: the chevet, into which are incorporated the ambulatory and the radiating chapels of Suger's chevet of 1144, and the transept and nave. The latter represent the final, "ideal" design for the rebuilding as conceived in 1231, while the former are dominated by the need to unify the remaining portions of Suger's structure with the new design as it appears elsewhere in the church.

The chevet is composed of three straight bays and a hemicycle and has a three-story elevation. In the two easternmost bays and the hemicycle simple cylindrical piers with attached shafts are used, and in the first bay east of the crossing, a new pier, composed of a cluster of attached shafts around a diamond-shaped core, is introduced (plate 13). The height of the arcade in the hemicycle preserves that of the twelfth-century ambulatory vaults behind, but it gradually increases toward the west where it joins the easternmost aisle of the transept, especially on the north side (plate 19). The triforium in the chevet is tall and narrow, consisting of pairs of trilobed arches enclosed by a larger relieving arch, and it is linked to the clerestory by mullions that rise from between each of the larger triforium arches (plate 19). In the turning bays, the clerestory is composed of two lights and a rosette, a pattern expanded in the straight bays to four lights and three rosettes (plate 20). This four-light window is retained throughout the clerestory in the transept and nave. The simpler design of the turning bays is a reduction of the four-light pattern to the much narrower dimensions of Suger's preserved hemicycle bays below. Likewise, the triforium arcading is reduced to two arches per bay in the closely spaced turning bays, half of the broader pattern of four arches in the wider intervals between the supports to the west. The design of the chevet elevation is thus determined by the existing twelfth-century ambulatory, and the resolved thirteenth-century program intended for the transept and nave is everywhere adjusted to the smaller proportions of Suger's hemicy-

Plate 18. The south aisle from the west.

cle. For all its elegance and refinement, the chevet is therefore composed of a series of compromises and adjustments between the old and the new programs, and the balance achieved between the two gives it a character distinct from that of the remainder of the new church.[42] The "ideal" design as established in the north transept arm was subsequently modified in the south transept arm and south side of the nave. These changes consist in the refinement of details, however, and the interior of the church as a whole is pervaded by a unity of conception and design.

The triforium in the nave continues the pattern established in the straight bays of the chevet: there are four arches per bay, each enclosing two smaller trilobed arches surmounted by a trefoil (plate 17). The pattern of the pointed arches in the triforium is repeated in the tracery of the clerestory, where each smaller pair of lights is surmounted by a large rosette enclosed in a larger arch. The design as a whole is then repeated on a larger scale with a third rosette in the center of the bay. A system of larger arches containing smaller ones is thus preserved in each story, with the openings sharing the same vertical members. But whereas the design of the triforium is essentially horizontal, that of the clerestory, dominated by the broadly opened arch, creates a vast opening in the upper wall surface paralleling that of the arcade below (plate 21). The decorative element in the triforium is the trefoil, a delicate, small-scale motif, while that of the clerestory is the monumental six-lobed rosette.

Particular to the disposition of St-Denis is the design of the aisles, which are enclosed by a blind trilobed arcade that supports a wall-passage placed between the responds and the aisle windows (plate 18). Unfortunately, the insertion of chapels on the north side in the early fourteenth century and the addition of the winter chapel on the south side between 1812 and 1832 obliterated the original thirteenth-century wall.[43] Elsewhere in the church this blind arcading has also been restored, having previously been dismantled when the floor level was raised in the entire church during the restorations of Cellerier and Debret. Fragments in the *dépot lapidaire* at St-Denis and the Percier drawings indicate that Viollet-le-Duc's restoration was accurate, but of course only the general design and not the details is of interest to us here.[44]

Trilobed arcading around the aisles was by no means unique to St-Denis. It existed along the nave of Amiens Cathedral prior to the insertion of chapels and can still be seen along the west walls of the transept and on the interior of the west facade. But at St-Denis the dado arcading is combined with a wall-passage, as is characteristic of Gothic buildings in the Champagne and in Burgundy, and it is conceived as framed by a rectangular molding to which it is attached at the apex of each of the trilobed arches (plate 18).[45] Whereas the arcading at Amiens (where there is no wall-passage) is bonded with the structure of the wall behind, at St-Denis this element is suspended as a screen in front of the wall, echoing its rectangular character with its own frame but elaborating the surface with trilobed arches.

The visual unity of the upper two stories is increased by the glazing of the

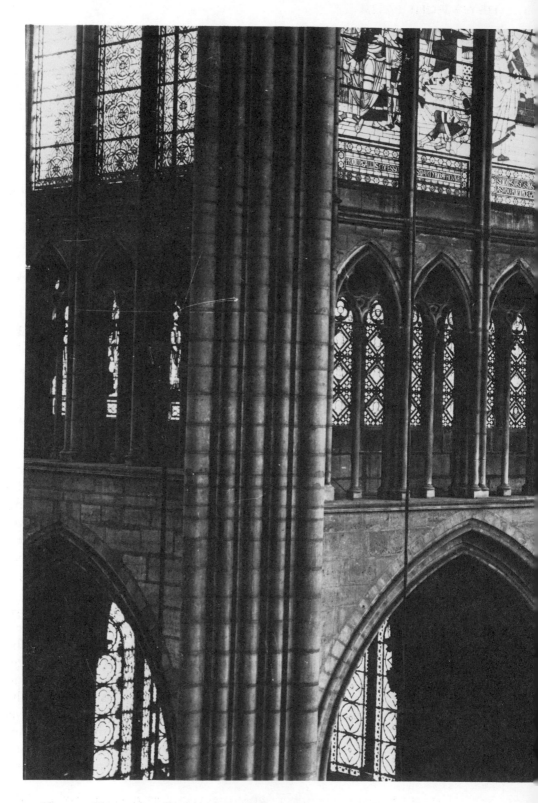

Plate 19. The north wall of the chevet from the west.

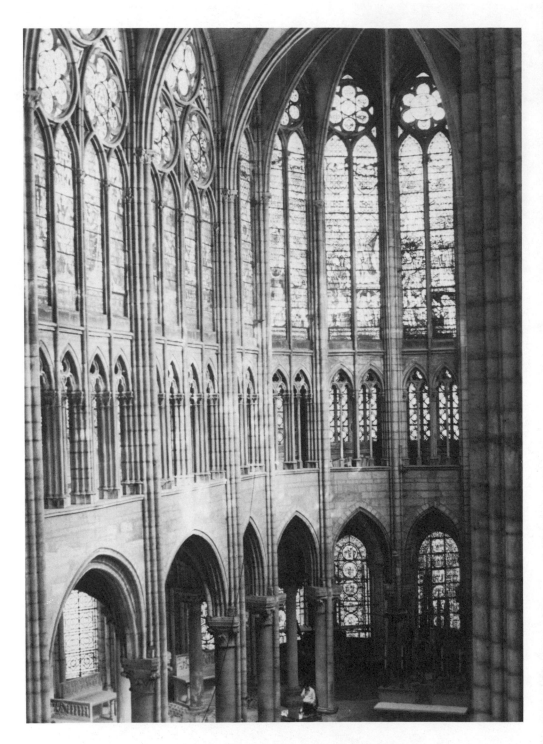

Plate 20. The north side of the chevet from the west.

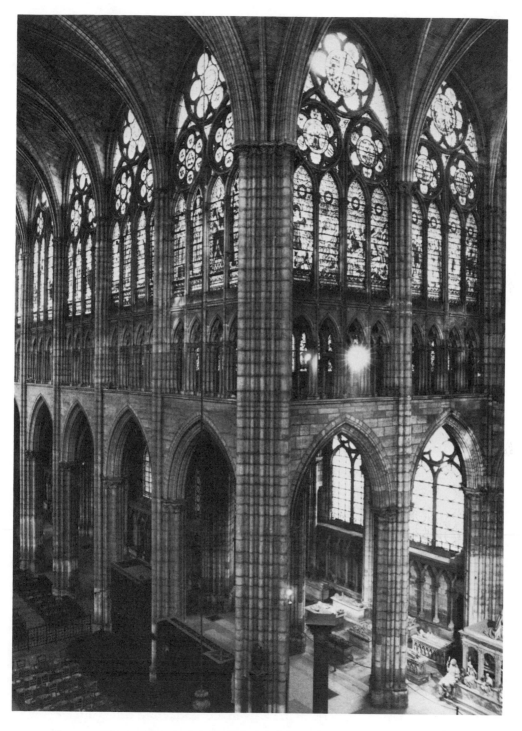

Plate 21. View of the west wall of the north transept arm and north side of the nave from the southeast.

triforium. This was accomplished by detaching the roofs over the aisles from the wall underneath the clerestory and placing openings in the back wall of the triforium that consist of double lancets and an oculus, a simplified version of each pair of trilobed arches on the interior (plates 22 and 23). The glazed triforium at St-Denis is one of the earliest examples of this form in a large-scale building and is executed in modest terms, with the small openings placed high in the back wall. In the eastern bays of the chevet which correspond with Suger's ambulatory they are supported by a relieving arch built underneath them in the wall (plate 20). Although somewhat conservative in its handling compared to the glazed triforia of only a decade later, this feature is one of the most important elements in the total design of St-Denis, as the light entering the interior at this level emphasizes the skeletal structure of the wall.

The innovations in the design extend to the interior walls of the transept terminals, which are now conceived as continuing the pattern of the elevation as a whole. The three large-scale blind arches preserve the height and proportions of the arcade in the aisles on either side (plate 12). Previously, transept terminal walls had generally been designed as separate and distinct surfaces, as at Chartres, Reims, Amiens, and Troyes. But at St-Denis, where the terminal wall was envisioned as a continuation of the elevation as a whole, there is a new approach to the problem. The transept arcade folds across the terminal wall as a pattern of blind arcading, while the triforium passage is slightly modified by the placing of additional trilobes in the spandrels, and the clerestory pattern of lancets and rosettes is transformed into rose windows of magnificent scale.[46] The diameter of the rose exceeds the height of the clerestory and equals the width of the central vessel. The tracery of the transept roses makes reference to the tracery elsewhere in the church by repeating the motifs of the six-lobed rosette and the trefoil arch.

The vaults reflect the difference between the chevet and the rest of the church. A consistent level for the crown of the vaults is maintained throughout the church, but as the main vessel in the chevet is much narrower and the vaults are slightly higher, the ribs to the east rise at a steeper angle than elsewhere (plate 1). Combined with the proportionately taller clerestory lancets and triforium in the chevet, this further heightens the intensity and emphasizes the verticality of this part of the church. The other vaults, however, eschew this steeper angle in favor of a flatter curve that gives the diagonal ribs a semicircular profile. This treatment of the vault enhances the effects of breadth and expansiveness of the nave and echoes the proportions of the lancets and rosettes in the clerestory.

The treatment of the vaults is intrinsic to the effect of the interior as a whole and must be counted among the most important spatial characteristics of this church. Instead of the steeply pointed vaults of Reims and Amiens, those at St-Denis deemphasize the vertical in favor of a broader and fuller interpretation of the interior volume, reminiscent of the spaciousness of the Early Gothic vaults of Sens Cathedral, for example.

The exterior of the thirteenth-century church of St-Denis is dominated

Plate 22. Exterior, the east wall of the north transept arm.

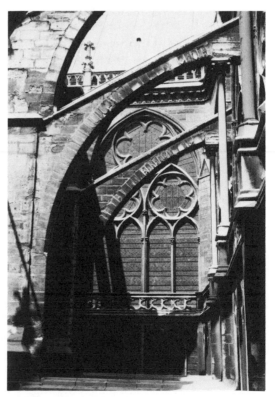

Plate 23. Exterior, the east wall of the south transept arm.

by the towers that flank the transept and support the fliers in the two bays of the transept and nave (plate 11). The buttresses in the chevet are planted above the spurs of wall that protrude between the radiating chapels (plate 24). Their slender proportions and flat, undecorated surfaces are determined by the slender twelfth-century wall buttresses on which they are planted.[47] The fliers consist of two levels of arches, the lower of which corresponds to the springing of the vaults and the upper of which rests against the wall beneath the roof. The flying buttresses in the straight bays of the chevet are supported by the eastern transept towers. On the north side the tower is part of the first program and is strikingly simple and austere in design (plates 11 and 24). Although it may seem awkward and incongruous in relation to the other three, more elaborate transept towers, the thin, flat surfaces of this tower are closely related to those of the flying buttresses around the chevet and, as will be seen in the following chapter, form part of the same campaign. On the west side of the north transept arm, the tower is considerably more ornate, with double lancet openings defined by a series of shafts and torus moldings on each of the four sides (plate 25). The southeast tower is similar to that on the northwest, but with polygonal shafts, and the one on the southwest returns to the rounded shafts of the northwest tower. The engraving of the abbey in *Monasticon gallicanum* indicates a raised roof over the southwestern tower of the type that frequently contained bells (plate 9),[48] and indeed, the inner walls at the top of this tower, unlike the other three, are canted outward to support a floor or heavy wooden truss for bells. All four transept towers have undergone complete restoration in the nineteenth-century, however-er, and most of the original features of their design and decoration are lost. As the moldings and capitals have been replaced, it is not worthwhile to discuss these features of the towers in greater detail.

The buttresses west of the towers and along the nave are different and far more elaborate in character than those around the chevet (plate 26). Although they could be interpreted as the design of another architect, it should be recalled that the slender, austere disposition of the eastern buttresses is determined by their placement above the spurs of twelfth-century wall buttresses. The nave buttresses were also completely restored by Debret and to a lesser extent by Viollet-le-Duc, but the restoration closely follows the original design. The up-permost part of each buttress is decorated with a pattern of blind, pointed, trilobed arches supported by detached colonettes and enclosed above by gables decorated by crockets and pierced by a small trilobe. The design is close to that of the rebuilt buttresses on the exterior of the chevet of Meaux as well as to some of the buttresses erected around the choir of Beauvais.[49] The octagonal pinnacle above each buttress echoes the design below by repeating the pattern of trilobed arches beneath gables, between each of which protrudes a small, grotesque figure. The conical roof is decorated with crockets.

The delicacy of the design of these buttresses is in keeping with a fully developed Rayonnant Gothic esthetic, and it is no coincidence that they begin in the third pier west of the crossing, where there were interruptions in the work

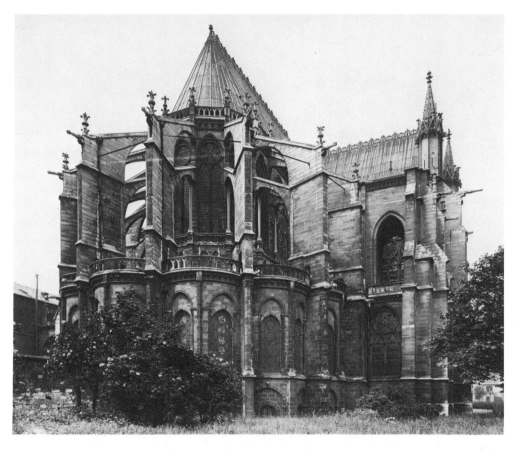

Plate 24. Exterior, the chevet from the east.

on both sides of the nave. The buttresses here are thus part of the new program begun in 1259 under Mathieu de Vendôme and are one of the few instances of a significant change in design from the original program.[50] In fact, the new disposition of the buttresses echoes the decoration of the upper transept facades, which culminate in pierced gables flanked by octagonal pinnacles (plate 25), larger versions of the small pinnacles that sit above the five Rayonnant buttresses on either side of the nave.[51]

The exteriors of the transept facades have already been mentioned in conjunction with the transept towers and more recently in connection with the pinnacles above the nave buttresses (plate 11). As an ensemble, they represent a new departure in the design of transept terminal walls and are the model for the transept facades of Notre-Dame, the northern one of which was begun about fifteen years later in 1250. At St-Denis the north transept arm (plate 25) is earlier and somewhat simpler in design than its counterpart to the south (plate 27). The northern transept rose is flanked by plain wall buttresses, the western one containing a stair tower. Wall-passages pass in front and in back of the rose—a

Plate 25. Exterior, the north transept arm.

Plate 26. Exterior, buttress on the north side of the nave.

Plate 27. Exterior, south transept rose.

doubling of the wall characteristic of monuments in the Aisne (Soissons, Laon, Longpont). The gable above is decorated with a blind rose composed of circles and trefoils and is flanked on either side by octagonal pinnacles that are the point of departure for the design of the upper parts of the buttresses along the nave. On the south side, the rose is flanked by two large-scale figures of kings carved within niches placed in the wall buttresses on either side of the rose (plate 27), and the gable is decorated with a large, rounded triangle of the type found in the west end of the aisles of Amiens and at the Ste-Chapelle.[52] As with the other parts of the exterior, these elements were completely restored in the early nineteenth century and are undergoing a second (in some cases a third) restoration at present.

Perhaps the most striking aspect of the transept terminals, aside from the detached towers, is the design of the rose windows. On the north side, the rose consists of trilobed arches that radiate from a central rosette, each then doubled in a second range of trilobed lancets (plate 25).[53] The outermost row is composed of a series of six-lobed rosettes that echo the central rose. The whole is contained in a square frame, with the spandrels filled with a glazed pattern of circles and trefoils on the bottom, repeated as blind tracery above. The rosettes with six lobes echo the design of the rosettes in the clerestory windows.

On the south side, the transept rose might be considered more archaic in style; it is a larger-scale repetition of the rose window in the palace chapel of St-Germain-en-Laye (plates 27 and 60). Here the design is essentially centripetal rather than centrifugal, for the trefoils around the circumference alternate with shafts that support arches that narrow as they converge toward the center. These are followed by a ring of six-lobed rosettes, each enclosed by spokes that radiate from the central rosette. Whereas the design of the rose on the north transept seems to emerge from the center, that of the south rose seems to move from the outside in. The latter takes its inspiration from the roses in the east and west walls of Laon and at Mantes, whereas the former seems to have been inspired by the rose in the west facade of Notre-Dame in Paris, probably under construction in the 1220s.[54] The north rose at St-Denis served subsequently as the inspiration for both transept roses at the cathedral of Paris.

The relationship between the design of the rose windows at St-Denis and at Notre-Dame is not limited simply to the tracery patterns. In both churches, the rose windows are set in a square, a design that seems to have been introduced first in the harmonic and balanced west facade of Notre-Dame in Paris. At the cathedral, the west rose is set in the square frame created by the horizontals and verticals inherent in the facade itself; the importance of the rectilinear frame for the rose is emphasized by the blind trefoils that are placed in the spandrels. At St-Denis, this approach is carried much further, with a more intimate and explicit relationship established between the circle and the square by the use of moldings to outline the enclosing frame and unite the two elements. Furthermore, the spandrels are now filled with tracery, and it is made clear that the rose is no longer conceived as an isolated element but rather as part of a larger rectilinear scheme, related in its proportions to other parts of the transept. This new treatment is emphasized by the narrow glazed band of the triforium, which continues across the terminal wall, so that the entire surface above the flat wall of the arcade level becomes a thin screen permeated by light (plate 12). The importance of this new approach is emphasized on the interior as well, for the transverse arch of the ribs is detached from the terminal wall, which continues upward to create the top of the square. Within a few years this feature was used at St-Germain-en-Laye and applied to the entire interior, with the vaults everywhere detached from the enclosing shell.[55] The square thus exists not only as a discrete unit on the exterior, but also as an active force on the interior, detaching the vaults of the transept from the terminal wall (plates 12 and 25).[56] These square units of the transept roses represent one of the modules of the interior proportions as a whole.

SCULPTURAL DECORATION

At St-Denis sculptural decoration plays a minor role in the interior. The carved surfaces of the capitals are secondary to the continuity of the architectural elements, such as the responds in the nave that rise without interruption to the springing of the vaults (plate 2). Capitals appear only at points of transition from vertical to curving surfaces; everywhere else, sculptural decoration is eliminated in favor of the architectural endoskeleton. Nowhere in St-Denis is there a counterpart to the richly modeled foliate capital that appears at Reims or the ornate floral rinceau beneath the triforium at Amiens.

St-Denis thus presents an attitude toward the relationship between architecture and decorative sculpture that is fundamentally different from that of the High Gothic monuments of the preceding decades. The austerity of the decoration recalls instead some of the churches of the preceding century in which sculptural decoration was subdued in favor of a tight linear system, as in the transept of Noyon Cathedral and the nave of Notre-Dame in Paris. The return to this type of decorative austerity establishes a shift in the relationship of architecture to sculpture: it is now the architectural elements themselves that are elaborated and that become inherently decorative, with the earlier system of pointed openings in the triforium transformed into trefoil arches and trilobes, and a dramatic elaboration of the pattern of the tracery in the clerestory. Sculpture has little place in the elaboration of surfaces; architecture itself takes over. Nowhere is this translation in the idiom of decoration more emphatically developed than in the transept facades of Notre-Dame, constructed in the middle of the thirteenth century. St-Denis represents an earlier stage of this change of interest but may be the first program in which the design is affected in the most fundamental way by this new sensibility in Rayonnant Gothic.

A certain restraint in the use of decorative sculpture may indeed have been indigenous to Paris and its environs. Certainly the cathedral of Paris and a number of smaller churches (for example, Larchant, Champeaux, and the chevet

Plate 28. The ambulatories and hemicycle on the north side of the chevet from the west.

of Gonesse) are characterized by an austerity in sculptural decoration.[57] Although the general occurrence of this phenomenon in the middle of the thirteenth century has been interpreted as a reflection of a certain Cistercian influence on the architecture of the time,[58] it seems much more plausible that the restrained treatment of capitals and other sculptural elements evolves from a new attitude toward architecture itself that ultimately derives from the invention of bar tracery. This attitude—like Rayonnant Gothic itself—has its origins in Paris.

Where sculptural decoration does occur at St-Denis, it has a tectonic quality, particularly in the early phases of construction. At St-Denis, the treatment of capitals can be divided essentially into seven groups which correspond with the campaigns of construction.

The first type is the simple crocket capital found primarily in the chevet and in the north transept arm (plates 28 and 29). Relatively long and attenuated leaves with pronounced spines rise from the astragal to the impost, where they swell into small and compact crockets. At times, the terminations are decorated with small flowers or with fernlike spirals. The base of the leaf is often notched at a point only slightly above the astragal, and the surface of the leaf is sometimes striated and sometimes carved as a flat and smooth surface (plate 29). The position of the crockets reinforces the angles of the abacus; this is striking not only in

Plate 29. Triforium capitals, chevet, bay 6N–7N.

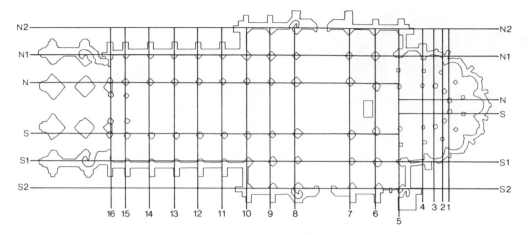

Figure 5. Schematic plan with designation of piers.

the small capitals of the triforium, but also in the large and monumental capitals in the piers of the hemicycle. The capitals in the hemicycle have broadly modeled and substantial crockets or leaves emerging from the astragal (plate 28). The positioning of the rolled ends of the crockets emphasizes the corners, and the ribbing of crockets and leaves picks up the strong modeling of the ribs in the ambulatory vaults and the moldings of the arcade, transmitting their downward thrust into the broad and sturdy forms of the piers below. Their simple forms are calculated to balance the large abaci above the solid columnar piers; they contrast vividly with the more elaborate and complex capitals of the intermediate supports in the ambulatory. In the triforium, the capitals are very similar to those in the dado arcading of the west side of the transept and against the west facade at Amiens, generally dated between 1230 and 1233.[59]

In the western bays of the chevet, the north transept arm, and the three eastern bays of the north side of the nave, this austere crocket style is mixed in with and often elaborated by a decoration of smaller leaves (plate 30). In the triforium at times the crockets themselves are treated as one long leaf that sweeps upward from the astragal to the impost (plates 31 and 32). More frequently, smaller leaves spring from the astragal in between each of the crockets, filling in the intervals with a lighter and more decorative motif. Even in this early group the small leaves tend to adhere to the curvature of the capital beneath (plate 29).

In the triforium of the south transept arm, in the south transept portal, and in the first three bays on the south side of the nave, these first two types become mixed with a more delicately cut and ornate leaf and crocket type (plates 33–35). The latter are distinguished from the earlier group by the undercutting of the leaves and their relative independence from the core of the capital. The most elaborate capitals in this area (plate 36) are close to those in the straight bays of the chevet of Amiens and to some of those in the Ste-Chapelle. At the same

Plate 30. Respond and capitals on the north side of the chevet, first compound pier east of the crossing (6N).

Plate 31. Triforium capitals, north transept arm, north wall.

Plate 32. Triforium capitals, north side of the nave, bay 9N–10N.

Plate 33. Triforium capital, south transept arm, west wall.

Plate 34. Triforium capitals, south transept arm, south wall.

Plate 35. South side of the nave, arcade capitals of pier 11S.

Plate 36. Triforium capital, south side
of the nave, bay 10S–11S.

time, the simple austere crocket type is preserved. Some badly weathered counterparts still survive in the remains of the Virgin Chapel of St-Germain-des-Prés,
constructed beginning about 1245.[60]

In the triforium of the central bays on the south side of the nave and
nowhere else at St-Denis there are some examples of a type of capital that became
popular around 1250. Consisting of a long leaf, the top of which turns inward as
though to enclose the abacus (plate 37), they are similar to some of the capitals
that appear in the crossing and north transept portal in the cathedral of Châlons-
sur-Marne, dated by Ravaux to circa 1249–61, and in the reworked straight bays
at Meaux, dated by Kurmann to circa 1253–75.[61]

Another type of capital that makes its appearance in the triforium of the
south side of the nave is what I call the rollmops capital, in which the leaves of the
crocket are rolled into a tight ball (plate 38). These too appear in other mid-
thirteenth-century structures, among them the cathedral of Châlons, in the
crossing as well as in the much-restored dado arcading in the nave.[62]

In the arcade on the south side of the nave of St-Denis, beginning with
the fourth pier west of the crossing and the aisle responds on the north side of the
nave (plate 39), and occasionally in the triforium, there is a return to the simple
crocket capital, but the forms are now treated in a harsher manner, with two
levels of crockets and strongly striated and stretched leaves that depart from the
astragal at an urgently oblique angle. These crocket capitals differ markedly

Plate 37. Triforium capital, south side
of the nave, bay 12S–13S.

Plate 38. Triforium capital, south side
of the nave, bay 9S–10S.

Plate 39. South side of the nave, arcade capitals of pier 12S.

from their predecessors in the chevet in the dry, crisp cutting of the stone and are very similar to a late capital at Notre-Dame (plate 40).

The final two groups are related to each other and can be seen in the west bays of the nave on the north side and in the triforium in bays 11–15 on the north and south (plates 41 and 42). Here the earlier principles of an essentially tectonic decoration are abandoned in favor of a simplified treatment of large, heavy leaf forms that create a strongly shadowed and vibrating surface. The first type is developed from the crocket capital. The forms culminate in roughly shaped, bulbous, leaflike forms that have a rather heavy appearance (plates 43 and 44). The contrast between the smooth surface of the lower third and the rounded forms above is deliberate and very striking. The leaves are deeply undercut and tend to establish a complex, heavily modeled surface that is parallel with that of the core of the capital inside.

The final type, found in a number of monuments of the third quarter of the thirteenth century, consists of small leaves and stems floating haphazardly on the surface of the capital (plate 45). Any pretense of continuity and order in the relationship of the capital to the abacus above is now abandoned in favor of a free-floating and deeply undercut surface. Similar capitals appear in the eastern parts of St-Urbain at Troyes and in the entrance to the chapel at St-Germer-de-Fly.[63]

Plate 40. Paris, Notre–Dame, capital of the first intermediate pier from west, north side of ambulatory.

Plate 41. Respond and capitals at 12N.

Plate 42. North side of the nave, arcade capitals of pier 14N.

Plate 43. Triforium capitals, north side of the nave, bay 13N–14N.

Plate 44. Triforium arcade, south side of the nave, bay 14S–15S.

Plate 45. Triforium capitals, north side of the nave, bay 11N–12N.

These different types of capitals coexist to some extent, except in the west bays of the nave, where there was a significant interruption of construction. This mixture of capital types results in part from the fact that a number of sculptors were working simultaneously, some with modern and some with archaic designs, and in part because some carved pieces remained in the workshop during an interruption of construction, not to be installed until the work began again. Earlier forms are thus often mixed in with later ones. Long interruptions, however, may well have resulted in the rejection of the older elements in favor of modern types of decoration. In the last two campaigns, for example, there are no capitals from the earlier program.

The design and planting of the abaci throughout the church change in accordance with the sequence of construction. This variation is particularly striking in the triforium and the clerestory, where much greater flexibility was permitted than in the arcade below.[64] Throughout the chevet, the north transept arm, and the three eastern bays of the nave, the abaci of the isolated shafts in the triforium are planted on the diagonal (plate 19), even though the plinths are parallel with the main axis of the church. Throughout this first part of the rebuilding, the abaci in the clerestory are consistently round (plate 20), as they are also at Reims Cathedral and at the palace chapel at St-Germain-en-Laye (plates 60 and 61).[65] In the east wall of the south transept arm, however, the abaci in the triforium and in the clerestory are planted diagonally, a disposition which continues throughout the south transept arm and the three eastern bays on the south side of the nave (plates 58, 59, and 63). The setting of the plinths is now also diagonal, and there is a complete consistency in the handling of these elements in the two upper stories of the elevation. The last phase of the work at St-Denis, in the five western bays of the nave, is characterized by the adoption of polygonal abaci in the triforium (plates 37 and 44), and the plinths are once again parallel with the axis of the nave. In the clerestory, the change in the tracery pattern means that the capitals of the central mullions are all at the same level and are now crowned with one star-shaped abacus.

The badly mutilated portal on the south transept arm (plates 46 and 47), the only thirteenth-century portal at St-Denis, presents a series of stylistic and iconographic problems that are beyond the scope of this study.[66] However, its design and decoration, with a low dado arcade of blind trefoil arches (the flat surfaces of which are decorated with the fleur-de-lys and castles of Castile), is consistent with the dominant architectural motif of the trefoil arch on the interior (plate 18). The doorjambs consist of thin, detached shafts alternating with concave recesses richly decorated with deeply cut, delicate ornament of leaves, vines, crockets, and fleur-de-lys (plate 47). Even in its severely damaged state, the quality of the carving is impressive. The capitals consist of crockets decorated with a profusion of leaves which spring up from the astragal and unite the capitals into a continuous undulating frieze.

The doorway is unusual in its rejection of both statue columns and tympanum[67] and stands early in a series of mid-thirteenth-century Parisian por-

Plate 46. The south transept portal.

Plate 47. The south transept portal, left jamb.

tals of the same type. The first of these is perhaps that of the palace chapel at St-Germain-en-Laye, probably carved between 1234 and 1238.[68] After the portal of St-Denis, which can be dated to the early 1240s,[69] the new type is adopted by Pierre de Montreuil in the portal of the Virgin Chapel at St-Germain-des-Prés, recently installed in the interior of the Cluny Museum in Paris (plate 74), and in the Porte Rouge of Notre-Dame.[70] Similar portals exist also in smaller churches in the area of Paris, for example, at Gonesse.

BASE PROFILES AND MOLDINGS

A discussion of the base profiles at St-Denis must be limited by and large to those in the hemicycle on the arcade level and in the triforium, as the changes in the floor levels of the nave and transept in the early nineteenth century obliterated original bases elsewhere. Nonetheless, the treatment of base profiles can be divided into five groups, again corresponding roughly with different building campaigns. But the significance of such distinctions is relative indeed; as Ravaux has recently pointed out in an article on Reims Cathedral, different types of base profiles are often deliberately incorporated into the design of the building depending on the context and scale of the architectural elements.[71] At Chartres, for example, bases with a rounded upper torus and bases with a depressed upper torus alternate in each pier with its attached shafts.

The thirteenth-century bases of the chevet at St-Denis consist of a high, depressed upper torus followed by a fillet, a relatively deep cavet followed by a second fillet, and a somewhat flattened lower torus that projects beyond the plinth below (figs. 6–8). Though the angle of torus and fillet varies slightly in each base, the profiles of the bases in the chevet form an essentially homogeneous group.[72]

In the triforium, the bases are by and large of a simpler type, as the cavet is usually eliminated (except in bays 1N–5N, the earliest phase of the work on this level), though occasionally replaced by beading. More often, the concave upper torus is followed by a small fillet in the center above a larger and strongly projecting lower torus. Bases of this type appear in the chevet and in the north transept arm (figs. 9–11).

In the three eastern bays on the north side of the nave and in the south transept arm, the bases undergo a subtle change: the general effect flattens and there are on occasion fillets and a shallow cavet also on the plinth beneath the base (fig. 12). The profiles here tend to be slightly more fluid and horizontal and are identical to those original bases preserved in the palace chapel at St-Germain-en-Laye, dated between 1234 and 1238 (fig. 13). Indeed, the similarities among some of the bases are so striking that it is tempting to assume that the same templates may have been used in both places (figs. 10–13).[73]

In the eastern bays on the south side of the nave, the fillet between the two tori begins to be eliminated; on occasion it is replaced by a slender notch. As

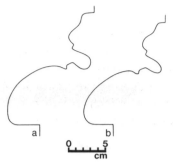

Figure 6. Base profiles, chevet hemicycle: (a) 2N; (b) 2S.

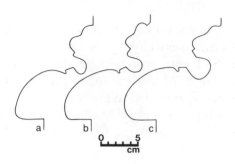

Figure 7. Base profiles, chevet: (a) 5S, east face; (b) 5S, west face; (c) 5N.

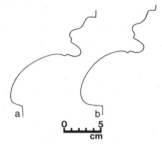

Figure 8. Base profiles, chevet: (a) 6N, north face; (b) 6N, west face.

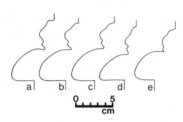

Figure 9. Base profiles, chevet triforium: (a–c) bay 1N–2N; (d, e) bay 1N–1S (axial bay).

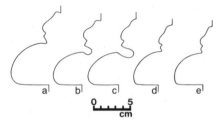

Figure 10. Base profiles, chevet triforium: (a) bay 5N–6N; (b) bay 4N–5N; (c–e) bay 3N–4N.

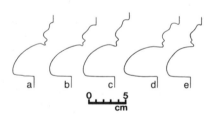

Figure 11. Base profiles, triforium: (a–d) north transept arm, east wall; (e) chevet, bay 6N–7N.

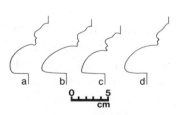

Figure 12. Base profiles, triforium of the nave: (a, b) bay 10N–11N; (c, d) bay 9N–10N.

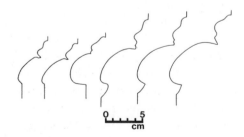

Figure 13. Bases from the chapel at St-Germain-en-Laye, unrestored, from window responds and dado arcading.

the nave moves east to west, this notch is eliminated completely (figs. 14–18), and the concave upper torus and convex lower torus simply abut, with the profile as a whole acquiring a flattened or slouching profile characteristic of the third quarter of the thirteenth century. Profiles of this type can be seen on the much-restored tomb of Dagobert at St-Denis (fig. 19), as well as at St-Urbain at Troyes, in the transepts of Notre-Dame, and in the reworked parts of the chevet at Meaux Cathedral. They also appear in the passageway to the Ste-Chapelle at St-Germer-de-Fly, which also dates to the late 1260s and 1270s.

The base profiles accord with the campaigns of construction suggested by the sculptural decoration described above, in general proceeding from the earliest forms in the chevet and north transept arm through the three eastern bays on the north side of the nave, the south transept arm, and finally, the south side of the nave. The latest forms can be found in the western bays on both sides of the nave.

Molding and rib profiles are, on the whole, standard for the time, with double-roll moldings in the arcade of the nave and transept (figs. 20 and 21) and slender rib profiles of a central torus flanked by fillets, cavets, and tori. There is, however, one significant exception to this standard pattern of profiles. In the chevet, the arcading above the cylindrical supports consists of four torus mold-ings separated by cavets (plate 28 and fig. 22). In the westernmost bays on each side, however, the double-roll molding is introduced. Although the presence of two types of arcade molding in the chevet may seem curious—and has been one reason for attributing the early stages of construction of the thirteenth-century church to two architects—it is in fact the only possible solution for the arcade molding in this part of the church. As will be demonstrated in the next chapter, the abaci above the cylindrical piers in the chevet are twelfth-century, thus determining to a large extent the form of the piers below (cylindrical rather than compound) and providing a limited surface from which the arches of the arcade can spring. In order to create a molding with visual interest that would fit on top of the older abacus, the architect at St-Denis adopted a profile that would project very little from the inner surface of the arcade. This solution has the happy effect of creating a consistent bundling of rounded forms that fits in well with the shafts rising from the pier to the springing of the vaults (plate 28). It also raises the height of the arcade almost to the level of the intrados of the twelfth-century vaults behind them, thus opening the hemicycle as much as possible to the ambulatory behind. As a result, the relationship between the new parts of the chevet and the older twelfth-century ambulatory and radiating chapels behind is singularly harmonious.

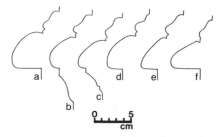

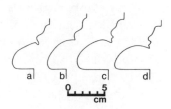

Figure 14. Base profiles, triforium: (a–d) south transept arm, east wall; (e, f) chevet, bay 6S–7S.

Figure 15. Base profiles, triforium of the nave: (a) bay 9S–10S; (b–d) bay 8S–9S.

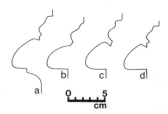

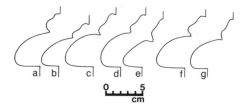

Figure 16. Base profiles, triforium of the nave: (a–d) bay 10S–11S.

Figure 17. Base profiles, triforium of the nave: (a–c) bay 14N–15N; (d–f) bay 13N–14N; (g) bay 12N–13N.

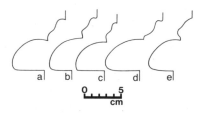

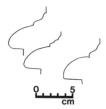

Figure 18. Base profiles, triforium of the nave: (a) bay 13S–14S; (b, c) bay 12S–13S; (d, e) bay 11S–12S.

Figure 19. Base profiles, tomb of Dagobert.

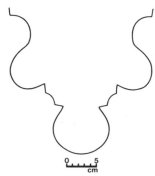

Figure 20. Diagonal rib in the thirteenth-century aisle vaults of the chevet.

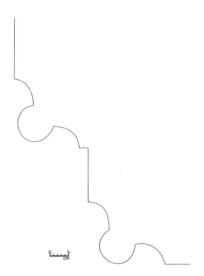

Figure 21. Arcade molding in the straight
bays of the chevet.

Figure 22. Torus molding of the hemicycle arcading in the chevet.

MEASUREMENTS AND PROPORTIONS*

The measurements of the thirteenth-century church are closely related to
those of the surviving parts of Abbot Suger's chevet and the two bays of his
narthex. As the discussion below will indicate, the new church was planned
from the start with the concordance between the new and the old structures as
the point of departure. The proportions of the interior do not, therefore, conform to a simple system of ratios between arcade, triforium, and clerestory, as
do the interior proportions at Chartres (where the height of the arcade equals that
of the clerestory), or Amiens (where the height of the arcade equals that of the
triforium and clerestory combined). At St-Denis, the vaults of the north and
south aisles of Suger's twelfth-century western bays determine the approximate
height of the thirteenth-century arcade. In the chevet, the arcade is gradually

*The following discussion is calculated on the basis of the present floor level in the interior,
which corresponds within several centimeters to the original level in the thirteenth-century building. Unless noted otherwise, the measurements include the framing moldings.

adjusted upward to move from the modest proportions of the original hemicycle to the larger ones of the thirteenth-century nave and transept (plate 13). In addition, the change in floor levels from the chevet to the transept adds 2.52 meters to the height of the elevation as a whole. Furthermore, the main vaults of the nave are only 4 meters higher than those of the central upper chapel in Suger's west facade, which prior to the installation of the nineteenth-century organ was visible (along with the rose window in the west facade) from the nave.[74] Thus the principles of unity and concordance explored above in terms of the interior design of the elevation as a whole also emerge in the proportions of the new church.

The point of departure for the proportions may well have been the interval between the western columns of Suger's chevet, which from center to center measure 10.50 meters. This unit is used for the height of the clerestory windows. The triforium equals one-third of the height of the clerestory, 3.50 meters, which also equals the height of the (restored) dado arcading in the aisles.

These dimensions are multiples of the "royal foot," variously defined as 32.47, 32.5, and 32.8 centimeters.[75] This unit, when multiplied by eleven, gives the dimension of 3.50 meters used for the height of the triforium and dado arcading.[76]

The total width of the nave equals the height of the vaults, which, though varying slightly from bay to bay, average 27 meters to the intrados of the keystone.[77] The aisles of the nave are half the width of the main vessel, which measures 13.30 meters from the centers of the piers. The aisle bays in the nave are thus slightly rectangular, measuring 6.08 meters east-west and 6.64 meters north-south.

As Crosby has pointed out in his discussion of the thirteenth-century church in L'Abbaye royale de Saint-Denis, the crossing is a great square, as is the transept as a whole (fig. 1).[78] The transept can be divided into nine equal squares, with the size of the bays and location of the piers determined by the three spatial units and the diagonals. From the centers of the crossing piers, the central space of the crossing measures 13 meters, but measured between the outer responds on the four main axes, the dimension is 12.20 meters. The latter figure corresponds to the height of the arcade in the transept and nave to the base of the triforium string-course and is repeated in the square frames of the transept roses, as well as in the height of the blind arcading of the lower half of the transept terminal wall below (plate 12). The square unit is repeated down the nave, as two bays of the arcade equal its height.

The rose windows rise higher than the clerestory windows (plate 12). But this difference in height is concealed because the transept terminal walls are detached from the vaults, so that the upper molding of the square frame rises above that of the transverse arch at the extremities of the transept.

The height of the triforium, about 3.50 meters in the transept and the nave, represents one-third of the height of the clerestory, as noted above. A division of the clerestory into thirds is, in fact, suggested in its tracery. The height of the triforium equals that of the shafts of the clerestory lights, 3.60 meters, a unit repeated twice more to include the tops of the lancets and the rosettes. As has been already stated, this dimension is repeated in the height of the dado arcading, and the correspondence between these two stories is further emphasized by the repetition of the pattern trilobed arcading. Furthermore, the same unit, 3.60 meters, established the width of each of the blind arches and of the portal in the south transept terminal wall (the different measurements on the north result from the incorporation of the older Valois door).

These proportions give the interior volumes at St-Denis a special character, setting this monument apart from other large-scale churches built in the early thirteenth century. The explicit rejection of verticality (Chartres, begun thirty years before, is ten meters taller) and the exploitation of lateral spaciousness result from the use of the square as the dominant unit: two bays of the nave equal the width of the main vessel between the outer responds, which in turn equals the dominant units of the crossing and transept. Most important, the total height of the vaults equals the total width of the building. These proportions indicate a fundamentally different approach from that in the recently begun cathedrals of Amiens and Reims. There is, then, not only a particular character to the elevation of St-Denis as a whole, with its sympathetic relation to earlier, twelfth-century structures, but also a profoundly different premise behind the formulation of the interior proportions.

As it has often been suggested that the early reconstruction at St-Denis is the work of two architects, it is important to note here that the correspondence of the vertical and horizontal measurements indicates that these two aspects of the design were considered simultaneously, that is, in my view, by the same architect. The unity between the old and the new work that is evident in the structure also emerges in the dimensions. The architect at St-Denis used the remaining parts of the structure erected by Suger as his point of departure for a new proportional system based on a tight correlation between the vertical and horizontal units. Thus the interval of 10.50 meters for the width of the twelfth-century main vessel as well as the width of 3.50 meters found in Suger's ambulatories is echoed in the disposition of the new church. Furthermore, the height of the arcade, 12.20 meters to the base of the triforium string-course, is close to the height of the central arch of Suger's twelfth-century narthex (12.70 meters), so that there was a harmonious junction between the new nave and the older western bays.

The proportions as established at the beginning of the reconstruction in 1231 were followed throughout the building, and a unity of conception pervades all aspects of the monument. The actual process by which the church was constructed, the working out of details, and the chronology of construction are the subject of the following chapters.

4 ❖

Construction

T HIS CHAPTER CONSIDERS THE SEQUENCE OF CONSTRUCTION AS REVEALED BY
the architectural evidence. Insofar as possible, I have attempted to recreate
the conditions that confronted the first architect and then his successors as they
undertook the various stages of the reconstruction: namely, what choices did the
retention of Suger's ambulatory and radiating chapels impose on the design as a
whole and on the earliest phases of the reconstruction? Why was work concentrated on certain parts of the church before others? What changes did the architects make during the process of reconstruction, and why? In order not to
obfuscate the evidence provided by the masonry itself, the dating of the campaigns between the beginning of the work in 1231[1] and the consecration of the
church in 1281 will be considered in the following chapter, in conjunction with a
discussion of the written documents.

THE HEMICYCLE

Prior to the reconstruction of the chevet, the upper stories of Suger's
work above the arcade were dismantled to the level of the arcade abaci, but the
ambulatory vaults supported by these abaci were kept in place.[2] It is reasonable
to suppose that at this point the Carolingian nave was closed off by a temporary
screen at either the eastern or the western crossing piers, so that services could
continue without interruption. Since the early campaign, as we shall see, comprised the chevet and north transept arm, it is probable that all of Suger's work
west of the easternmost straight bay of the chevet on the north side of the church
was also demolished, along with whatever survived of the Carolingian north
transept arm (fig. 23).[3]

It has been suggested that the upper stories of Suger's chevet were pulled
down because they were in poor condition. This theory is based on two considerations: Abbot Eudes' statement in a document of 1241 that the church was
rebuilt because the old one threatened ruin, and the physical evidence of the
reconstructed crypt and hemicycle piers.[4]

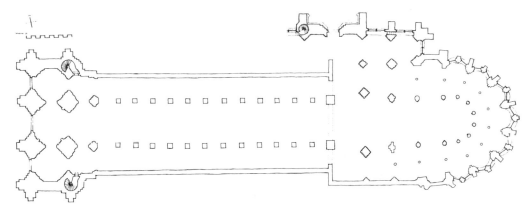

Figure 23. Plan of the church during the first stages of reconstruction, with the Carolingian nave intact.

The argument implies that had the upper stories of the twelfth-century church been stable, they would have been preserved in the new church. But Eudes makes no distinction in the documents between Suger's structure and the Carolingian nave, and the insertion of new piers in the chevet and crypt does not necessarily mean that their predecessors provided inadequate support in the building for which they were designed.[5] As the Carolingian nave was already crumbling in Suger's day, it is possible that Eudes may have been referring to the old nave, not to Suger's chevet.[6] The remaining parts of the chevet presently contain no indications of structural instability which would account for the reconstruction, and Suger himself attested to the solidity of his structure when he described the unfinished twelfth-century vaults as withstanding gale force winds.[7] There is thus little reason to assume that the upper parts of Suger's chevet were in a state of imminent collapse less than a century after their completion. The only possible evidence to the contrary is provided by the documents: the *Grandes Chroniques de France* states that the church was reconstructed because the vaults were collapsing.[8] As the Carolingian basilica had a wooden roof, those vaults can only have been Suger's. However, Suger of course erected vaults in the west end of the church as well as at its east end, and indeed several of these were rebuilt in the thirteenth century. Furthermore, the text in the *Grandes Chroniques* is derived from the terser description of Guillaume de Nangis, who makes no reference to vaults.[9]

Whatever the condition of Suger's chevet, it seems highly probable that the upper stories were rebuilt in the interests of internal homogeneity. The principles of harmony and unity of design are, after all, among the dominant characteristics of the plan and elevation, as has been indicated in the preceding chapter. Suger's ambulatory and radiating chapels were preserved because they did not interfere with the homogeneity of the main vessel, concealed as they are behind the arcade of the hemicycle (plate 13). On the other hand, the upper stories of the twelfth-century chevet must have appeared low and dark compared to the projected design for the transept and nave. If the ancient Carolingian structure was to be replaced at long last, it would have seemed incongruous indeed to permit the area of the altar and sanctuary, in every sense the culmination of the interior vessel, to be the least impressive part of the church.

Though little can be said about the elevation erected in the twelfth-century and dismantled in the thirteenth,[10] it can be assumed that the twelfth-century main vaults would have been considerably lower than those erected in the thirteenth century.[11] The new hemicycle piers were therefore inserted to support a taller structure. It is also probable that the original supports of the chevet arcade were monoliths, like those in the surviving twelfth-century intermediate supports in the ambulatory of St-Denis itself (plate 28) as well as in the chevets of Senlis, Noyon, Mantes, Gonesse, and Vézelay.[12] This type of support is fragile and prone to splitting or cracking under the weight of the upper stories. Such damage occurred in the hemicycle of Noyon and may also have been one of the reasons for the reworking *en sous-oeuvre* of the piers in the hemicycle at Meaux.[13] The decision to replace the monoliths of the hemicycle at St-Denis at the beginning of the reconstruction is therefore hardly surprising. Certainly by this time the limitations of monolithic columns in other buildings were already evident, even if those columns were still in good condition at St-Denis itself. Although relatively slender monolithic columns may have sufficed for the twelfth-century elevation, it is most unlikely that they would have been adequate for its taller thirteenth-century replacement.

The process of the reconstruction of the chevet is revealed by a close examination of the abaci (figs. 24 and 25). That these are twelfth-century is clear from the fact that the abaci above the cylindrical piers with one engaged shaft and the abaci above the piers with three shafts are identical in their dimensions; in other words, these identical abaci were intended originally for identical supports, Suger's columns.[14] It has already been pointed out on several occasions that the abaci have been recut to permit the shafts that rise from the base of the columns to continue to the vaults without interruption.[15] This recutting has been done skillfully on some piers and clumsily on others, suggesting that the work was done in place, perhaps in haste, and by a series of workmen, some evidently more skilled than others (plates 48 and 49).

The variations in the abaci also suggest that Suger's columns were replaced one by one: the abacus could have been supported by a heavy wooden falsework while the original column was slipped out and the drums of the new, stronger pier erected underneath. The primary advantage of this system was the retention of the lower beds of the twelfth-century vaults in place in conjunction with some centering under the ambulatory ribs. Furthermore, the falsework and centering could be reused in each support as work proceeded around the hemicycle. Although the variations in the cutting of the abaci do not permit a precise

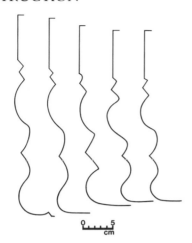

Figure 24. The twelfth-century abaci
of the hemicycle.

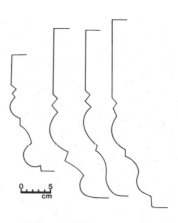

Figure 25. The twelfth-century abaci in the
intermediate ambulatory columns and
chapels of the chevet.

identification of the sequence of the work through the chevet, it does seem as though at least in the straight bays the work on the south side may have been accomplished before that on the north. The outer shafts in the piers of the straight bays on the south are more embedded in the abacus than those on the north, where the edges are chamfered in order to permit the outer shafts to emerge more strongly. On both north and south, the further projection of the central shaft beyond the abacus is achieved by the addition of a separate piece of stone (plates 50 and 51).

Although the exact process by which the hemicycle piers were replaced must remain conjectural, this type of work was by no means unusual in medieval monuments.[16] In fact, at St-Denis the work *en sous-oeuvre* was not nearly as ambitious as that subsequently done at Meaux or in the nave of Rouen, for example, inasmuch as the upper stories at St-Denis, unlike these others, had been demolished. The falsework therefore supported only the abaci and the ambulatory vaults resting on their upper surfaces.

Before the chevet supports were replaced, four new piers were added to the crypt, their locations corresponding to the straight bays of the chevet above. These new crypt piers replaced twelfth-century supports that had been erected as part of Suger's building. They are planted in roughly the same locations as their twelfth-century predecessors and were inserted because of the greater weight of the new elevation and wider diameter of the chevet piers immediately above them. Like the new supports in the chevet above, these new crypt piers were designed to carry a heavier superstructure and need not be taken as an indication of instability in the earlier church.[17]

Although the proportions of the hemicycle abaci seem heavy, especially in relation to the more slender columns of Suger's program, their size was determined by the substantial diameters of the transverse arches and diagonal ribs of his vaults, which descend to the upper surface of the abacus (plate 28). As the retention of these would have made it impossible to reduce significantly the

Plate 48. The chevet arcade, 2N.

Plate 49. The chevet arcade, 3N.

Plate 50. The chevet arcade, 4S.

Plate 51. The chevet arcade, 5S.

size of the abaci, little would have been gained by replacing them. The only further modification of their form was the recutting to allow the shafts of the new piers to rise without interruption and the chamfering of the edges.

The retention of the twelfth-century abaci had certain inevitable consequences for the new arcade molding, which had to be fitted onto the space remaining on the upper surface of the abaci (plate 49). Since this molding had to be relatively flat in profile, a solution was found in the disposition of four equal-sized tori, each of the first three projecting further from the core, and the fourth tucked slightly behind the others (fig. 22). This unusual design is virtually identical with the treatment of the moldings of the arches that open into the lateral nave chapels of Notre-Dame, especially on the north side, where the chapels were inserted between 1220 and 1250.[18] The context in which this molding appears at Notre-Dame is not unrelated to the conditions at St-Denis, as at the former, too, it forms part of a remodeling of an older structure. At Notre-Dame, the enclosing arched molding had to rise from slender responds carved for the most part from the existing fabric of the wall and refaced, in order to permit as much light as possible to filter from the chapels to the already dark double side aisles. A molding of multiple tori was ideally suited to such circumstances, as it permitted the arch to rise as high as possible, to present a visually interesting profile, and yet not to obscure the light from the chapel windows. The adoption of a similar profile at St-Denis also allowed the new arches of the arcade to rise as high as possible to the intrados of the earlier vaults behind them.

The arcade arches, spandrels, and responds that rise from the abaci are entirely thirteenth-century, though they abut the twelfth-century ambulatory vaults. Indications that the columns were replaced one by one are perhaps also to be found in the seams visible in the masonry to either side of the responds as they rise from the abaci. After each pair was replaced, the lower beds of the continuing shafts above the abaci and adjoining arches of the arcade were put into place; indeed, the lower three beds of each are cut as one piece (plate 52). This may well have been done even before the abaci were recut.[19] The masonry suggests that the arches of the arcade as well as the continuing shafts of the responds were erected before the spandrels were entirely filled in and the masonry continued to the base of the triforium. The disjunctures in the chevet masonry by and large disappear at the level of the third coursing of masonry beneath the triforium (plate 52), indicating that this level was completed only when all the cylindrical piers were replaced and the compound piers on the north side erected.[20] The three upper beds of masonry in the chevet were thus part of a second phase of work on the chevet, which included the construction of the triforium and eventually of the clerestory. This took place in conjunction with the construction of the upper stories on the east and the north wall of the north transept arm.

The new supports in the hemicycle consist of a cylindrical pier with one attached shaft in the turning bays and three attached shafts in the straight bays. These shafts, bonded with the drums of the piers, rise without interruption through the capital and abacus, where they are joined by the more slender shafts supporting the wall-rib (plate 52). In the turning bays, the piers and their plinths

Plate 52. View of the chevet from the southwest.

Plate 53. Superimposed twelfth- and thirteenth-century plinths at 3N.

Plate 54. Beaumont-sur-Oise (Oise), north side of the nave.

sit on rough polygonal foundations, the remains of Suger's twelfth-century plinths (plate 53). Unlike the abaci above, the chamfered corners of these older plinths in the turning bays are original and correspond to those under the intermediate supports of the double ambulatory (plate 28). In the straight bays, the twelfth-century plinths are no longer visible.

The proportions of the new chevet piers, with a diameter of approximately 65 centimeters in the turning bays and 76 centimeters in the straight bays, are considerably heavier than those of the slender columns of Suger's ambulatory behind them.[21] The effect of their greater width is mitigated by the vertical accent of the engaged shaft or shafts that rise through the capital and abacus (plate 20).

The prominent capitals of the chevet piers consist of either strongly defined and broadly carved crockets or large, smooth-edged leaves.[22] The full and fleshy quality of these capitals balances the strong proportions of the piers below.[23] Similar types of capitals appear in various churches of the Ile-de-France of the same period, but the strong modeling and austere simplicity of the capitals at St-Denis are surely also designed to respond to the particular esthetic conditions impinging upon the new work in the chevet, the most conspicuous being the ponderous twelfth-century abaci (plate 49 and fig. 24).

Although the new cylindrical piers in the chevet have been condemned as "clumsy" and "lacking in grace,"[24] the fact remains that with the retention of the square abaci, the possibilities beneath were limited indeed, and the new piers represent an elegant solution to the complex problems of incorporating the old program with the new. The columnar form of the piers repeats the disposition of the intermediate ambulatory columns, and the engaged shafts applied to the thirteenth-century supports recall the forms of the detached shafts applied to the walls within and between the radiating chapels (plate 28). The engaged shafts also connect the pier with the wall and vaults above, a principle developed further in the design of the supports of the transept and nave. The columnar form, dictated by the retention of the square abacus, was thus nonetheless integrated with the elevation by the addition of engaged shafts; the distinction between the hemicycle supports and those in the rest of the new church is therefore less dramatic than might initially appear.

To summarize, analysis of the first part of the rebuilding demonstrates that the character of the early work was determined by the preserved parts of the chevet but was designed in relation to the character of the projected elevation elsewhere in the new church. As will be seen in a following chapter, these hemicycle supports probably reflect the influence of Parisian, and to some extent northern, sources, such as the small church of Beaumont-sur-Oise (plate 54). Although designed only for this particular part of the new church at St-Denis, the chevet piers may have had some impact on the design of a number of smaller churches in the area, among them the unfinished nave of Gonesse, and, farther afield, the western bays of Mantes and the chevet of Ourscamp (plate 55).[25] But these relationships are complex and will be discussed in the broader examination of the influence of St-Denis at the end of chapter 6.

Plate 55. Ourscamp (Oise), ruins of the chevet, north side.

THE WESTERN BAYS OF THE CHEVET

The chevet at St-Denis is not homogeneous. In the last pair of piers prior to the crossing, the form of the support changes from a cylindrical core with one or three attached shafts to a diamond-shaped core enclosed by fourteen attached shafts (fig. 1 and plate 13). Base profiles, capital style, abaci, and the arcade molding undergo various degrees of transformation in response to the new type of support to which they are attached. These western piers introduce the new design to be maintained throughout the remainder of the interior. Building activity probably began on the south side of the chevet with the reconstruction of the hemicycle piers and the recutting of the twelfth-century abaci, proceeded counterclockwise and was concentrated largely on the north side of the chevet, the north transept arm, and the three eastern bays on the north side of the nave (fig. 26). The south side of the chevet was completed last. It is likely that work on the east side of the north transept arm began even while the hemicycle columns were being replaced.

The new piers represent the initial stage of the new design of the elevation first introduced in its fully resolved form in the north transept arm. And yet in some respects, these piers are still dominated by the special conditions that prevailed in the chevet: the accommodation of the new program to the old. The compound piers are introduced at the point at which the twelfth-century ambulatory is replaced by the eastern aisle of the new transept.[26] This juncture is therefore a point of transition from the established conditions of the eastern bays of the chevet to the new plan of the rest of the church, emphasized by the change in axis of the wall as it spreads from the narrower proportions of Suger's main vessel to the new wider dimensions of its thirteenth-century replacement. Because of this deviation in the axis of the wall, the new piers are highly visible from the nave, and their design unites them with the rest of the new program (plate 1).

Most studies of St-Denis state that the new type of pier introduced in the western bays of the chevet is the work of a new architect.[27] The distortion in the new double-roll arcade molding as it descends on its eastern side to the abacus of the westernmost cylindrical pier has been seen as additional evidence of this (plates 13 and 51).[28] But the retention of the twelfth-century abaci in the eastern bays of the chevet meant that the support beneath was limited to a cylindrical form, as noted above. And the use of the older abaci also had implications for whatever was above: the arcade molding had to be conceived with a sufficiently flat profile to fit on their upper surfaces (plate 49). The new arch in two orders, on the other hand, which intimately responds to the grouping of shafts around the new pier (plate 13), had to be flattened in order to descend on its far side to the smaller and more compact surface of the twelfth-century abacus (plate 51). The proposal that a change in architects occurred at this point in the rebuilding must

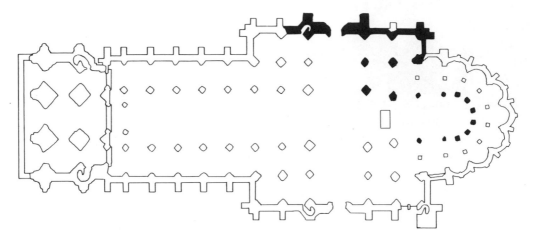

Figure 26. First phase of construction.

therefore be abandoned in favor of the idea that there was one architect who imposed his own design on the interior after he had passed to the west of the older ambulatory. This transition corresponds to that from the sacred and contained spaces of the chevet to the large-scale and open volumes of the transept and nave below. As at Canterbury Cathedral, the changes in level of the church were responded to by varying the type of pier.[29] The forms themselves, the individual elements of the elevation, thus reflect the significance and function of the space.[30]

  The compound piers are thus a point of transition in every sense, and that process, which involved all aspects of the elevation, was by no means a simple one. The western piers of the chevet respond to the forms already established to the east, anticipate the forms and elevation to be introduced to the west, and must be considered in terms of both.

  The compound piers of the chevet also initiate the adjustment of the width of the main vessel from the narrow proportions of Suger's chevet to the ample volumes of the thirteenth-century nave. This was done by planting the crossing piers at the new width and setting the walls of the first bay of the chevet at an angle. While the chevet of Suger's church was 10.50 meters wide between the centers of the supports, the distance between the centers of the new crossing piers is 13 meters. The disalignment between Suger's chevet and his west facade is reflected in the sharper angle of the chevet wall on the north side and the deviation in the positioning of the intermediate pier in the eastern aisle of the north transept arm (see the plan, fig. 1, and plate 13).[31]

  The more complex problem in this early phase of construction was the adjustment from the height of Suger's arcade arches to that of the projected elevation of the transepts and nave.[32] To some extent this was facilitated by the

2.52 meter change in level from the chevet to the transepts, but this difference in height was not in itself sufficient to accommodate the new higher level of the arcade introduced in the transepts.[33]

The western bays of the chevet, then, make the transition from the original height of Suger's arcade to the new proportions of the thirteenth-century elevation, as well as the transition to the new width of the nave (plate 13). This transition is handled differently on the north side from the south, however. Although the preoccupation with unity of design that characterized the earliest work on the reconstruction remains a dominating principle on both sides, on each the solution is perceived in a different way.

The fourteen shafts of the compound piers in the last bay of the chevet correspond to the five ribs of the main vaults and the wall-rib, the three shafts on either side support the moldings of the arcade, and the three shafts facing the aisle rise to the diagonal and transverse ribs of the aisle vaults. Every element in the vaults is thus predicted in the design of the support, a concept fundamentally different from that of the simple cylindrical columns that originally existed in Suger's chevet. The compound pier, with its emphasis on linearity, separation of parts, and yet the unity of the whole, anticipates the character of the elevation above.

To summarize, with the introduction of the compound pier, the arcade molding inevitably undergoes transformation. Instead of the earlier arrangement of four equal-sized tori, there is now the more usual disposition of an arch in two orders (figs. 21 and 22). As a result, the character of the arcade becomes more sharply defined, with the upper molding enclosing the lower and enlivening surface of the wall above the arcade arches (plate 20). This new molding, however, cannot fit on the westernmost twelfth-century abaci and is therefore flattened (plate 51).

There are also subtle modifications in the capitals and bases of these new piers. The former are now decorated with smaller, deeply cut, elegant crockets with small leaves springing from the astragal (plate 30). It should be emphasized, however, that this is not so much a change in design as the adaptation of the form of the capital to the smaller scale of the shafts attached to the pier (plate 13). Whereas the large capitals above the piers to the east responded to the more massive cylinder below and to the heavy abacus above, here the smaller capitals correspond to each of the slender shafts attached to the pier. The bases are also adjusted to correspond to the new type of pier.[34] Although the indented upper torus and deep cavet of the bases closely resemble those found in the eastern part of the chevet, the forms here tend to become more fluid, and the fillet that precedes the cavet is reduced to a notch (figs. 6 and 8).

The abaci in these compound piers are now of a standard thirteenth-century type and contrast with the preserved twelfth-century abaci to the east (figs. 24 and 27 and plates 30 and 48): a strongly projecting torus and fillet followed by a deep cavet—a type of abacus found consistently in monuments of

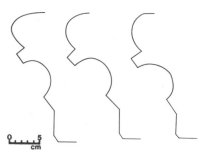

Figure 27. Abaci profiles of the first compound piers of the chevet and the
northeastern crossing pier.

the late 1220s and 1230s, such as Royaumont. The profile emphasizes the strong
contrast between the recessed and projecting parts, making the upper torus seem
to float above the dark void below.

The aforementioned details all result from the introduction of a new type
of pier; they do not in themselves denote the presence of a second architect or a
change in the program. The profiles of the bases and abaci of these piers as well as
the carving of the capitals respond to the scale and character of the elements in the
new compound supports.

The compound pier on the north side of the chevet may well be earlier

Plate 56. Bases and plinths at 6S.

than that on the south, however. Its plinth is consistent with the height of the plinths of the cylindrical piers with engaged shafts to the east (varying from 58 to 64 centimeters). On the south side, the plinth of the eastern shaft of the compound pier is 84 centimeters tall, while the others all measure 59 centimeters (plate 56). The taller plinth introduced in one of the shafts of this southern compound pier corresponds to the height of the plinths of the piers to the south, toward the chapel of Saint Louis.[35] The capital of the compound pier on the south is cut in a drier, flatter style than that on the north, a style more closely related to the capitals on the south transept arm than to those on the north side of the first campaign.

These seemingly minor details, as will be seen in the following pages, form part of a larger argument that the chevet remained incomplete on the south side for some years.[36] Although the crossing piers were constructed at the same time or soon after the hemicycle piers were replaced and the first compound pier on the north was erected, work on the corresponding compound pier on the south seems to have been delayed. After the replacement of the hemicycle piers the early phases of the reconstruction were concentrated on the north side of the chevet and north transept arm. These observations correspond to strong indications in the upper stories as well that the south side of the chevet is later in date than the north side.

THE UPPER STORIES OF THE CHEVET AND THE NORTH TRANSEPT ARM

The chevet, north transept arm, and the three eastern bays on the north side of the nave form one campaign. There are no indications of significant interruptions in construction, and the work generally proceeded from east to west. Indeed, the construction of this part of the church seems to have advanced with extraordinary rapidity and to have been virtually complete within ten years of its inception.

The fully developed elevation is introduced in the north transept arm for the first time. While the component parts had appeared in the western bays and upper stories of the chevet, the resolved elevation with its proper proportions emerges only in the transept and nave. The modifications of design that take place between the elevation of the chevet and that of the north transept arm reveal the extent to which the chevet consists of compromise solutions between the old and the new work, rather than the fully resolved, "ideal" elevation elsewhere.

In the north transept arm, the compound piers are reduced from fourteen to twelve shafts by beginning the shafts that support the wall-rib at the base of the triforium, rather than allowing them to descend to the ground as they do in the compound piers of the chevet (plates 13 and 21). The pier thus has four equal sides: it is a perfect diamond in plan. The piers of the transept and nave are thereby more slender, increasing the openness of the arcade. This reduction of the piers to twelve shafts also has important implications for the setting of the wall in the upper two stories. The truncated shafts that stop at the triforium set the wall plane of the triforium and clerestory behind that of the arcade spandrels (plate 21).

The reason for the heavier compound piers in the chevet also lies in the disposition of the wall in relation to the supports. In the eastern bays of the chevet, the shafts supporting the wall–rib descend to the top of the abacus, and the walls of the arcade, triforium, and clerestory are therefore set back only to the depth of the clerestory mullions (plate 52). When the first pair of compound piers was introduced in the westernmost bay of the chevet, this arrangement of the wall planes could be preserved only by allowing the shafts in question to descend to the ground, thereby creating a heavier pier with fourteen engaged shafts (plate 13). If the shafts had been stopped at the base of the triforium, as elsewhere in the building, the triforium and clerestory in this last bay would have been set further back behind the plane of the wall of the arcade, exaggerating the diagonal setting of the walls. This distortion, already pronounced on the north side, would have had to be made even greater to accommodate the deeper plane of the wall of the upper two stories. The last pair of piers in the chevet are therefore not an "experimental" introduction of this new type of support,[37] but rather, once again, a response to the particular conditions of the chevet.

However, a preliminary hint of the imminent change in the treatment of the outer shafts supporting the wall–rib appears in the chevet on the eastern side of the crossing piers. On the north, the shaft is stopped at the base of the triforium, thus adding to the outward twist of the wall. This distortion is diminished on the south, where the shaft is continued in a slightly flattened form to the level of the impost (plate 57). The truncation of this shaft was necessary as its continuation to ground level would have created heavier crossing piers on the east than on the west. The continuation of the shaft on the south to the level of the impost resolves, however, the problem revealed by the greater twisting of the northern wall. As the evidence presented in the following pages will show, this solution is one of many further indications that the south side of the chevet was completed after the north.

The masonry in the spandrels of the arcade as well as details of the construction of the triforium and clerestory suggests the sequence of the work. In the chevet, the height of the arcade on the north side is increased in each of the straight bays between the hemicycle and the crossing; a decision had been made to reach the dimensions of the north transept arm gradually by raising the height of both arcade and triforium slightly bay by bay (plate 13). This leads to some awkward jumps in level in the molding at the base of the triforium in relation to the responds (plate 19). The upper beds of masonry of the arcade level are bonded from the north side of the chevet through most of the north transept arm, with the exception of the lower beds of stone on the west side of the last cylindrical pier, where dislocations result from adjustments to the new arcade profile. The narrow band of masonry passing around the circumference of the chevet slightly below the base molding of the triforium has been interpreted as the original level of the triforium before the supposed change in program or architects.[38] This band of masonry corresponds to the floor level of the triforium passage, however, which rises when the base molding of the triforium steps above the first compound pier on the north side (plate 19). The narrow band continues until the west wall of the north transept arm (plate 12) and is abandoned in the nave. The points at which this element disappears in the north and south transept arms are related to the construction and level of the triforium passage and provide important indications of the sequence of the work on these parts of the church.

On the south side of the chevet there are more frequent breaks in the masonry of the spandrels above the piers.[39] But the abrupt changes in the height of the arcade itself, so pronounced on the north side, are not present on the south (plate 57). Rather, the changes in level are eliminated, and a change in the proportions of the different levels of the elevation occurs only at the corner of the wall between the western bay of the south side of the chevet and the adjacent transept wall. The continuous adjustments visible in the arcade and in the rising base of the triforium on the north are simply absent on the south; instead, the transition appears as a fait accompli on the east side of the south transept arm.

The modifications to the design of the south side of the chevet suggest a taste for greater regularity and homogeneity within that part of the church. In this connection, it is perhaps worth recalling that the shift in the axis of the wall on the south side is also greatly reduced. Likewise, the planting of the intermediate pier in the eastern aisle of the transept, off-axis on the north side, is more closely aligned with the transept on the south.[40] The construction of the arcade on the south is dominated by the principle of retaining the essential proportions of the twelfth-century arcade up to the juncture with the transept, while on the north the new proportions are attained virtually within the chevet itself. The treatment of details indicates a significant delay in the completion of the upper stories on the south side as well.

The triforium in the last bay of the south side of the chevet is constructed differently from that in the north, though its design remains of course the same. On the north side of the chevet as in the north transept arm and in the first three bays on the north side of the nave, the central grouping of double-mullioned shafts descending from the clerestory is composed of six or seven beds of stone (plate 19). In the last bay on the south side of the chevet, however, these shafts are cut in one or two long pieces (plate 57). This tendency to reduce the number of separately cut parts is continued throughout the construction of the rest of the church—that is, in the south transept arm (plate 58), on the south side of the nave (plate 63), and in the western bays of the nave on the north side.

Other details in the triforium also suggest later completion of the south side of the chevet. These consist largely of what seem to be "trial" forms in the handling of the bases and plinths, appearing at first as isolated variations on the standard disposition established on the north side but presently adopted as a

Plate 57. The western bays on the south side of the chevet, triforium level.

second, improved arrangement in the east wall of the south transept arm. These variations occur not only in the height and width of the plinths, but also in the planting of one of the plinths on the diagonal in the third straight bay east of the crossing piers (4S–5S), a disposition adopted in the east wall of the south transept arm and continued to the fourth bay west of the crossing on the south side of the nave (plate 58).[41] Both plinth and abacus are now planted on the same axis, whereas before the abacus was planted on the diagonal while the plinth was parallel to the axis of the nave (plates 19 and 58).[42]

In the realm of more subtle distinctions, there are also some variations in the carving of the triforium capitals on the south side of the chevet which become more elaborate and deeply cut. A certain mixture of capital types occurs throughout much of the church, however; such elements were often carved in the workshop long before they were inserted into place.[43]

In the back wall of the triforium, behind the responds that descend to the compound pier of the chevet on the south side (6S), there is a major break in the bonding of the masonry. In the triforium arcade to the west of this pier, a new plinth, lower and wider, is consistently used (plate 57). A recollection of the first system of higher, narrower plinths is still attached to the eastern face of the

Plate 58. The triforium in the east wall of the south transept arm.

Plate 59. Exterior, clerestory on the east wall of the south transept arm.

southeastern crossing pier, however; this pier may have been erected as part of the first campaign, which otherwise concentrated for the most part on completion of the north side (plate 57).[44]

There are also interruptions in the upper wall of the south side of the chevet above the clerestory lancets on the exterior of the building, where there are breaks in the masonry that correspond in their location to the breaks and changes in the masonry of the triforium below. This occurs in the bedding of the masonry on either side of the wall buttress at 5S and in the central part of the wall between 5S and 6S. The masonry around the corner on the east wall of the south transept arm is, however, continuous with that of the last bay on the south side of the chevet. The partial adoption of imposts planted at an angle in the mullions of the clerestory windows at the juncture of the south transept arm with the chevet, instead of the previously used rounded imposts, indicates that these changes in design were anticipated during the completion of the chevet but not adopted until the "new territory" of the south transept arm had been reached (plate 59).

The evidence indicates that the western bays of the chevet on either side were constructed simultaneously with the transept arms on either side, first on the north, in a campaign that included the entire north transept arm and three eastern bays on the north side of the nave, and then on the south in the corresponding parts of the church. The logic of this procedure becomes evident when the structure of the church is considered. The detached towers flanking either transept terminal carry the fliers that support the upper walls and vaults of the western bays of the chevet and the transept as well as the eastern bays of the nave (plate 11). These walls could not be erected to their full height without the simultaneous construction of the transept towers, which were to carry the fliers that stabilize the upper parts of the structure.[45] But the towers, of course, could be erected only above the completed structure of the northern and southern extremities of the transept aisles below. The western bays of the chevet and the eastern bays of the nave must therefore have been constructed in conjunction with the transept towers that support their upper walls; hence the erection of the north side of the chevet and eastern bays of the nave could occur only in conjunction with the north transept arm, and the same was true on the south. The construction of the church in the area of the crossing depended upon the erection of the four transept towers and can therefore be divided essentially into four quadrants, the first two on the north and the second two on the south.

The northeastern transept tower is thus part of the early phase of the reconstruction of the north side of the chevet and the eastern side of the north transept arm. Its singularly austere surfaces, unarticulated by any sort of decorative molding, should be seen in relation to the design of the flat, planar surfaces of the buttresses around the chevet that rise from the slender spur walls between Suger's radiating chapels (plate 24).[46]

Aside from the change in proportions from the chevet to the north transept arm, the carving of capitals, bases, and all other details is identical. The

first interruption in the masonry on this side of the church takes place in the north
wall between the two aisles on the western side of the transept.[47] A seam in the
upper wall on the arcade level is also visible on the western side of the north
transept terminal wall (plate 12). This means that the spiral stair on the western
side of the north transept terminal formed part of the first campaign, providing
convenient access to the upper stories of the chevet and the eastern and northern
walls of the north transept arm (fig. 26).[48] While work was carried out on these
upper parts of the elevation, construction soon picked up again on the western
parts of the north transept arm and the outer walls of the aisle on the north side of
the nave.[49] The erection of the arcade on the west side of the transept and the
three eastern bays on the north side of the nave as well as the upper parts of the
elevation in this part of the church was simultaneous with the construction of the
northwestern transept tower (fig. 28).[50]

   The reason the work on the north side was completed before that on the
south is related to the older structures at the site. Suger's church was intended to
have a nonprojecting transept, and the width of his building continued the
alignment of the outer wall in the last pair of rectangular twelfth-century chapels
in the chevet. The present thirteenth-century transept thus falls well outside the
fabric of Suger's and whatever remained of its Carolingian predecessor, at that
time presumably on relatively open terrain.[51] Work on the north transept arm
and the north side of the nave could have been carried to a considerable height
with little or no disturbance to the main vessel of the Carolingian church, aside
from the chevet (fig. 23). The disalignment of the piers in the eastern aisles of the
north transept arm may be the result of early and rapid building on this side as
well as the preservation of the older structure of Suger. Most of the older
transept and the monks' choir in the nave could thus continue to be used for
regular liturgical services while work was carried on in an area well outside
(fig. 23).

   Conversely, the delay in the completion of the south side is the result of
the location of the conventual buildings. These would have been directly connected to whatever had been completed of Suger's nonprojecting transept and its
Carolingian predecessor (plates 9 and 10). The construction of the south transept
arm thus entailed the partial destruction and disruption of the monastery itself; it
is easy to understand a certain desire on the part of the abbot and the monks to
have completed a major part of the new church before inflicting great upheaval
on the conventual buildings.[52] As the western bays of the chevet are an integral
part of the eastern range of the transept on either side, the completion of the
south side of the chevet was delayed until the terrain could be cleared for the
rapid construction of the entire south transept arm.

   If this was indeed the case—and both the masonry and the documents
strongly support such an argument—then the chevet could not have been vaulted as part of the first campaign, since throughout that campaign the south side
remained incomplete. Indeed, the vaults in the chevet could have been erected
only after significant portions of the south transept arm were in place. (Although

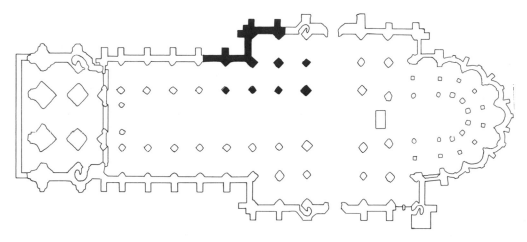

Figure 28. Second phase of construction.

the repeated restoration of the vaults makes the sequence of their construction most difficult to determine, the probabilities will be examined in chapter 5.) The chevet could have been used, however, even though the vaults were not completed, as happened at Cologne and Clermont-Ferrand cathedrals.[53]

The adjustments in the design of the chevet from east to west are, then, calculated as a transition from the predetermined height of the arcade in the hemicycle to the desired proportions and elevation elsewhere in the church.[54] The particular character of the hemicycle was established by the low vaults of Suger's ambulatory combined with the new height of the thirteenth-century vaults. The first pair of compound piers introduced the new type of pier while partially preserving the general proportions and treatment of wall planes in the hemicycle. As the height of the clerestory had to be maintained for reasons of internal unity (plate 1), the only part of the elevation that could expand to compensate for the lower level of the arcade was the triforium. As a result, this part of the elevation has an elastic quality in the eastern parts of the church; it is stretched to form a tall, vertical element in the hemicycle and then contracted to a smaller-scaled element in the transept and nave (plate 19). A comparison of the dimensions of each of the stories in the chevet with those in the rest of the church makes this clear: in the chevet the arcade is 8.91 meters tall (to the base of the triforium in the axial bay); the triforium is about 5 meters tall; and the clerestory is about 10.50 meters tall. In the north transept arm, on the other hand, the lowered floor level and the raised height of the arcade bring it up to 12.20 meters, while the triforium is reduced to about 3.60 meters and the clerestory remains at 10.50 meters. In the chevet, the height of the clerestory exceeds that of the arcade by about two meters; with the taller triforium, this part of the church thus acquires a much tighter and more vertical effect (plate 13).

On the west wall of the north transept arm, the narrow band of masonry beneath the triforium that had passed around most of the chevet and through the east and north walls of the north transept arm is abandoned (plate 12). As has been observed in the preceding pages, this is the point at which a seam in the masonry indicates a break between the construction of the lower story and the inception of work on the upper two levels around the chevet and the eastern side of the north transept arm.[55] Construction in this part of the church (that is, the western aisles and western arcade of the north transept arm) probably began during the work on the upper stories to the east, as the handling of details is completely consistent with the earlier parts of the reconstruction. The north-western crossing tower belongs to this second phase of work on the north transept arm, and its forms are significantly different from those of its counter-part to the east (plate 25). While the eastern tower seems to have been designed in relation to the flat, thin surfaces of the flying buttresses around the chevet, its western counterpart, with twin lancet openings enclosed by shafts and moldings on either side, presents a more advanced design consistent with the two towers of the south transept arm.

A further deviation in the treatment of certain details in the three eastern bays on the north side of the nave also suggests a slightly later date for this part of the building than for the west wall of the north transept arm. This is the absence of plinths and bases for the shafts supporting the wall-rib at the point where they descend to the base of the triforium (plate 17).[56] This detail exists only in these three bays of the church; the bases and plinths reappear immediately when work is subsequently picked up in the remainder of the chevet and the east wall of the south transept arm.

The design of the north transept terminal wall once again involves ac-commodation of the new design to older elements in the church, for this wall incorporates the twelfth-century Valois Portal (plates 12 and 25). The three large blind arches that decorate the lower half of the terminal wall are not of equal size, as they are on the south; rather, the central arch is reduced in size to correspond to the smaller, older portal.[57]

As noted previously, the north transept rose, with its elegant design of centripetal petals, is derived from that in the west facade of Notre-Dame in Paris, usually dated to circa 1225 (plate 12).[58] The more elegant, slender design of the tracery at St-Denis suggests that the installation of the tracery here may have been delayed until the 1240s.[59]

The construction of the north transept arm, including the reuse of the Valois Portal in the terminal wall, is consistent with the attitude toward the preservation of earlier segments of the church already noted in the chevet. Here too we are confronted with a design that involves some compromise between the ideal solution (as embodied in the design of the south transept terminal wall) and the desire to preserve certain parts of the older structure.

THE SOUTH TRANSEPT ARM

As has been noted in the preceding pages, the completion of the south side of the chevet was undertaken only in conjunction with the construction of the east side of the south transept arm. While some of the piers may have been planted while work was in progress on the north, most of the construction in this part of the church seems to have taken place only once the north side of the nave and north transept were largely complete (fig. 29).[60] This sequence is indicated by the experimentation with and then tentative adoption of new forms in the triforium of the last bays of the chevet on the south side, prior to their consistent use in the south transept arm (no hint of these forms appears on the north) (plate 57). In other words, although some of the piers in the south transept arm may have been begun while work was still going on in the north, the triforium and clerestory as well as the arches and spandrels of the arcade were probably put in place only when work on the north side of the nave was essentially finished.

The few changes in the triforium introduced in the westernmost bay on the south side of the chevet are subtle indeed; others, far more striking, are adopted only in the east wall of the south transept arm. Here the modifications are closely related to contemporary work at the palace chapel at St-Germain-en-Laye, built by Louis IX and completed about 1238 (plates 60–62).[61] As other authors have pointed out, the similarities between St-Denis and St-Germain-en-Laye are so close that they can be considered the work of the same architect,[62] and it seems likely that the work on the smaller chapel provided an opportunity to refine some elements established a few years earlier in the chevet and north transept arm of the abbey church.

The reasons for the delay in the completion of the south side of the chevet and the south transept arm have been enumerated above. The modifications of the program that take place are all refinements of the original program and, once adopted, continue to be used in the subsequent work. Evidence of such modification can be seen not only in the diagonally planted plinths and imposts mentioned above, but also in the preference for constructing the central shafts of the triforium arcade in each bay in larger, *en délit* pieces that enhance the verticality (plate 58).

The major transformation, however, is in the clerestory, where a third mullion is added to the pair of central mullions that rise from the base of the triforium to the clerestory lancets (plate 59). Here the central mullion continues above its companions in the tracery of the clerestory to absorb the stilting of the arches in the earlier design (plates 22 and 23). At the same time, capitals with abaci planted on the diagonal are added to the outer shafts of these lancets next to the wall buttresses corresponding to their partner in the center (plate 59). A mixture of old and new forms appears in the first bay south of the southeastern

Plate 60. St-Germain-en-Laye, palace chapel, rose window.

Plate 61. St-Germain-en-Laye, clerestory tracery.

Plate 62. St-Germain-en-Laye, exterior.

crossing pier in the combination of rounded and diagonally planted abaci within the same window.

These changes have significant implications for the design of the clerestory. The system of double central mullions tended to emphasize the separateness of each of the larger lancets; they were united only by the large central rose above them and the enclosing wall-rib (plate 21). The addition of a third mullion pulls the entire design of the clerestory into a cohesive whole (plates 23 and 59). Furthermore, the descent of the third mullion to the base of the triforium emphasizes the bundling of the shafts within the bay and the plasticity of surfaces characteristic of the elevation elsewhere (plate 58). The adoption of diagonally planted abaci in the clerestory repeats the new setting of these elements in the triforium, resulting in greater internal consistency in the treatment of details.

These refinements are reflected in the much-restored palace chapel of St-Germain-en-Laye, constructed between circa 1234 and 1238.[63] When the palace chapel was begun, work on the abbey church had already been in progress for three years, and the essential disposition of its elevation was established. At St-Germain, the treatment of the dado arcade and wall-passage is almost identical to that at St-Denis (plates 18 and 60). The elevation of St-Germain-en-Laye is thus a small-scale and slightly elaborated version of that of the abbey church. The much smaller size and the different function of the chapel naturally led, however, to certain modifications in detail and changes in proportion. These are most visible in the diameter of the responds, now very slender, the use of a third central mullion in the windows, and the treatment of the outer wall as a rectangular panel, with large trilobes sitting in the spandrels of the arch above the lancets (plates 61 and 62). The proportions of the lancets are also much taller than those at St-Denis.

In spite of these refinements, the treatment of details confirms the relatively early date of St-Germain-en-Laye and reinforces its close ties to St-Denis. Base profiles are identical to those in the chevet and transept triforium on the north side of the abbey church (figs. 9, 10, and 13). Capitals and imposts are also the same, consisting largely of crockets with small leaves, and the imposts in the windows are still circular (plates 60 and 61).

The intricate connections between the two buildings and the relatively well established dates of the chapel permit it to be dated slightly later than the earliest parts of St-Denis, but probably before the completion of the chevet on the south side and the work on the south transept arm, the eastern parts of which may have been begun while the palace chapel was still under construction. Attribution of both structures to the same architect is highly plausible, and, most important, many of the modifications in design in the chapel are subsequently incorporated into the continuing work in the south transept arm at St-Denis.[64] St-Germain-en-Laye thus confirms the early dating of the first campaign as well as the rapidity with which work progressed at St-Denis.

Construction of the south transept arm followed the pattern established

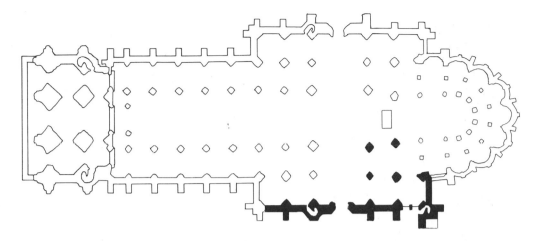

Figure 29. Third phase of construction.

on the north, with the erection of the responds and staircase in the southwest corner of the south terminal wall before the upper walls on the east side and the terminal wall were completed (fig. 29). The aisle walls were erected to the southwest corner of the transept, where there is a joint in the masonry, and at the same time the southwestern crossing pier and the arcade on the west side of the transept were begun.[65]

As on the north a second phase of the construction of the south involved the completion of the west walls and the first three bays of the arcade on the south side of the nave[66] as well as the upper stories of the south and west transept walls (fig. 30). The south transept rose was part of this campaign: its almost exact

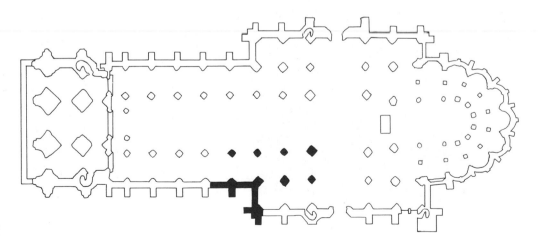

Figure 30. Fourth phase of construction.

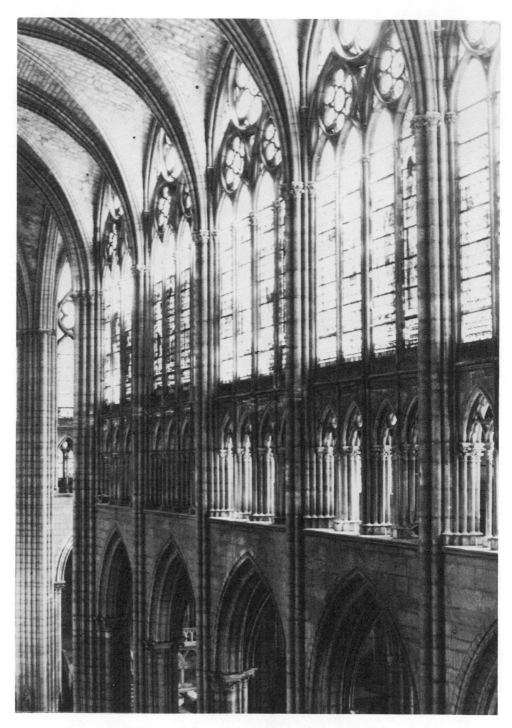

Plate 63. Eastern bays on the south side of the nave.

repetition of the tracery pattern of the rose at St-Germain-en-Laye illustrates once again the close connections between these two royal buildings (plates 27 and 60).[67]

The handling of details in the south transept arm is consistent on all three sides, and the treatment of the capitals and abaci in the clerestory continues the new disposition of the tracery pattern as begun on the east wall. Capitals on the whole show lighter, more deeply cut leaves springing from the astragal (plate 34), and the bases in the triforium tend to flatten, with the cavet now usually eliminated entirely (fig. 14). All these details are later in date than the corresponding elements on the north and reflect a general trend in the architecture of the later 1230s and 1240s. The homogeneity of the structure suggests that this part of the building was also built in one rapid program essentially continuous with that on the north.

THE SOUTH SIDE OF THE NAVE

The construction of the chevet and transept seems to have taken place rapidly and continuously: the seams in the masonry denote points at which the laying out of the lower story was temporarily interrupted while work proceeded on the upper stories, and the slight changes in capital and base types are only such as can logically be expected to appear over a period of ten or fifteen years.[68] The first interruption of any significance appears at the juncture of the south transept arm with the south side of the nave, where there is a vertical seam in the masonry between the southwest crossing pier and the south wall of the nave at the level of the triforium and clerestory. Whereas the earlier work had proceeded in a pattern that essentially radiated around the crossing, construction on the south side seems to have been interrupted at an improbable and unanticipated point that left the monks' choir in the three eastern bays of the nave incomplete. Indeed, the masonry at this point indicates that the interruption was sudden, that it lasted for some time, and that it occurred in the middle of a campaign originally intended to include at least the three eastern bays on the south side of the nave.[69]

A number of major changes in the program are now introduced. By far the most prominent is the difference in the proportions of the clerestory lancets and rosettes. The former are now elongated, and the latter shrink in scale to become a much less prominent part of the design (plate 63). These changes alter the character of the clerestory: the breadth and amplitude of forms in the original design are now exchanged for a much more attenuated and vertical interpretation of the tracery pattern (plate 2). The original disposition had reflected the taste for spaciousness characteristic of all aspects of the first program, while the new design represents a transformation of that approach into the more metallic forms that came into fashion in the later 1240s and 1250s, forms that might be seen as characteristic of the so-called Court Style.[70] The homogeneity of the interior so marked in the elevation of the abbey church is maintained in the

Plate 64. St-Germain-des-Prés, fragments from the Virgin Chapel.

number and order of the individual parts of the tracery, but the change in their proportions constitutes a considerable modernization of the original. The new clerestory recalls the vertical proportions of the wall-passage arcading in the transept terminals of Notre-Dame or the new lightness of proportions in the Virgin Chapel at St-Germain-des-Prés; in both, the mullions are consistently reduced to an extremely thin vertical accent, giving the structures new, brittle character (plate 64).[71]

At the same time, the capitals in the responds at the springing of the vaults and in the clerestory are treated in a new way: instead of the fuller, fleshier crocket capitals with leaves springing from the astragal, a stiffer, harsher style with tall, striated crockets is introduced. This type is used also in the continuation of the arcade on the south side of the nave to the juncture with the west bays built by Abbot Suger, a continuation that must be regarded as part of the same campaign that completed the upper two stories of the elevation on this side (plates 18 and 39). The same type of capital appears in the responds of the north aisle from the point at which the first campaign on this side of the nave was terminated to the western bays of Suger's narthex on the north. This brittle, new style is in keeping with the dry elegance of the new tracery pattern in the clerestory and corresponds to the type of capital often found in work of the third quarter of the thirteenth century—for example, the reworked piers in the chevet of Notre-Dame, one of which has been dated by Marcel Aubert to circa 1250–70 (plate 40).[72]

To summarize, after the south transept arm and the arcade on the three eastern bays of the south side of the nave were complete, work was interrupted for some time, leaving the upper stories of the eastern bays of the nave incomplete. This meant that the new monks' choir, located in the three eastern bays of the nave, was still unuseable, and the old Carolingian choir may have remained intact within it (fig. 31). Later, a new program was initiated to construct the triforium and clerestory in these three eastern bays on the south side, and at the same time, the south aisle and arcade were continued to the juncture with the south side of Suger's narthex (fig. 32).[73] As the capital style and other details of the aisle wall on the five western bays of the north side of the nave are identical, this wall may have been constructed at the same time. The complete reworking of the wall masonry between the aisle responds on both sides of the nave (fig. 2) makes a precise identification of the campaigns here most difficult, however.

The design of the triforium in the three eastern bays on the south side of the nave remains the same, however. The variety in the treatment of capitals and bases suggests that some parts may already have been in place or at least carved and ready to be placed by the workshop when construction was interrupted. There are some indications that the triforium elements (bases, capitals, etc.) attached to the main responds are more archaic than those of the arcading within each bay, which may indicate that the responds had been erected for several bays above the triforium string-course prior to the interruption of the work. While

Figure 31. The interruption of construction at the juncture of the south transept arm with the upper stories of the south side of the nave.

some of the capitals show the combination of crockets and small leaves seen previously in the south transept, others have the drier, stretched crocket type found in the arcading on the south side of the nave and the south aisle (plates 18 and 39), and a third, more infrequent type consists of one long leaf that sweeps upward from the astragal to the abacus above (plate 37). These capital types can be correlated with the handling of bases (figs. 15 and 16); those with a fillet between the upper and lower torus are intermingled with others with a taller and more depressed upper torus with no fillet preceding the cavet. The mixture continues throughout the three eastern bays of the south side.

This evidence suggests that some elements of the triforium were put into place prior to the interruption of the work and that others may have been waiting below in the workshop ready to be inserted as soon as the construction recommenced. These details may also be indications of an abrupt and unexpected interruption of the work on this part of the church.

THE COMPLETION OF THE NAVE

The completion of the nave is difficult to establish with certainty, as both the lower and upper stories have suffered especially from restoration. The sequence of the work must therefore be based to a large extent on the carving of the capitals, the treatment of the bases and plinths in the triforium, and the coursing of the masonry in the spandrels of the arcade on both sides.

The capitals in the nave indicate two campaigns: the first, as noted in the preceding pages, comprised the south wall and south arcade from 11S to 16S and the north wall from 11N (1) to 16N (1). These parts of the church have in common the austere, strongly striated crocket type of capital described above. A

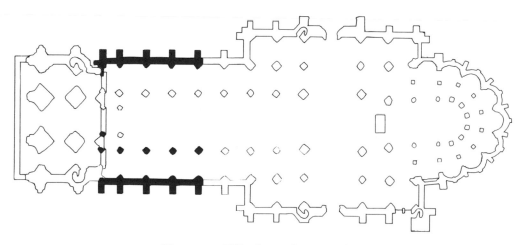

Figure 32. Fifth phase of construction.

second type of capital, appearing in the arcade on the north side (bays 12N–15N) and in the triforium and clerestory on both sides of the nave from bays 12 through 15, is composed of a flattened, smoothed crocket form that presses against the core of the capital until it erupts at the top with heavy, rounded projections (plates 41–44). The upper parts of the leaves often form an outer plane parallel with that of the center and are deeply undercut, creating a strong contrast of light and dark and a somewhat vibrant surface. Very few capitals of the earlier, striated type are found even in the western bays of the triforium. On occasion, a second variety of the later capital appears, one with a wandering, twiglike stem twisting horizontally across the surface and erupting in small, crudely cut leaves that no longer adhere in any way to the main axes (plate 45). Both types appear in other monuments in France dated after 1260, such as the chapel at St-Germer-de-Fly and the chevet and transept of St-Urbain at Troyes.

The nave was thus completed in two major campaigns. The first comprised the monks' choir in the first three eastern bays of the nave and extended the south aisle to join the newly constructed transept and chevet with the older west facade and narthex erected by Abbot Suger. The second finished the arcade and the upper stories in the five western bays on both sides of the nave as far as the juncture with Suger's narthex and upper chapels (fig. 33). The surviving capitals and bases in the triforium of these five western bays are consistent and correspond to those in other monuments erected in the 1260s and early 1270s. In these western bays of the nave, a number of details in the triforium have been modernized. The abaci are now polygonal, with a flat side facing the nave and the triforium passage (plate 44). This change is reflected in the plinths, which are again planted parallel to the main axis of the nave. Polygonal plinths and abaci had been used at Amiens since the 1230s and were a standard element in the context of the triforium and other small-scale arcading in many other monuments.[74]

At the same time, the openings in the back wall of the triforium were modernized: their edges were now more sharply chamfered and the general effect larger, lighter, and more generous. This new disposition is introduced on both sides immediately to the west of the wall buttress behind the supports at 11N and 11S.

The change in campaigns in this part of the church is further confirmed by a considerable change in the axis of the wall on both sides. This shift, equally pronounced on the north and south sides of the nave but visible only within the triforium passage, aligns the axis of the eastern parts of the church with that of the western.

The other new element is the design of the flying buttresses and their supports along the nave. The only previous freestanding fliers existed around the chevet, as the upper walls and vaults of the crossing, transepts, and eastern bays of the nave were supported by the transept towers (plate 11). While the fliers around the chevet were extremely flat and slender, doubtless because they rested

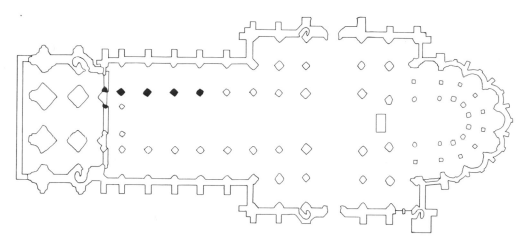

Figure 33. Sixth phase of construction.

on the relatively small spurs of wall between Suger's radiating chapels, those added upon completion of the nave in the last campaign are much more in keeping with the design of *culées* in other contemporary monuments. They consist of three gabled blind arches on each side, with an additional blind arch enclosed by a gable facing the outside. The arches stand on *en délit* shafts that support a sharply pointed trilobe enclosed by a larger pointed arch. Each gable is pierced by a small trilobe and capped by crockets and finials.[76] The whole structure is surmounted by delicate octagonal pinnacles similarly decorated with trilobed arches beneath gables.[77] Gargoyles project from between the gables, and the conical caps of the pinnacles are decorated with an abundance of crockets and topped by finials. The fliers, as before, rise in two ranges, with the lower applied to the point directly behind the springing of the vaults and the upper interrupting the crocket molding at the cornice beneath the roof. The lower flier is sustained by a tall and slender *en délit* shaft that is set on the outer passage on the clerestory level.

The treatment of these buttresses along the nave is similar to that at a number of other churches of the 1250s and 1260s: octagonal pinnacles of the same type appear above the plainer buttresses in the work of Gautier de Varin-froy at Meaux[78] as well as the Virgin Chapel at St-Germer-de-Fly, begun about 1261.[79] Also similar to St-Denis is the blind arcading that decorates the octagonal stair towers at St-Germer-de-Fly.[80] Probably both monuments were influenced by the transept of Notre-Dame in Paris, particularly the south transept arm, begun about 1258, although the use of octagonal pinnacles at the cathedral perhaps goes back in turn to the transept of St-Denis itself, in the work completed in the 1230s and 1240s on both sides.[81] The buttresses around the chevet of Beauvais are also decorated with an identical type of blind arcading supported by detached shafts, recently dated by Stephen Murray to the late 1250s and 1260s.[82]

The juncture of the west facade with the new, thirteenth-century nave takes place with a shorter west bay, now mostly obscured by the large organ loft erected in the 1830s. As noted above, the arcade piers and aisle responds were built in conjunction with the bays that precede them to the east. The triforium and clerestory in this shorter bay may have been the last parts of the new church to be put into place. The bases in the triforium are the most extreme examples of the flattened type found in its five western bays, and the capitals exemplify the heavy, clumped decoration arranged in horizontal bands typical of the last campaign. In this last bay, the clerestory tracery is unique and corresponds to its smaller dimensions. It consists of three narrow lancets—the central one the tallest—rising to the base of the large central rosette. Two shorter rosettes are placed above the shorter outer lancets, however, so that the general three-rosette disposition existing throughout the church is nonetheless maintained. These windows, now blocked by cement slabs, are probably the last parts of the church to be erected: certainly their capitals, with leaves curling up over the impost and spreading out in a plane parallel to that of the central cores, are the latest in date to be found in the church, anticipating similar types that appear in the chapels added around the chevet of Notre-Dame in Paris in the last decades of the thirteenth century.[83]

SUMMARY

An analysis of the structure and sequence of campaigns permits several fundamental conclusions that contradict previous literature on St-Denis:

1. The earliest work on the hemicycle supports was designed in conjunction with the western bays of the chevet, the transept, and nave, and all this was the work of one architect. The difference in pier types between the hemicycle and the remainder of the church to the west results from the decision to preserve Suger's ambulatory and radiating chapels. The various anomalies in the arcade moldings are the function of the retention of Suger's square abaci that support his twelfth-century ambulatory vaults and do not in themselves denote a first architect who was almost immediately supplanted by a second.

2. The chevet was not completed immediately, but rather the south side remained unfinished for some time, probably until the late 1230s, while work continued apace on the north side of the chevet, the north transept arm, and the eastern bays on the north side of the nave. The delay resulted from the fact that the conventual buildings were located on this side of the church (fig. 23).

3. The sequence of construction was organized to permit the continued use of the monks' choir in the eastern bays of the Carolingian nave until construction of the new choir was essentially complete. Parts of the new transept and refurbished chevet were put into use while work proceeded on the south

transept arm and south side of the nave. Until the south aisle was completed, the Carolingian nave served as access from Suger's west facade and narthex to the new transept and reworked chevet.

The sequence of construction can be divided into the following campaigns:

1. Demolition of the upper stories of Suger's chevet and the replacement of the hemicycle piers, which included the recutting of the twelfth-century abaci *in situ*. At the same time, the foundations for the north transept arm may have been established.

2. Construction of the arcade spandrels in the chevet in conjunction with the eastern and northern walls of the north transept arm. This phase included the spiral stair at the west corner of the north transept terminal wall (fig. 26).

3. Completion of the upper stories of the chevet and the east side of the north transept arm in conjunction with the lower walls in the west side of the north transept arm and three eastern bays on the north side of the nave (fig. 28).

4. Construction of the upper walls on the west side of the north transept arm and three eastern bays on the north side of the nave in conjunction with the northwest crossing tower. Probably at the same time, the arcade on the south side of the chevet was completed, along with the eastern side of the south transept arm. This included the east and south transept walls to the southwest corner, including the spiral stair on this side of the transept (fig. 29).

5. Completion of the upper chevet walls on the south side and east side of the south transept arm, including the southeastern transept tower. The chevet vaults could then have been put in place.

6. Construction of the western side of the south transept arm and the outer wall and arcade in the three eastern bays on the south side of the nave. Although the triforium and clerestory on the west side of the south transept arm were finished, the corresponding walls on the south side of the nave were left incomplete. The vaults of the crossing and south transept arm would also therefore have remained incomplete (figs. 30 and 31).

The work described above took place in one long, continuous campaign, in spite of minor changes in program. The completion of the nave, however, seems to have taken place relatively slowly, in two major phases of construction:

7. Completion of the triforium and clerestory in the first three bays on the south side of the nave, and the erection of the arcade on the south side to the juncture with Suger's narthex. This would have permitted the vaulting of the south transept arm and possibly of the monks' choir in the three eastern bays of the nave, inasmuch as completion of the southwestern transept tower, which supported the vaults and upper walls of this part of the church, formed part of this campaign as well. The reworking of the vault in the easternmost of Suger's west bays (narthex) on the south side also seems to have been accomplished at

this point. In addition, this campaign seems to have included the wall and responds in the western bays on the north side of the nave (fig. 32).

8. The last campaign completed the church. It involved the erection of the arcade in the five western bays on the north side of the nave and the triforium and clerestory on both sides, including the vaulting of the five western bays of the nave. There are some indications that the vaulting of the monks' choir may have been delayed until this point (fig. 33).

5 ❖

Dating and Chronology
THE BUILDING AND THE DOCUMENTS

N̲O COUNTERPART TO ABBOT SUGER EXISTED TO RECORD AND DESCRIBE THE reconstruction of the abbey church in the thirteenth century. The major source for the documentation of the reconstruction is the chronicle of the events that occurred at the abbey, the *Chronicon Sancti Dionysii ad cyclos paschales,* which exists in two versions. The first provides only a laconic statement to the effect that the renovation of the chevet was begun in 1231, then refers to the translation of various relics and the moving of certain tombs, and mentions the consecration of the church in 1281. The second version of the *Chronicon* enlarges upon the first and describes to some extent the progress of the work but is considered slightly less reliable. Both versions of the *Chronicon* are expanded upon in the chronicle of Guillaume de Nangis and in the *Grandes chroniques de France.*

Aside from these sources, occasional indications of the various phases of the reconstruction appear only in texts on other subjects. Most of these texts are charters and legal documents that make passing references to altars, chapels, or donations for the fabric of the church. The one lengthy passage in a text that specifically refers to the rebuilding, a description of the collapse of a scaffolding and the deaths of many men, tells us nothing of where in the church the calamity took place.[1]

Nonetheless, the thirteenth-century reconstruction of St-Denis is unusually well documented for a medieval church, especially in the early phases. As the work initiated by Abbot Eudes Clément faltered under one of his successors, stopped under another, and thrived under the third, the discussion of the campaigns can be divided into the abbacies of Eudes Clément, 1228–45; Guillaume de Massouris, 1245–54, and Henri Mallet, 1254–58; and Mathieu de Vendôme, 1258–86.

THE CONSTRUCTION UNDER EUDES CLÉMENT, 1231–45

In the first version of the *Chronicon Sancti Dionysii* the entry for the year 1231 states quite simply: "Hoc anno renovatum est capitulum Beati Dionysii."[2] The second version was probably written somewhat later, perhaps circa 1260.[3] It summarizes all the work done while Abbot Eudes was in office prior to his appointment as the archbishop of Rouen in 1245:

> Hoc anno cepit Odo abbas renovare capitium ecclesie Beati Dyonisii Aryopagite in Frantia, et perfecit illud usque ad finem chori, hoc excepto quo[d] turris ubi sunt cinbala a parte revestiarii non erat perfecta, nec voltatus erat chorus, sed a parte Sancti Ipoliti totum erat perfectum, et etiam voltatum erat a parte vestiarii.[4]

The meaning of this text is generally clear: during the abbacy of Eudes Clément, work on the reconstruction began in the chevet and was taken to the end of the choir (by which should be understood the liturgical choir in the three eastern bays of the nave, where the monks' stalls were located),[5] with these exceptions: that the bell tower on the side of the *revestiarium* was not completed nor the monks' choir vaulted, but on the side of the altar of Saint Hyppolytus (the north transept arm), all was finished, and the vaults were in place in the area near the *vestiarium*.

A more precise understanding of this text hinges on the meaning of the various terms for the different parts of the church. The term *capitium* clearly refers to the chevet, and *chorus* to the three eastern bays of the nave, where the thirteenth-century stalls were in place until their reconstruction in the eighteenth century (see Félibien's plan, plate 3). But the use of the terms *revestiarium* and *vestiarium* is problematic. Although scholars have felt that both terms refer to the vestry (or sacristy), it seems highly unlikely that different terms would be used within the same sentence to designate the same place.[6] And indeed, the text itself makes a distinction between the location of the *vestiarium*, which was vaulted, and of the *revestiarium*, where the tower was still incomplete.

Unfortunately, additions to the east side of the south transept arm and the reworking of the wall adjoining the cloister on the south side make it impossible to determine the location of the vestry in the thirteenth century.[7] But the term *revestiarium* can be used to designate a treasury as well as a vestry;[8] therefore, in our text it almost certainly refers to the twelfth-century treasury located in the angle between the south transept arm and the nave (plate 3), a room demolished when Cellerier and Debret constructed the winter chapel along the south flank of the nave. This treasury is clearly visible in Félibien's plan; it was entered from the south aisle of the church. A description of the interior of the church in 1517 distinguishes the sacristy from the treasury:

Sacristia, a latere dextro versus monasterium, ditissima, post quam ab eodem latere, camera thesauri posita in loco eminenti, ad quam per cocleam marmoream ascenditur XX gradibus.[9]

The plan of St-Denis by Scamozzi (plate 65), though often unreliable, also shows an area marked as the *sacristia* to the south of the monks' choir in the location where the stairway rose to the treasury, at the east end of the south side. As the treasury contained a large number of sacred and precious vessels and vestments used in the mass, the terms for treasury and sacristy (or vestry) were interchangeable.[10]

One further piece of evidence confirms the location of the *revestiarium* as identical with that of the old treasury on the west side of the south transept. The text from the *Chronicon* mentions the *turris ubi sunt cinbala a parte revestiarii,* a tower with bells in this part of the church. In the view of the monastery in *Monasticon gallicanum* (plate 9), dated to 1687, the roof of the southwest transept tower is double-storied, the type of structure frequently employed to contain bells.[11] None of the other towers had this type of raised roof, and it can be assumed that only the bells that tolled the hours of the offices for the monastic community would have been placed in this tower, above the cloister.[12] The *revestiarium* and the *turris ubi sunt cinbala,* left unfinished at Eudes' departure for Rouen in 1245, were thus located in the same part of the church, the west side of the south transept arm. Moreover, although three of the four transept towers have stairs, only the interior of the southwest tower contains on the inside a strong projection of the upper walls in order to support a wooden floor or truss from which the bells were suspended. The southwest transept tower could thus probably have replaced in function the bell tower once located in the Carolingian crossing.[13]

If all this is indeed correct, the text of the second version of the *Chronicon* indicates that in the south transept arm, the work on the east side (where vestries are usually located) was complete, but that the tower flanking the treasury on the west side, the vaults of the monks' choir, and possibly the adjacent south upper wall of the nave were still unfinished (fig. 31).[14] This corresponds to the indications in the masonry described in the preceding chapter and to the observation that the towers were erected simultaneously with the upper walls and roof at the junction of the crossing and the nave. Certain charters issued by Eudes Clément in 1241, to be discussed below, indicate that at that date, altars in the chevet, crossing, and north transept arm were put into use, but there is no mention of corresponding altars in the south transept arm, then under construction. The seam in the masonry between the southwestern crossing pier and the triforium and clerestory on the south side of the nave suggests that this upper wall also was probably unfinished in 1245.

The second version of the *Chronicon* presents one further problem: exactly what is meant by the term *perfecit?* Does it mean that the parts of the church mentioned were vaulted or merely that the walls were erected to their full height

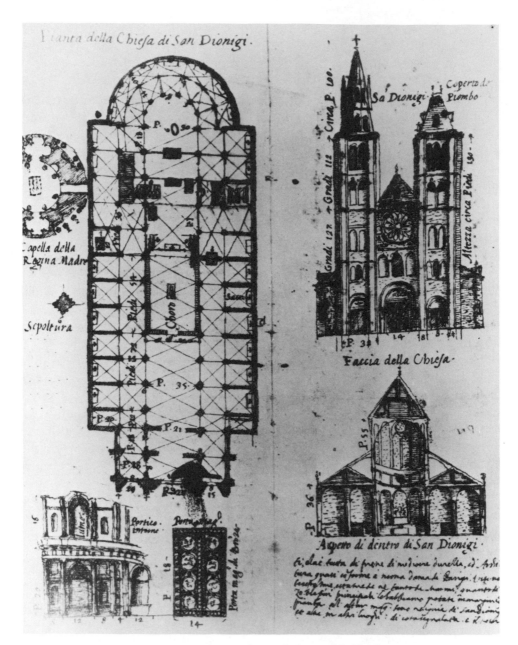

Plate 65. Scamozzi, plan and views of St-Denis.

and now supported the roof?[15] The distinctions in the text would seem to suggest that except where they are specifically mentioned as incomplete, the vaults were in place, and that the area in question was complete. Thus the chevet and the north transept arm were vaulted at this time, but the south transept arm and the choir were not, except for the vaults in the east aisle of the south transept arm (*et etiam voltatum erat a parte vestiarii*). The main vaults of the south transept arm could not have been put into place until the southwest transept tower was complete, and we know specifically from the text that this tower and the vaults of the choir were not yet finished. What had been completed by 1245 was, then, the transept on the north and the chevet, including their vaults, while the crossing, the south transept arm, and the eastern bays of the nave remained incomplete. The archaeological evidence of the stones themselves, discussed in the preceding chapter, confirms this.

The rapid pace of the construction of the first parts of the new church is suggested not only by the text discussed above, but also by entries in both versions of the *Chronicon* for February 1236 which state that the relics of Saint Hyppolytus were transferred from an altar in the middle of the old nave to a new chapel in the left part of the new work:

> Hoc anno in Purificacione Beate Marie translatum fuit cum magna sollempnitate corpus Sancti Ypoliti ab oratorio quod diu fuerat in media navi ecclesie in novum oratorium in sinistra parte novi operis.[16]

In the eighteenth century, this chapel was located in the first aisle west of the north transept terminal wall, a position which would correspond to the general indications provided by the text.[17] This is confirmed in the inventories of the treasures of the abbey of 1401 and 1505.[18] The location of this altar beside the spiral staircase located on the west side of the north transept terminal wall, a staircase which would have been used as a main source of access to the upper stories during construction, would suggest that most of the work in the north transept arm was complete by 1236.[19]

The attentive reader might wonder at the rapid pace of the work. But Abbot Suger himself has provided us with evidence that, in exceptional circumstances, work could be pressed "both summer and winter."[20] Equally rapid construction seems to have taken place at Chartres, which was rebuilt from east to west in the span of about twenty-seven years, and there is the contemporary parallel of the abbey church of Royamont, which was founded in 1228 by Louis IX and consecrated in 1236.[21] Money, much more than time, was the critical element, and St-Denis in the early thirteenth century apparently had no lack of the former.[22]

In 1241, Abbot Eudes issued three charters in which feasts were instituted in the new parts of the church.[23] He mentions the main altar (located in the first bay of the chevet east of the crossing), the matutinal altar (on the west side of the crossing), the altar of Saint Eustache (traditionally located in the northeastern corner chapel of the north transept arm), the retroaltar (in the chevet), and the altar dedicated to the Virgin Mary in the crypt.[24] The texts imply that large parts of the new church were being put into active use and that a new liturgy was being formulated for the vastly expanded space of the abbey church at the same time that work was picked up on the south transept arm and the south wall of the nave.[25] This supposition is confirmed by the gradual rededication, beginning in 1243, of the radiating chapels.[26]

The texts of 1241 bear examination in greater detail. In one of them, Eudes Clément speaks of his acquisition of property for the abbey, part of it land restored to the jurisdiction of St-Denis through litigation. The abbot spent a total of 30,000 *librae* on court costs and on the extraordinarily expensive repairs to the church (*sumptuosissimis expensis in reparatione ecclesie nostrae*).[27] His labors on behalf of the monastery justified the foundation of an anniversary in his memory, to be celebrated on the date of his death.[28]

Unfortunately, the text of 1241 does not specify the amounts spent in litigation, acquisition of new property, and repairs to granges as opposed to the construction of the new church. But even if Eudes spent only 40 to 50 percent of the sum on the reconstruction of the church (and it seems probable that he spent much more), the expenditures would amount to 12,000 to 15,000 *librae*. By comparison, during the first five years of construction at Westminster, £10,702 were spent on the new church, a sum that roughly corresponds to the expenditures calculated above for the first ten years of work at St-Denis.[29]

The accounts of the *Grande commanderie,* which detail the income and expenditures of the monastery, exist only for 1229–30 and then pick up again with 1280–81, a lacuna that coincides with disturbing proximity to the dates of construction of the new church. The charter of 1241 is thus the only record of the cost of construction, and it is highly enigmatic in character.

In spite of the litigation carried on by Abbot Eudes, there is no reason to suppose that the abbey was short of funds. Historically, St-Denis was one of the wealthiest abbeys in France, and in the preceding decades the monastery recovered from the financial difficulties of the second half of the twelfth century and had been the beneficiary of a number of important relics and other gifts from Philip Augustus as well as other patrons.[30] Abbot Eudes' efforts to consolidate the properties of the abbey parallel those of Abbot Suger in the previous century, and Eudes himself makes it clear that the litigation was related to the vast expenses incurred in the reconstruction of the church. According to Guillaume de Nangis and the *Grandes Chroniques,* Blanche de Castille and Louis IX were consulted on the decision to reconstruct the church, and it is possible (though not imperative) that they contributed significantly toward its construction.[31]

There are also texts in the cartularies concerning donations for the construction or dedication of altars. The first of these texts, dated June 1231, mentions the donation of a tithe for the erection of an altar at St-Denis.[32] The cartularies in 1237 and 1238 record further gifts or settlements *ad opus dictae ecclesiae* or *ad opus fabrice ecclesie*.[33] Although exact amounts are not given, the fact that these donations were contested by the heirs surely suggests that they involved property of considerable value.

Documents of this type unfortunately never specify the part of the work that was in progress; indeed, the texts could hardly be vaguer. Yet they do in a general way confirm that work was in progress, that an office of the fabric existed, and that construction was paid for not only from the abbey's own resources, but also by some private donors, possibly including the king.[34] Although Matthew Paris in his *English History* stated that Abbot Eudes left the abbey of St-Denis "irremediably in debt" and that he obtained the archbishopric of Rouen through simony, these remarks can probably be dismissed as malicious gossip.[35] All other indications suggest that Eudes was an able and energetic administrator whose sharp attention to the maintenance of the abbey's properties and whose close ties with the royal family assured an income sufficiently ample to support the monastic community and the reconstruction of the church. In the necrology of the abbey published by Félibien, it is recorded that Eudes Clément *in spiritualibus et temporalibus multipliciter ampliavit,* praise accorded few abbots in the abbey's long history.[36]

How can we apply the indications that the documents provide to the evidence of the campaigns of construction visible in the fabric of the building itself? The location of the beginning of the work is firmly stated in both versions of the *Chronicon* as well as by Guillaume de Nangis and the *Grandes Chroniques de France,* and the discussion of the reconstruction in the previous chapter indicates that this took place in the hemicycle with the replacement of Suger's columns. The subsequent construction in the north transept arm and on the north side of the nave is confirmed by the dedication of the altar of Saint Hyppolytus in 1236 on the west side of the north transept arm. This probably meant that the western aisles of the north arm had been vaulted and perhaps that the upper stories were completed as well. It therefore seems likely that work then progressed on the completion of the three eastern bays on the north side of the nave and the clearing of the site (involving the partial destruction of the conventual buildings on the northern and eastern sides of the cloister) on the south side of the chevet and the south transept arm, probably between the years 1237 and 1240. The charters issued by Abbot Eudes in 1241 indicate that the crossing, the chevet, and the north transept arm were sufficiently complete to be put into use while the south arm, probably blocked off by a screen, was under active construction. In any case, the vaulting of the north transept arm and the chevet took place prior to 1245, when Eudes left for Rouen. By that time, four years later, most of the south transept arm and the arcade on the first three bays of the nave must also have been largely finished.

Thus, as the description above suggests, work on the church took place essentially in quadrants radiating around the crossing. The only one of these left unfinished at Eudes Clément's departure was that on the southwest side of the transept (fig. 31). Construction of the chevet and transept in these quadrants is confirmed by the different designs of the transept towers, no two of which are alike. These towers, as noted in the preceding chapter, are an integral part of the structure, performing an essential function in supporting the upper walls of the elevation, the roof, and the main vaults on the interior; they were therefore of necessity erected simultaneously with the upper walls to either side of them.

The progress of the reconstruction and the planting of the new piers of the nave outside the nave of the old Carolingian church meant that the latter could have remained in use between 1231 and 1241. Presumably, a temporary wall could have been erected at the western crossing piers of the eighth-century nave and between the supports of the arcade on the north side, closing off the *chantier* from the main body of the old church, in which services continued to be sung (fig. 23). The arrangement would have been not unlike that which is still visible at Beauvais, with the remains of the old church abutting the incomplete new one high above it. The documents issued by Eudes Clément in 1241, with their enumeration of the processions and services to be performed at various altars, seem to indicate that parts of the rebuilt chevet and the entirely new north transept arm could by that time be used for regular services, though it is not unlikely that the old nave was kept intact until the new choir on the south side was complete.[37]

This continuity of use during construction is an important aspect of the rebuilding, and various events and ceremonies that took place at St-Denis in the 1230s and 1240s must be imagined as having taken place either in the old nave, truncated at the Carolingian crossing, or in the old nave and the newly opened thirteenth-century north transept arm and chevet. The famous episode of the loss of the Holy Nail must, for example, have occurred in the old Carolingian nave, as by 1232 not enough of the new structure would have been complete for the new parts of the church to be in use.[38] The burial of the king's uncle, Philip Hurepel, in the following year may have taken place in a temporary location or else, (as seems less likely) in the middle of the *chantier,* as his tomb was on the north side of the crossing, next to that of Philip Augustus.[39] On the other hand, the great ceremonies and processions that took place in 1244 for the health of Louis IX when he was seriously ill could have been set in the newly opened north transept arm, crossing, and chevet.[40] The church is described as having been decorated with brightly colored hangings; these may have been suspended from the triforium in the chevet, perhaps not unlike those in the painting of the *Mass of Saint Giles* in the National Gallery, London (plate 7).[41]

By the end of Eudes Clément's tenure as abbot, therefore, much of the eastern part of the new church was complete. This means that the mutilated but still beautiful south transept portal dates to the first years of the 1240s. But construction of the south side of the nave, which included the entrance to the earlier (twelfth-century) *revestiarium,* was still not finished. Its completion became the responsibility of Clément's successor, Guillaume de Massouris.

THE CONSTRUCTION UNDER GUILLAUME DE MASSOURIS, 1245–54, AND HENRI MALLET, 1254–58

The departure of Eudes Clément in April 1245 did not interrupt construction.[42] But progress was impeded by the loss of an energetic administrator who had ably directed the fortunes of the abbey for fourteen years. His replacement by two successive abbots (the second of whom was deposed for ineptitude) within a period of only twelve years led to a slowing of the work. As other authors have suggested, the king's absence during the crusade of 1248–54—and the expenses associated with that unsuccessful enterprise—also had repercussions on the financial resources of the abbey and on the pace of the work,[43] leading to a significant interruption in the late 1240s.

The church as it stands today suggests no major interruption of the work between the abbacies of Eudes and Guillaume. Indeed, it is probable that the construction of the south aisle and of the remaining portions of the south transept arm were already under way and that work continued on these parts of the church without pause. But between 1245 and 1254, the work does seem to have proceeded much more slowly, and it may have been interrupted for some years by Louis's crusade. It appears not only that Guillaume de Massouris, for all his virtues, was a somewhat less impressive administrator than Eudes Clément, but also that the times themselves had changed, largely for the worse.[44] The early work had been carried on in the decade of affluence, energy, and optimism of the early years of Louis IX's reign. But the later 1240s, which saw the departure of the king on crusade in 1248 (an enterprise that elicited considerable misgivings on the part of his contemporaries and family) and a series of legal difficulties at the abbey itself, led to a period of stagnation. Beginning in 1246, a series of further complications occurred: that year a number of monks fled the monastic community, abandoning their vows;[45] there are other contemporary suggestions that the observance of monastic rule had become quite lax;[46] and in 1250–51, Abbot Guillaume became embroiled in a series of legal suits against local lords who had usurped the abbey's property.[47] In addition, beginning in 1245, severe taxes were imposed in support of the crusade.[48] Further expenses connected with this disastrous venture were incurred in 1253, during King Louis's captivity, when the abbot equipped a ship laden with supplies for the king and his retinue.[49]

In spite of the great wealth of St-Denis, the documents suggest that Abbot Guillaume had problems raising the funds to pay for both the heavy new taxes and the continuation of construction on the church. The taxes levied in support of the crusade may well have induced the abbot in 1248 to enfranchise the inhabitants of a number of villages belonging to St-Denis for the sum of 1,700 *livres*.[50] A papal bull of Innocent IV in 1246 confirmed the abbey's right to

inherit all the goods and property of the monks, an important source of income.[51] Guillaume's litigation over properties that had been usurped by local
lords is reminiscent of that of Abbot Eudes in the preceding decade, and the latter
linked his action directly to the expenses incurred in the reconstruction of the
church.[52]

Difficulties and financial obligations notwithstanding, several documents suggest that the *chantier* was continued and confirm the evidence of the
structure itself that work proceeded, albeit slowly. The chapel of St. Maurice in
the chevet was dedicated in 1245; the chapel of St. Hilaire in January 1247; and
that of St. Cucuphas probably in 1248, continuing the pattern of gradual refurbishing and reconsecrations established by Abbot Eudes.[53] The altar of the
Virgin Chapel was reconsecrated in 1253.[54] In May 1250 there was also a donation for the construction of the church, a gift from one Eugène Albate for the
conventum et fabricam ecclesie beati dyonisii.[55] A charter of 1251 mentions quarries
belonging to the abbey, and a charter of 1247 refers to Pierre de Montreuil as
cementarius de Sancto Dyonisio.[56] The precise role of this famous architect in the
construction of St-Denis is difficult to determine and not immediately relevant
here (see below, Appendix 2). What is important is the indication that Pierre de
Montreuil was probably present at the abbey and that construction in some part
of the monastery was in progress.[57]

Abbot Guillaume's efforts to keep the workshop going, even in the face
of numerous difficulties, were probably not maintained by his successor, Henri
Mallet, who was elected to office after Guillaume's death in March 1254.[58]
Abbot Henri was deposed by papal bull in 1258, after a short abbacy in which
bad economy and administration prevailed.[59] Robert Branner's statement that
no work took place during this period is probably correct,[60] though it should be
noted that the documents pertaining to Abbot Henri's deposition make no
reference whatsoever to interruption of work on the church; the grounds against
him are purely financial and administrative. The difficulties began within the
first year of his abbacy, and it seems likely that the disorder infecting the abbey as
a whole applied to the workshop as well.

It is not possible to determine with perfect precision how much of the
church was completed during the tenure of these two abbots. From 1245
through about 1248 the work undertaken by Abbot Eudes was continued,
though perhaps at a somewhat slower pace. The completion of the south transept arm can probably be dated to these years.

Work was probably interrupted during the years of the crusade, beginning in 1248.[61] When in the last years of Guillaume's abbacy the decision was
made to renew construction, the south aisle was extended to the juncture with
Abbot Suger's western bays and facade (fig. 32), and the upper stories of the
monks' choir were completed. Certainly an interruption of some significance is
indicated by the seam in the masonry just to the west of the southwest crossing
pier as well as by the transformation in the proportions of the rosettes and lancets
in the clerestory.[62] The triforium and clerestory in these three eastern bays of the

nave probably date to the years 1252–54. The change in design is consistent with forms introduced in the north transept terminal wall at Notre-Dame, in which lancets are elongated into attenuated and brittle elements. This change in proportions, typical of the mid–thirteenth century, appears also in the windows of the eastern chapels added to the north side of the nave of Notre-Dame, generally dated to c. 1245–50[63] and is echoed in the tracery pattern in the galleries of the west towers[64] as well as in the clerestory patterns of the chevets of Troyes and Le Mans cathedrals.[65] The shorter lancets with the larger, broader rosettes of the earlier parts of St-Denis were well out of date by the late 1250s, and the transition from the older to the newer and more elegant proportions occurs simultaneously in many other churches whose construction spanned decades from the 1220s and 1230s to the 1250s and 1260s.[66] At Amiens, for example, the pattern of pairs of lancets and large, ponderous rosettes used in the aisles and west wall of the transept is transformed in the western bays of the chevet on the level of the aisles into an elaborated pattern of four narrower and taller lancets supporting three equal-sized rosettes.[67]

The new tracery pattern at St-Denis may have been introduced by Pierre de Montreuil, who was documented as being present at the abbey in some capacity in the late 1240s and who might still have been involved with the construction in the 1250s. If he was in any way involved in the work on the western parts of the south transept arm, he might have been constrained to maintain the earlier tracery pattern, but the inception of work on the new territory of the upper stories on the south side of the nave after an interruption of a few years provided the opportunity to introduce a modification in the tracery.[68] Certainly the second pattern was used in the refectory and Virgin Chapel at St-Germain-de-Prés, built by Pierre de Montreuil beginning in 1239.[69] Other monuments in and around Paris reflect this new sensibility, rejecting the spaciousness of the forms introduced in the early work at St-Denis in favor of a tighter, flatter type of design. Indeed, even in the chapel at St-Germain-en-Laye, built in the mid-1230s, the change has begun to take place (plates 60–62).[70]

The fact that the upper stories in the first three bays on the south side of the nave were finished prior to the subsequent campaign that completed the arcade of the nave on the north side as well as the upper stories in the five western bays on both sides suggests that another interruption took place after the completion of the monks' choir in the early 1250s. It seems likely, therefore, that work was indeed interrupted during the abbacy of Henri Mallet, as Branner has suggested, even though we have no proof of this.[71] The changes in capital style and in the treatment of the imposts and plinths in the triforium, however, all give rise to the supposition that completion of the five western bays of the nave took place in one long program that was the work not of Henri Mallet but of his far more illustrious successor, Mathieu de Vendôme.

Two questions remain. Was the choir perhaps still unvaulted during the abbacy of Henri Mallet, thus leaving the monks without a proper setting for their offices? Is it possible that the protracted delay in the completion of this part of the church was one of the reasons for Mallet's dismissal? Neither the masonry nor the documents provide a clear answer. However, the fact that the royal tombs, sculpted in the preceding decades,[72] were not installed until the early 1260s suggests that the area around the crossing in which those tombs were placed was not completed.

CONSTRUCTION UNDER MATHIEU DE VENDÔME, 1258–86

Guillaume de Nangis states clearly that Abbot Mathieu de Vendôme brought the construction of the abbey church to completion:

> monasterium namque illius abbatiae, longe a retroactis temporibus incoeptum et miro ac sumptuoso opere constructum, fere a media parte usque ad ultimum consummavit.[73]

This is reiterated in the *Grandes Chroniques de France:*

> Lequel abbé Mahieu, le moustier de Saint-Denis, de moult de temps commencié de merveillable et constant euvre par l pou de la moitié, une partie jusques au derrenier consomma et parfist.[74]

The election of Mathieu de Vendôme also marked a general improvement in the fortunes of St-Denis. Once again the monastery was led by an abbot who was a familiar of the king and court and who became, by virtue of his role as regent during the second crusade of Louis IX and later as counselor to Philip III, one of the leading political figures of his generation.[75]

After the unsuccessful abbacy of Henri Mallet,[76] Mathieu de Vendôme seems to have taken matters in hand directly upon his election. In the next few years there is evidence of the immediate renewal of work on the nave. This was not the end of the abbey's vicissitudes, however. A text in the *Flores historiarum* describes a disaster that took place in the part of the church then under construction:

> Circa ejusdem anni curricula in partibus contigit Gallicanis infortunium lacrimabile, et maxime religiosis in aeternum lamentabile. In ecclesia etenim sancti Dionisii, Francorum apostoli, fabrica quaedam nova, sullevata in altum, lignis fuit convexis et insimul ligatis suffulta quamplurimis. Cumque die quadam plures de conventu, associatis sibi et secularibus, causa considerandi laborem subter ambularent, ecce tonitrus magnus irruit et horribilis, qui vehementer lignorum struem concutiens resoluta junctura ea funditus diruit, et multos tam religiosos quam seculares in terram conquassatos extinxit. Unde multorum relatu

asseritur advenientium, quod monachi ejusdem monasterii usque ad XIV, seculares vero quamplurimi, illo solo ictu perempti sunt infortunato. Quare magna, nec mirum, ex insolito suscitabatur in Francia lamentatio, cum vita mutatur in mortem, et gaudium convertitur in luctum.[77]

The ambiguity of the terminology here suggests that the event was described by an author far from the scene, one who probably did not himself know where in the church the misfortune took place.[78] The interpretation of the passage must therefore remain somewhat vague. If the description is generally correct, the location of the scaffolding in a high place (*sullevata in altum*), sufficiently high for monks and visitors to walk underneath it, would seem to suggest the type of hanging scaffolding suspended from the triforium customarily used in construction of the upper stories and the vaults.[79] The number of monks killed is surely exaggerated (indeed, it would seem to be contradicted within the text itself, in which it is said that *plures de conventu, associatis sibi et secularibus* were inspecting the new construction).[80] Could the scaffolding that collapsed have been the one used to construct the vaults in the three eastern bays of the nave (the monks' choir), the upper walls of which were completed only in the early 1250s, or did the disaster take place further west, in the construction of the remainder of the nave? There is no mention of the calamity in any other source, including the *Chronicon,* and the only conclusion that can be drawn is that in 1259, work was going on in the upper stories of the nave. If the collapse took place in the vaults over the monks' choir, it is probable that the lower parts of the building would have been protected by some sort of provisional roof.[81]

In 1259 the tombs of abbots Suger, Henry, Peter, Adam, Hughes, and some others were moved to the south transept arm.[82] These were complemented by the program of royal tombs, unique in medieval sculpture, that were installed in the crossing, beginning probably in 1264.[83] The latter may have been part of the original design for the new church as conceived in the years just prior to 1231, and the great volumes of the transept arms were created to provide adequate space for this series of royal tombs.[84] The gisants of the Capetian and Carolingian kings replaced what was probably an unprepossessing assortment of earlier tombs; indeed, there is evidence that a few of the royal tombs were not marked or commemorated even in Suger's day.[85]

One further indication that work had recommenced on the nave and that the office of the fabric was again in operation is a charter of November 1261 that includes tithes *ad opus ecclesie;* it is the first such donation since 1250.[86]

As noted in the previous chapter, no significant breaks occur in the construction of the five western bays of the nave, and the carving of capitals and bases is handled consistently throughout this part of the church. Hence it is likely that the work progressed without interruption, with the construction concentrated first on the completion of the vaults of the south transept arm and monks' choir in the three eastern bays of the nave prior to the erection of the five western piers on the north side of the nave and the construction of the upper levels of the elevation on both sides.[87]

The church was consecrated only in 1281. The single source for this date is the statement in the *Chronicon: Consoumatum est novum opus ecclesie Beati Dyonisii a domino Matheo abbate.*[88] No other surviving document mentions the consecration, and we do not have any indication of who attended the ceremony. It is surprising, moreover, that the completion of the nave should have taken twenty-two years. With the completion of the transept and monks' choir, however, the essential parts of the church were thus in place: all areas with altars at which services were performed were east of the third bay west of the crossing, and the earlier construction of the south aisle to the juncture with Suger's western bays and facade provide the essential link to the completed parts of the new church. Thus, in the liturgical sense, the church was complete long before the nave was actually finished, and perhaps there was less pressure therefore to push on with the construction, which could be done, to borrow Suger's phrase, "only betweenwhiles."[89] In addition, the retention of Suger's west facade gave the church a completed appearance when approached from the west.

Nonetheless, the two decades between the renewal of the work under Mathieu de Vendôme and the consecration in 1281 seem like a curiously long period. There are three possible explanations for this, one of which has already been suggested above: the work in this less essential part of the church simply proceeded more slowly. But there are other considerations as well. Although the completion of the church may have been initiated in 1258 with considerable vigor, including the "putting to rights" of the crossing and transept, with their full complement of the tombs of the royal predecessors as well as those of illustrious abbots, new tithes may have once again affected the work. In 1262 taxes were imposed for the rescue of the Latin Empire of Constantinople, and in 1263 a tithe was decreed for Charles d'Anjou.[90] Louis IX's vow to go on crusade in 1267 led to a new tithe imposed on the clergy for a period of three years.[91] Only the Knights Templar, the Hospitallers, and the Teutonic order were exempted, presumably because of their military contributions to the undertaking.[92] Subsequent taxes imposed by Gregory X in the mid-1270s may have affected the finances of St-Denis as severely as they did those of so many other churches and abbeys.[93]

Finally, the church may have been completed long before its consecration in 1281. Delayed consecrations were by no means infrequent, even for monuments of great importance, and all of the altars and chapels had been reconsecrated many years before.[94]

The death of Louis IX in 1270 must have dealt a severe blow to St-Denis, as it did to all France. With his last words the king expressed the wish to be buried at St-Denis but that his sons be buried at Royaumont, clear evidence of his vision of the former as the necropolis only of kings.[95] The king had been involved with the reconstruction of the church beginning in 1231 and had made many visits to the abbey over the years, scrupulously observing the annual feasts and other traditions associated with it.[96]

The suggestion has been made that Philip III sought to disassociate himself from his father's projects after he ascended the throne. The canonization of Louis was initiated by Gregory X in 1274, but Philip took no active role in the procedure until 1280.[97] The formal public inquest into Louis's life and miracles that had taken place in the twelve years since Louis's death formed an important part of the evidence. Is it possible that the church was finally consecrated because the inquest into the canonization, parts of which took place in the abbey church, was about to begin? No certain answer is possible at present, and the architectural evidence suggests only that work took place without major interruptions, while capital style and base profiles resemble those in other monuments of the 1260s and the 1270s. I suspect that the church was finished sometime in the 1270s but that consecration was postponed for various reasons until 1281.

SUMMARY

The reconstruction of St-Denis began only three years after Eudes Clément became abbot, suggesting that plans for the rebuilding of the church may have been initiated when he came into office in 1228. By the time he departed in 1245, the chevet, the north transept arm, the three eastern bays on the north side of the nave, and most of the south transept arm were completed (fig. 31). His successor, Guillaume de Massouris, completed the south transept arm, and in the early 1250s, after a brief interruption, finished the upper two stories in the three eastern bays on the south side of the nave and the south aisle to the juncture with Suger's western bays. The vaults of the monks' choir may have been left incomplete at his death in 1254. Henri Mallet's years as abbot (1254–58) were troubled ones, and he was removed from office by papal decree. Both the fabric of the building and the documents suggest that perhaps no further construction took place during these four years. Work was picked up again with the election of Mathieu de Vendôme as abbot in 1258, and as soon as possible the royal tombs were installed in the crossing. Completion of the nave was slow, however, as taxation for the crusade of 1270 and further taxes imposed by Gregory X in 1274 probably affected the finances of St-Denis. It is also probable that the nave was completed at least a few years before the consecration in 1281.

6 ✤

Sources and Influences

S T-DENIS IS THE PRODUCT OF A CENTURY OF REFLECTION ON THE WALL, THE vault, and the nature of Gothic architecture. Its design recalls many of the ideas of the preceding century in the first Gothic of Abbot Suger and his contemporaries and rejects the codified interpretation of the style in the great High Gothic cathedrals of Chartres, Soissons, Amiens, and Reims.[1] There is a revival of forms that had made an appearance in the first Gothic monuments of the 1130s and 1140s as well as of a number of structural elements that had remained for the most part locked in a provincial context. The new attitude toward Gothic design and the complex variety of sources at St-Denis indeed suggest that there was a fundamental reconsideration of the style—a reconsideration that results in the variant of Gothic known as Rayonnant. This chapter examines these sources as well as the artistic context for the thirteenth-century church. The dating and chronology discussed in the preceding chapter form the point of departure for this process and are indispensable in situating the design of the new church where it belongs: that is, in 1230 or early 1231.

Before entering into an extensive analysis of the relationship of this church to the architecture of its time, we should recall that the chevet is dominated by the principle of adjustment from the proportions of Suger's ambulatory to the new, "ideal" proportions of the transept and nave. It is this latter elevation and these proportions that were sought by the architect of the first program; as we have seen, the bays to the east of the crossing are by and large a compromise between the givens of Suger's chevet of 1144 and the elevation of 1231. The discussion here will therefore concentrate on the transept and the nave rather than on the chevet.

I shall focus first on the design of the elevation as a whole and then proceed to consider the parts. To some extent, the discussion is limited by the restoration of St-Denis and the complete or partial loss of a number of major monuments that were, or may have been, related to its program. A further complication lies in the absence of positive dates of construction for a number of contemporary buildings of comparable scale, not to speak of the even more limited documentation for smaller parish churches.[2] Moreover, the treatment of tracery patterns and other details by the 1230s rarely permits the identification of the place of origin and training of a medieval architect; if such identification was possible in the preceding century, as many scholars have maintained, it is no longer viable in the thirteenth.[3] The design of St-Denis is the result of wide exposure to sources in Normandy, Picardy, Burgundy, the Ile-de-France, and the Champagne. To attribute the architect's great originality and receptivity to a wealth of ideas simply to the accidents of place of birth and the good fortune of travel is to do him an injustice. Certainly these were factors, but so must have been drawings, notebooks, and the eternal resource of discussion and conversation.[4] The skeptical reader need only consider the conscious revival of elements from twelfth-century Gothic in the design of St-Denis to obtain some small sense of the process of reflection and study behind the disposition of this church.

The three-story elevation goes back, of course, to Chartres and before that to various (now mostly destroyed) monuments in the Aisne.[5] The simplified elevation introduced on a monumental scale at Chartres had come to characterize all large-scale buildings in Picardy, the Champagne, and the Ile-de-France after 1200.[6] But the handling of the proportions at St-Denis differs from the prototypes; at Chartres, as at Reims and Soissons, the arcade and the clerestory are of equal height, whereas at St-Denis, the system of proportions is more complex, responding as it does to the incorporation of large parts of the old church into the new structure. The repetition of the same dimension for arcade and clerestory at Chartres and Soissons is rejected at St-Denis by linking the triforium and clerestory through shared mullions; when combined with the glazing of the triforium this creates a certain ambiguity as to whether there are two stories or three. In other words, the proportions of the elevation are tied to the treatment of the parts, and once the triforium and clerestory are no longer handled as separate units, their relationship to the arcade below also undergoes a transformation.

It is therefore not possible to reduce the elevation of St-Denis to a simple ratio between the parts. The adoption of a taller arcade in relation to the height of the clerestory recalls the proportions of a series of churches in earlier Gothic architecture of the twelfth century, such as those at St-Germain-des-Prés or possibly at St-Denis itself.[7] But aside from the linkage of the upper two stories and the adjustment to the dimensions of the preserved parts of the twelfth-century church, is it possible that the new proportions of St-Denis develop in response to what may have been perceived as a certain static quality in High Gothic proportions? Certainly those at Chartres and Soissons are generally abandoned in a series of monuments in the second quarter of the thirteenth century, as in the nave of Châlons-sur-Marne and in the chevets of Tournai and Le Mans cathedrals, where the height of the arcade is increased to create a vertical diminution of scale that exaggerates the effects of perspective as the walls rise above the visitor to the church.[8] Actual height is thus replaced by the illusion of height.

While at St-Denis the proportions of the arcade to the triforium and clerestory are roughly 3 : 1 : 2½, those at Amiens, at Châlons, and in the chevet of Tournai are expanded to 4 : 1 : 3. One wonders whether the overwhelming presence of the nave arcade at Bourges may not have found a distant reflection in this new interest in an enlarged lower story.[9]

Within the elevation itself, there is the suggestion of a similar reexamination of the High Gothic formula, of a continuous search for new and more complex relations between the parts. One factor here is the linkage of the clerestory and triforium, as we have seen. The tracery is designed to permit the continuation of the clerestory mullions as part of the triforium arcade. The two stories are also structurally united by the treatment of the shaft underneath the wall-rib, which descends only to the base of the triforium (plate 21), thus setting back the wall plane of the upper stories behind that of the arcade (plate 2). This detail emphasizes the unity of the triforium and clerestory, adds to the complex textures of the wall surfaces, and slightly expands the volume of the nave as the wall moves upward.

The treatment of the shaft beneath the wall-rib at St-Denis is anticipated in the nave of Amiens (plate 66). However, the reasons for the truncation of this element at the base of the triforium at Amiens seem to be different from those at St-Denis, as at the former the cantonnated pier inherited from Chartres is still very much in evidence. At Chartres the descent of the wall-rib to the arcade abacus creates an effect of weight and plasticity, also visible at Reims (plate 67). At both Chartres and Reims, the responds project vigorously from the spandrels of the arcade, modeling the interior volume and creating a sharp division between the bays. Amiens is a much thinner, lighter structure, and perhaps no detail in its design is more telling than the truncation of these shafts at the base of the triforium, setting the plane of the wall of the upper two stories back slightly instead of themselves projecting into the main vessel.

However, the effect of the recessed wall plane resulting from the interruption of the shafts is in fact deemphasized as much as possible at Amiens. While at St-Denis the triforium is clearly set on a horizontal platform resting on top of the thick arcade wall (plate 63), Amiens uses a number of devices to distract the eye from the recessed upper wall. The most dramatic is the richly modeled floral *rinceau* passing along the base of the triforium and over the nave responds (plate 66). Also, the triforium itself is set back on a steeply canted *glacis* that makes the transition from one layer of depth to the next. (This is barely visible from below in the nave.) A third device unites the shaft of the wall-rib to the colonettes of the triforium arcade, for the shaft is given a common abacus with its neighbors, even though it has no capital (plate 66). The long shaft beneath the wall-rib is thus absorbed into the arcading of the triforium.

All this differs considerably from St-Denis, where the shaft descends with unencumbered independence from the springing of the wall-rib to the base of the triforium (plate 17). One can probably therefore reject the nave of Amiens

Plate 66. Amiens, eastern bays on the north side of the nave.

Plate 67. Reims, the north side of the nave.

as a source for this disposition at St-Denis,[10] turning instead to what may be a common source for both monuments:[11] the treatment of wall-ribs and their supporting shafts in the churches of Normandy, for example at the Cathedral of St-Pierre at Lisieux or the abbey church of La Trinité at Fécamp.[12] In both churches, the wall-rib stops at the base of the middle story, although at Lisieux that descent is interrupted by the horizontal continuation of the triforium abaci across the shafts, a disposition reflected at Amiens, as seen above. At Fécamp there is a passage in front of the clerestory (plate 68), but in spite of this the two upper stories are unified by the treatment of the respond supporting the wall-rib. The two upper stories are enclosed and contained by a double-roll molding, the outer of which descends to the base of the gallery, while the inner stops at the clerestory platform. Three separate layers in depth are thus drawn into a scheme in which each story is enclosed by its own framing arch as well as that of the story beneath it.[13]

The treatment of these elements reflects an interest in the integration of the elevation that characterizes many Norman churches going back to the eleventh century, in England as well as in France. One need only consider the completely different treatment of the planes of the wall and the handling of the shafts in the Cathedral of Paris and in many smaller churches in the Paris area to sense the Norman preference for the treatment of the wall as a mass of stone penetrated at different levels and depths, yet united by the vertical accent of continuous shafts.

Linkage of course exists elsewhere as well. It appears, for example, in the second bay of the chevet of Vézelay in a rather idiosyncratic form. Much more important is the use of this disposition at St-Remi at Reims, copied at Notre-Dame-en-Vaux at Châlons-sur-Marne and at the abbeys of Essomes and Orbais.[14] But the handling of the shaft under the wall-rib at St-Denis seems distinctly Norman in that it is interrupted at the base of the triforium, thus creating the staggered planes of the wall in the elevation. In the Champenois examples, on the other hand, the wall-rib descends to the column in the arcade below, and the entire height of the elevation remains on the same plane.[15]

The connection between St-Denis and Normandy is reinforced by the treatment of the pier at St-Denis. Here again, the concept of unifying the elevation is the point of departure: the cluster of shafts around a diamond-shaped core rises to support individual elements of the ribs and moldings above. The compound pier had been characteristic of Romanesque and continued to appear in some Early Gothic monuments, as in Suger's western bays at St-Denis itself, in the alternating supports of buildings such as Noyon, Senlis, Sens, Mantes, St-Julien-le-Pauvre, and in innumerable other churches.[16] But in the 1160s, the compound pier was generally supplanted by the column, and even the famous *pilier cantonné* of High Gothic owes its origin more to the columnar support than to the compound pier. With only a few exceptions, Normandy tended to remain stubbornly faithful to the compound support. It is an alternative to the High Gothic formula as established at Chartres, for it presumes not that the wall and support are separate entities, but rather that the wall and arches in all the complexity of their parts are compressed and continue downward to form the compound pier.

The return to the compound pier at St-Denis can be seen as the resolution of a long investigation of the relationship between the pier and the wall it supports. The variations in the design of the supports in the nave arcade at Laon suggest an attempt at continuity between column and wall by the addition of shafts around the column. The architects of Reims and Amiens experimented further in the context of the column with attached shafts as established at Chartres.[17] But ultimately the search for unity of the elevation and the cylindrical support were irreconcilable, for there was no way the cylindrical support could accommodate the complexity of moldings and ribs of the arcade and aisle, not to speak of the responds of the main vaults. The handling of these elements in the turning bays of the chevet could become particularly difficult, for the narrower intervals between the supports led to the elimination of the shafts on the sides of the pier, which then left no support for the heavy moldings of the arcade above. This problem caused the master at Beauvais to perch his arcade molding in the hemicycle on strongly projecting corbels planted high in the pier.[18]

The pier at St-Denis provided the solution. As in the case of the treatment of the wall-rib, it is tempting to suppose that Norman buildings may have been the inspiration here as well. Piers of this type were ubiquitous in Normandy and can also be found at Amiens (St-Nicolas) and in the Vexin at the church of St-Sauveur at Les Andelys.[19] In Normandy this form was entrenched long before the appearance of the rib-vault, but like double-wall construction it was particularly suited to that method of covering the main vessel. The shafts that rise from the base of the pier establish a constant against which the wall planes of the arcade, triforium, and clerestory levels are set in a series of changing relationships (plate 68). This is true at Lisieux, at Fécamp, in the nave of Rouen, and in the choir of St-Etienne at Caen, to name but a few examples. If one of the outstanding characteristics of Gothic architecture consists in the membrane of connections between vault and wall, so that the whole creates a unified skeletal framework, then the Norman pier, which with simplicity and clarity carries the weight of the vault down to the floor, is the ideal and magnificent solution.

The columns with attached shafts in the hemicycle are related to the compound piers in their design, for in each the dominant principle is the continuity of the responds down through the support. But aside from the particular conditions at St-Denis that determine their form, the new hemicycle piers and their component parts reflect a certain Parisian character that can be related to corresponding elements in churches in Paris and its environs (plate 54). Although the tradition of simple cylindrical supports established in the twelfth century at St-Denis itself—and then at St-Germain-des-Prés and Notre-Dame—had proved tenacious, some efforts were made in the last decade of the twelfth century to integrate the support more fully with the wall and vaults above. The western bays of Notre-Dame (plate 69), with their experiments in

Plate 68. Fécamp, the north side of the nave.

Plate 69. Paris, Notre–Dame, the western bays on the south side of the nave.

pier types, reflect this concern and give evidence of the struggle to achieve a vertical integration of the elevation that culminates in the piers at St-Denis, at Mantes, and in the nave of Gonesse. It seems likely that both the work at the west end of Notre-Dame and the new piers at St-Denis were influenced by the piers of Soissons and Chartres cathedrals, although at St-Denis the single attached shaft or triple shafts exist only on the inner face of the support, suggesting that the connection with Soissons is the more compelling.[20] The slenderness of the pier at Soissons provided a possible model for the slightly more elaborate column with shafts at St-Denis. But in the latter the uninterrupted shaft permits a direct link between the pier and the wall and vaults, a principle that becomes even more pronounced in the compound piers.

Another unusual feature in the design of the lower story at St-Denis is the use of a wall-passage around the nave and transepts (plate 18).[21] Though the wall-passage is common in the churches of the Champagne and Burgundy, it is new in the Ile-de-France, where the aisle wall has been treated as a thin, unpenetrated membrane. The passage sets the aisle windows in a wall plane behind that of the responds, splitting the wall into two parallel planes and thus expanding the width of the aisle by swelling the space out to the sides. This type of wall-passage, normally referred to as *Champenois,* appears frequently in the area for which it is named, as well as in Burgundy.[22] But of course it had its ultimate origins in Norman double-wall construction and in the elegant experiments with this idea that take place in the Oise and the Aisne in the transepts of Noyon, Soissons, and Laon cathedrals.[23] The insertion of a passage circumnavigating the walls of the church at the arcade level probably derives from the axial chapel of St-Remi at Reims, and it was soon picked up and used in Reims Cathedral.[24] But St-Remi seems also to have been the inspiration for a series of churches in Burgundy where this feature is adopted as an integral part of the design, as at Auxerre, the chevet of Notre-Dame in Dijon, and smaller churches such as St-Martin at Clamecy.[25]

The adoption of this aisle passage at St-Denis marks the first time it is used in the churches in or around Paris. This is not surprising, for the thinness of structure characteristic of Parisian architecture, particularly of the cathedral of Notre-Dame, was antithetical to the doubling of the wall that became characteristic of Gothic design elsewhere.[26] The design of the wall-passage at St-Denis is not simply copied from either Burgundian or Champenois sources, however; rather it takes certain features from each region and blends them into a new variation on the theme.

Wall-passages had developed differently in the Champagne and in Burgundy, though St-Remi may have been the inspiration for both dispositions. At the Burgundian cathedral of Auxerre, for example, the aisle responds tend to conceal the spur of wall behind, and the passage from one bay to the next is created by the abrupt interruption of this wall at a high level. The two layers of wall are separated by a flat ceiling above, creating a narrow, rectangular volume of space in front of the aisle windows. There is an explicit separation of the two planes of wall, repeated in the clerestory of the chevet, where the passage is partially vaulted. On both levels the effect of two thin parallel screens of wall is striking.

The Champenois approach is exemplified at Reims Cathedral (plate 67) and in related monuments, as at the Cathedral of Toul and at smaller churches, such as Rieux. At Reims, the responds, instead of concealing the transverse wall behind, are molded into its face, thereby augmenting its mass. In an attempt to unify the shafts and the buttressing wall behind them, the foliate design of the capitals continues as a sculpted frieze back to the windows (plate 67). This of course has the effect of exaggerating the width and substance of this connecting mass of masonry. The wall-passage thus produces massive, three-dimensional modeling of the wall, rather than the superposition of two thin and brittle layers of stone, as at Auxerre. The responds are also bonded in with the dado arcading by the continuation of the horizontal molding across the shafts. The heaviness of the Reims solution and the unity of the front and back planes is reinforced by the arch over the window, here so thick that it almost becomes a transverse vault. This arch is placed slightly lower than the wall-rib and the webbing of the aisle vaults; its conspicuous form focuses attention on the weight and plasticity of the wall, unlike Auxerre, where instead the eye is caught by the voids and confused by the constantly changing relationship of the two surfaces. The small passageways passing from bay to bay at Reims are placed low and seem dwarfed by the great mass of masonry they penetrate.

At St-Denis, the transverse wall is set back behind the responds, and the vaulted covering over each bay of the passage is tucked upward behind and above the wall-rib, forming a recessed canopy (plate 18). As at Auxerre and the chevet of Clamecy, the wall-rib clearly separates the spatial plane of the aisle wall from that of the window, emphasizing the lightness and elegance of the structure, rather than the more massive, tunnel-vaulted effect at Reims.

Other elements suggest Champenois sources. Specifically, the shafts are consistently bonded with the transverse wall behind, not cut in *en délit* pieces as in the Burgundian monuments.[27] As at Reims, all the aisle responds rise from the ground level and culminate in a common abacus; none are set on the passage itself. Furthermore, there is an attempt to unify the level of the capitals of the responds with those of the window by linking them through the horizontal continuation of the abacus across the transverse wall (plate 18). The use of the prolonged abacus here is not exclusively Champenois, however, for it appears in the transept chapels, transept terminal walls, and the rebuilt east end of Laon as well as in the clerestory of Fécamp (plate 68). It is perhaps also related to St-Remi, where the abaci in the axial window extend halfway back to the window.[28]

The design of the wall-passage at St-Denis thus combines a number of elements borrowed from both Burgundian and Champenois sources. So does the dado arcading which enlivens the thick lower wall. Trilobed arches appear in Burgundy in churches such as Notre-Dame in Dijon, but also in various structures without passages in the east of France, such as the chevet of Mon-tiérender,[29] as well as in the nave of Amiens.

The freedom with which the master designed the wall-passage at St-Denis is echoed at St-Germain-en-Laye, where the Burgundian variant of a rectangular passage is revived, in contrast to the vaulted passage at the abbey church (plates 60 and 61). As the palace chapel is a much smaller structure, the architect at St-Germain-en-Laye may have felt freer to lighten the wall and to exploit the idea of parallel screens. In any event, the screen effect here is taken even further than in Burgundian monuments, for the back windows are con-ceived as rectangular panels, with trilobes placed in the spandrels (plate 62).[30] The light structure and delicate play of planes in the wall make the vaults seem to float above the interior, suspended only by the slender responds (plates 60 and 61). It is a small-scale refinement of the design of St-Denis that returns to the Burgundian esthetic of paper-thin double walls and floating vaults.[31]

Further innovations in the design of the triforium and clerestory at St-Denis, aside from the linkage of the two stories discussed above, consist in the glazing of the triforium and in the tracery patterns of the clerestory. Here too the sources of inspiration are older models and regional solutions characteristic of Normandy and the Champagne. These are combined with a lightness of struc-ture frequently seen in churches of the Aisne, Paris, and the surrounding regions. It is no coincidence that linkage and glazing appear simultaneously at St-Denis, since they had already been associated in earlier programs and in more modest contexts, as in the ambulatory of Beauvais.

The design of the triforium, composed of pairs of narrow arches en-closed by larger pointed arches, is reminiscent of the treatment of this element at Sens, at St-Germain-des-Prés, in the chevet of Gonesse, at Lisieux and Bayeux, and possibly in the earlier chevet of St-Denis itself as built in the 1140s. This general principle of grouping elements within enclosing arches had recently been revived at Amiens and in the Cistercian church of Royaumont. At Amiens, however, there were three smaller openings within each larger arch, with a total of six smaller openings per bay, so that the importance of the triforium as a horizontal band of small-scale openings tended to be maintained nonetheless. Royaumont, begun in 1228, is a much more likely source for the design of the triforium at St-Denis, and the design there may have been derived from the prehurricane program in the cathedral of Troyes.[32] About the latter we can say very little, but at Royaumont the triforium seems to have consisted of pairs of trilobed arches enclosed by a lancet, each pair surmounted by a trefoil.[33] In the south transept arm, the triforium was glazed on the west side facing the cloister.

The experiments that take place in the design of the triforium during the years between 1220 and 1235 suggest that the role of this part of the elevation as it had been designed during the previous decades was being reconsidered, and the new approach to the triforium as larger units linked to the clerestory can be seen as a reaction to the continuous horizontal arcading of Chartres, Reims, Soissons, and numerous smaller churches. The tendency to group elements under larger

enclosing arches—rather than to repeat a long series of small-scale openings—
may also reflect a certain Parisian taste for combining forms into a more unified
design, often within larger relieving or enclosing arches, as in the gallery of
Notre-Dame and the triforium at Royaumont. The predilection for such groupings goes back early, to the first monuments of the Gothic style, as in the
triforium of Sens, at St-Germain-des-Prés, and possibly also at St-Denis.[34]

Trilobed arches in the context of the triforium had made an early appearance in the chevet of Noyon, and they also appear in the triforium and dado
arcading in the chevet of Montiérender. At St-Denis there is a correspondence
between the arcading of the dado beneath the wall-passage and the triforium; this
might also have been intended at Reims, if we can trust Villard d'Honnecourt's
drawing. At Amiens the blind arcading below the aisle windows was decorated
with trilobes, as was the triforium in the ambulatory of Beauvais, the former
begun in 1220 and the latter only a few years later. Indeed, trilobed arches soon
became a standard feature of Rayonnant Gothic design: they are ubiquitous in
the facade of Amiens, now recently redated to between 1236 and 1241,[35] in both
levels of the Ste-Chapelle, in the transepts and west towers of Notre-Dame, in
the cathedrals of Tours and Troyes, in the destroyed church of St-Nicaise in
Reims, and at Royaumont. They also appear in any number of small-scale
churches of the time, as at Cambronne, St-Séverin and the destroyed church of
the Holy Innocents in Paris, La Chapelle-sur-Crécy, and as far south as the
chevet of the church of Riom in the Puy-de-Dôme.

The triforium of St-Denis is extraordinary not only for the elegance of its
design, but also for the fact that the arcading is set off by a series of windows set
in the back wall of the triforium passage (plate 22). For the first time such glazing
occurs as an integral part of the design of a large-scale monument, though a
variety of experiments of this kind can be found in more modest settings.[36]
Glazing this part of the church required only a small further step in buildings
where there are no aisles in the transepts—as at St.-Léger in Soissons—for in
these no roof obscured the back wall. But until the south transept arm of Royaumont, this possibility does not seem to have been explored, and glazing of a wall-
passage was generally confined to the terminal walls of the transept or nave.[37]

The earliest examples of this experimentation with increased light and
the reduction of mass seem to appear in the Oise. Small scale and rather eccen-
trically placed openings can be found in the back wall of the triforium of St-Leu-
d'Esserent, and a further modest example of about 1210 can be seen in the church
of Mello, south of Beauvais (plate 70). At Beauvais Cathedral this idea is used in
the low triforium passage in the aisle and ambulatory of the chevet.[38] Perhaps
one should also consider the transept of Noyon Cathedral, where the series of
superimposed arcades with and without windows anticipate this Rayonnant
Gothic sensibility.

The glazing of the triforium was not simply a question of inserting a new
range of windows into the elevation. It established a whole new relationship
between light and masonry. At St-Denis, light now filters in from the width of

Plate 70. Mello (Oise), exterior.

the aisle at the arcade level, through the narrower triforium passage above, and finally, it defines the space itself in the clerestory (plate 1). Perhaps this feature, more than any other, defines the character of the Rayonnant Gothic esthetic, for the slender masonry supports are continuously set off by a light-permeated wall, emphasizing the slenderness and delicacy of the stone elements.

Glazing the triforium required a new approach to the roofs over the aisle vaults. Originally the triforium had developed as a method of decorating the blank area of wall between the clerestory and the arcade that resulted from the disposition of the aisle roofs abutting the main vessel at the base of the clerestory windows. In the rare instances where there were no aisles, as on the west side of the south transept arm of Royaumont, the glazing of the triforium presented no difficulties, and it is not surprising that it appears first in this context. But elsewhere, in the more customary arrangement of a main vessel flanked by aisles, peaked roofs had to be placed over the aisles and ambulatory, a disposition still visible at Amiens and Strasbourg. The original roofing of St-Denis appears quite clearly in a number of pre-nineteenth-century sources as well as in Debret's restoration drawings (plates 4 and 11).[39]

The tracery in the clerestory of St-Denis is anticipated in the nave of

Amiens (plate 66). In each, there is a pattern of four lancets with rosettes above.[40]
But here the similarities end, for at Amiens the treatment of the mullions,
capitals, and abaci is different, and the proportions of the whole far more slender.
The lower lancets and heavier rosettes at St-Denis are much closer in spirit to
those at Reims Cathedral, as is the handling of details: paired mullions with
circular abaci, for example. Indeed, the proportions of the clerestory elements
are the most archaic feature of the new design at St-Denis, for elsewhere, in all
the other major programs of the 1230s, 1240s, and 1250s, including St-Germain-
en-Laye, the lancets are tall and slender and the rosettes quite small. Normally
the latter occupy only a third or a quarter of the total height of the clerestory, but
at St-Denis they occupy fully a half. As we have seen in the preceding chapters,
this is the one element of the thirteenth-century elevation of St-Denis that undergoes a major change in design, and in the western bays of the nave the more
elongated *parti* is adopted (plate 17). The original clerestory pattern at St-Denis is
one of the most unusual features of the church, but the broad and ample forms
can be seen as characteristic of the general treatment of the interior volumes as
well as consonant with the concepts of harmony and unity which pervade the
new design as a whole. The large, ponderous rosettes at St-Denis recall the great,
round openings in the clerestory of Chartres Cathedral, repeated in the chevet of
Auxerre Cathedral—in both of these also the rosettes give the upper windows
considerable force and monumentality.

     Certain features of St-Denis, such as the planting of the transept towers
over the outer aisles, remain without specific sources. Transept towers in themselves are not, of course, new; they exist at Laon, Chartres, Rouen, and Reims,
among other examples. But by the second quarter of the thirteenth century this
feature had often been abandoned (at Amiens, for example), and at St-Denis the
separation of the towers from the main mass of the transept gives them a particular prominence in the exterior massing, dramatically emphasizing the square
transept. This unusual disposition finds its closest model in the fourth-century
basilica at Trier, which had been much rebuilt by the thirteenth century. In any
case, the transept towers mark this as an especially significant part of the church,
and it is indeed in the center of that volume that the royal tombs were located.
The fact that their disposition remains unique in Gothic architecture may con-
stitute an oblique confirmation of the function of this part of the church as a royal
necropolis.[41]

     As the transept towers are separated from the main vessel by one bay,
they are ideally placed to support the main vessel's fliers, thus avoiding the
complex and awkward juncture of fliers and buttresses at the angle of nave and
transept found at Chartres, Amiens, Beauvais, and Reims. The detached towers
are also placed in such a way as to avoid blocking the clerestory windows in the
outer bays of the transept arms, as they tend to do at Chartres, for example. Only
in the buttresses added to the chevet towers of St-Benoît-sur-Loire and in the
chevet towers at Chartres are there arrangements that seem to anticipate the
treatment of the towers and fliers at St-Denis. At St-Benoît this was possible

because the towers were planted over chapels off the ambulatory and thus were separated from the main vessel; at Chartres the chevet towers are over the outer aisle.

The buttresses around the chevet of St-Denis are unusual in their flat, undecorated quality, but, as pointed out in a previous chapter, their character was established by their position above the wall buttresses set between Suger's chapels. There is a precedent for their slender and austere structure in the chevet of Mantes, however. The buttresses along the nave date only to the last phases of construction, that is, between circa 1260 and the completion of the church in 1281. They are close to the design of the buttresses at Beauvais and at Meaux and may well have been copied from the new programs recently initiated in both churches.[42]

The influence of St-Denis on the architecture of the thirteenth-century appears in both small-scale copies of the parts and in larger attempts to reproduce the elevation as a whole. A reduced version of the abbey church appears in the palace chapel of St-Germain-en-Laye, a shrinking of a large-scale elevation analogous to the reduction of the chevet of Amiens to dimensions of the Ste-Chapelle. Elsewhere, Dionysian influence is especially strong in the years 1230–50, although certain elements, such as the compound pier, continued to be used long afterward.[43]

Major portions of two cathedrals are large-scale copies of St-Denis. The earliest is probably the chevet of Troyes, rebuilt after it was destroyed by a hurricane in 1228 (plates 71 and 72). Troyes has been cited by Robert Branner and others as the source of the design of St-Denis, but the treatment and carving of its parts indicate that the cathedral is later, not earlier, than the first stages of the rebuilding of the abbey church.[44] Since various improvements in design take place at Troyes that are subsequently introduced at St-Denis only in the later phases of the late 1230s—in the south side of the chevet and the south transept arm—the rebuilt upper stories of Troyes must be later in date, even if certain aspects of its design may have been anticipated in the elevation as it was begun before 1228.[45] Work was interrupted after the destruction caused by the hurricane and then resumed, perhaps as early as 1235–36. The design of the triforium at Troyes may also have been influenced to some extent by the galleries in the upper stories of the west facade at Notre-Dame, perhaps under construction in the late 1230s (plate 73). The elongated lancets of the clerestory tracery reproduce the pattern of St-Germain-en-Laye rather than that found in the transepts of St-Denis, a change in proportions eventually adopted at St-Denis itself in the clerestory of the south side of the nave, begun in the early 1250s (plates 62 and 63).

Troyes reproduces only the upper two stories of St-Denis, however; its arcade formed part of an earlier campaign begun before 1208.[46] A full, three-story copy of St-Denis appears in the nave of Strasbourg, built between circa

Plate 71. Troyes, Cathedral of St-Pierre, the north side of the chevet.

Plate 72. Troyes, Cathedral of St-Pierre, triforium on the south side of the chevet.

Plate 73. Paris, Notre-Dame, the south tower from the west.

1236/37 and 1274.[47] Here the essential elements and proportions of the elevation of St-Denis are reproduced with only relatively small modifications. These modifications are interesting, however. The piers of Strasbourg consist of sixteen shafts; this design is found in the compound piers of the chevet of St-Denis. The shaft underneath the wall-rib at Strasbourg descends to the base of the triforium, while the triple shafts for the transverse arch and two further shafts for the ribs descend to the floor. The truncation of the wall-rib shafts at the base of the triforium and the resulting recession of the wall represent the only attempt to unite triforium and clerestory, inasmuch as the former is conceived as a rectangular panel framed above and below by heavy, horizontal moldings with no further linkage. The striking unity of the upper two stories at St-Denis is thus abandoned at Strasbourg, although at the latter a vestige of St-Denis' connecting mullions remains in the double shafts in the center of the triforium in each bay.

The treatment of the triforium at Strasbourg is related to the galleries in the transept terminal walls of Notre-Dame, with polygonal shafts culminating in barely projecting capitals.[48] The insertion of quatrefoils above the trefoil arches is reminiscent of a similar device seen in a variety of churches in Paris and its environs: for example, St-Séverin, Gonesse, Cambronne, Cormeilles-en-Vexin, and Brie-Comte-Robert.[49] The decoration of the interior, especially the rinceau of small leaves at the top of the triforium, recalls similar floral moldings at the chapel of St-Germer-de-Fly, at the Ste-Chapelle, the triforium of Beauvais, and other midcentury monuments. The decorative character of the triforium and the concentration on sculptural ornament are in strong contrast to the austerity of St-Denis.

Yet in other respects Strasbourg is extraordinarily close to St-Denis. A wall-passage circumnavigates the aisles with a dado arcade (modeled on that in the radiating chapels of Amiens and the Ste-Chapelle). The greater width of the bays permits the use of four-light windows in the aisles, resulting in a neater correspondence between the tracery patterns in the aisles and the clerestory above.[50] Similarly, the shaft supporting the wall-rib stops at the base of the passage, so that the same interruption of elements occurs here as in the elevation as a whole. As a result, the responds project less vigorously from the wall than they do at St-Denis, a disposition that seems reminiscent of both Normandy (plate 68) and Burgundy.[51] Capital styles at Strasbourg are also very like those in the nave of St-Denis: one finds stiff, brittle crockets resembling those in the south aisle at St-Denis (plate 39); patterns of oak leaves in clusters, found also in the triforium of the five western bays of the nave at St-Denis (plate 45); and patterns of deeply undercut leaves forming an outer plane parallel to that of the inner core of the capital itself (plate 44).[52] Unlike those at St-Denis, the ribs at Strasbourg are consistently keeled or provided with a fillet.

On the exterior, the openings of the back wall of the triforium are identical to those at Troyes, with the spandrels glazed. The tracery of the upper rosettes is pointed in the clerestory and rounded (as at St-Denis) in the aisles, while the buttresses rise to the outer walls with only one flier, above which an engaged column on a polygonal dosseret rises to articulate the bay divisions in the upper portion of the clerestory wall.

At both Troyes and Strasbourg, elements derived from St-Denis are combined with details copied from other monuments in and around Paris. The St-Denis elevation was thus modernized in each of these buildings to incorporate the slightly more recent monuments under construction in the 1230s.

Although the unique arrangement of the transept towers at St-Denis remained without any tangible impact on the architecture of succeeding decades, the treatment of the interior transept terminal walls was another matter. The large blind arches of the same height and dimensions as the arcade that wrap around the lower half of the wall seem to have been inspired by the transept of Chartres, particularly on the north. At St-Denis, however, the principle of uniting the transept terminal wall with the rest of the elevation is more fully resolved, as the band of the triforium is carried directly across the terminal wall, while the transept rose occupies the space allotted the clerestory (plate 12). Aside from the rose, all other parts of the design of the north and south transept terminals carry through the proportions and general arrangement of the rest of the elevation. This results in a clarity and simplicity of design very different in character from the narrow and compressed transept terminal walls with their stacking of levels of Reims, for example. The particularly happy design of the transept at St-Denis results from the correlation of the width of the transept vessel with the height of the rose level: it cannot be coincidental and again emphasizes the remarkable unity of conception of the thirteenth-century program. The width of the main vessel in relation to the height of the vaults gives the rose an impressive new scale, making it the dominant element in the design of the transept as a whole. At the same time, the glazed arcading below makes this greatly expanded rose seem to hover and float in the wall, held in place only by the curving arch of the vaults above.

In the design of the north transept rose, the architect of St-Denis once again reveals the brilliance of his conception of the new church. The design of the north rose, a set of radiating trilobed arches that subdivide, culminating on the outer rim with a ring of sexlobed rosettes, explicitly recalls the tracery patterns of the triforium and clerestory on the interior. The simplicity and elegance of this rose may well derive from the recently completed one in the west facade of Notre-Dame. The somewhat elaborated design of St-Denis is then re-echoed in the rose of the new north transept terminal wall of the cathedral. Although the radiating petals in the north transept arm of Notre-Dame culminate in inscribed, pointed trilobed arches, the inspiration here—as well as in the treatment of the terminal wall as a whole, with its large-scale blind arches flanking the portal—is St-Denis. As at St-Denis, the transept rose at Notre-Dame floats above the thin screen of the glazed triforium passage directly beneath it. Although the forms at the cathedral have become thinner and more elongated, giving this structure an almost flat, metallic effect, the composition of the wall derives from the abbey church. In the south transept facade at Notre-Dame these tendencies are carried even further, linking the lower wall with the arcading of the passage beneath the rose by thin continuous shafts that appear on both interior and exterior.[53] A later version of this approach can be seen in the cathedral at Meaux. At Notre-Dame, as at St-Denis, the transept roses are inscribed in a square, with the spandrels rising above the transverse arch of the vaults. The continuation of the mullions to link with other levels on the south transept reflects the sensibility for interlocking all levels of the elevation that appeared at St-Denis in the elevation as a whole—a concept antithetical to the strict horizontal divisions established in the chapels of Amiens and in the Ste-Chapelle.

The compound pier, revived and given new life at St-Denis, was perhaps the most influential part of the new design. On occasion, as at the Cathedral of Clermont-Ferrand, the transition from cylindrical supports with attached shafts to compound piers, as in the chevet of St-Denis, is repeated "verbatim." Compound piers also appear at St-Urbain at Troyes, St-Sulpice-de-Favières, the nave of Semur-en-Auxois, St-Gengoulf at Toul, the chevets of Evreux and Cologne, and any number of other churches.[54] The linear extension of the ribs and arches to the structure of the pier was ideally suited to the skeletal structure of the wall.

The wall-passage in the aisles was copied, as we have seen, at Strasbourg, and perhaps via Strasbourg reappears in the aisles of the nave at Freiburg-im-Breisgau.[55] Closer to home, it is repeated in the aisles and apse of St-Sulpice-de-Favières, a pilgrimage church to the south of Paris. At Favières the model of St-

Germain-en-Laye was also important, for the outer wall in which the glass is set is again conceived as a rectangular panel, with blind tracery in the spandrels.[56] The dado arcading, now consisting of trefoil arches inscribed in a pointed arch, repeats the formula of the chevet of Amiens, of the Ste-Chapelle, and, as we have seen, of Strasbourg. The slender, widely spaced compound piers emphasize the breadth of the space in a manner similar to that at St-Denis, and the doubling of the aisle walls enhances this effect. At St-Sulpice, the spaciousness of the nave is increased further by raising the arches of the arcade to the base of the triforium.

The wall-passage in the aisles of St-Sulpice is handled in much the same way as at St-Denis, with the five responds descending to floor level and the impost continued back across the transverse wall. There are further similarities in the treatment of the bases, plinths, capitals, and openings of the wall-passage behind the responds. Indeed, the affinities between the western aisles at St-Denis and the aisles of St-Sulpice suggest that the latter dates to the late 1250s or 1260s, and not the 1240s or as late as 1270, as has been suggested.[57]

At St-Sulpice-de-Favières, the four-light tracery pattern is repeated in the aisles but not in the clerestory windows, where the tracery consists of pairs of trilobes surmounted by a trefoil, repeating almost exactly the pattern in the triforium. The windows in the west wall of each aisle recall the tracery in the westernmost bay of the nave of St-Denis. As at Strasbourg, there is a complete rejection of linkage at St-Sulpice, once again in favor of rectangular panels framing the triforium arcading.

The glazed triforium had, of course, existed before it was introduced at St-Denis. But nowhere had it been used as extensively as in the interior of the abbey church, where it became an extension of the clerestory and created the effect of the wall as a luminous membrane. At Troyes and at Strasbourg, the glazed triforia are clearly modeled on that of St-Denis. The glazed triforia of Amiens, Tours, and Beauvais, on the other hand, derive from independent sources. At St-Sulpice-de-Favières, the treatment of the triforium as a series of rectangular panels derives in part from St-Denis (the transept roses), but more immediately from the palace chapel of St-Germain-en-Laye. Favières also closely resembles St-Denis in the treatment of the wall-passage and tracery in the aisles.

The cylindrical supports of the hemicycle at St-Denis likewise seem to have exerted some influence on the architecture of the following decades. Although it is impossible to establish absolutely the precedence of St-Denis or Mantes, the introduction of cylindrical piers with three shafts in the west bays of the collegiate church would seem to suggest that this solution to the integration of wall and support held considerable significance.[58] The chevet of Ourscamp, rebuilt beginning about 1232, reproduces the hemicycle supports of St-Denis in the context of a reduced, two-story elevation (plate 55).[59] They reappear in the unfinished nave of Gonesse and in the meager remains of the Templar Chapel of Mont-de-Soissons.[60] The origins for this type of pier may be located in the Soissonais, although the surviving examples in the Aisne tend to be somewhat

later in date than St-Denis. Wherever this type of support is introduced, octagonal abaci are substituted for the reused twelfth-century square abaci in the
chevet of St-Denis.

The unusual proportions of the four-light clerestory of St-Denis, rejected in almost every other "copy" of the elevation in favor of slimmer and
taller forms, do reappear in a number of smaller churches, for example, in the
aisles of St-Martin-aux-Bois, in the reconstructed east wall of the parish church
of Angicourt, and in several other monuments of the Oise and the Aisne.[61] After
St-Denis, such windows appear in the straight bays of the chevet of Amiens,
though with taller lancets, and in the nave chapels of Notre-Dame and the
refectory and chapel of St-Germain-des-Près, begun in 1239 and 1245, respec-
tively, by Pierre de Montreuil.[62]

One further element of the design of the nave and transept of St-Denis
seems to have had some impact on thirteenth-century architecture. The low,
broadly pitched main vaults, so striking in the abbey church, also appear in the
chevet of Troyes, in the nave of Strasbourg, and in the chevet of Evreux.[63] This
new spaciousness is directly antithetical to the earlier sensibility at the cathedrals
of Reims and Amiens and can also be seen as a reconsideration of Early Gothic (as
at Sens).

The rapid evolution of the Gothic style in the middle of the thirteenth
century meant that many aspects of the design of St-Denis were surpassed long
before the abbey church was complete. Even Troyes, in many respects a copy of
St-Denis, exaggerates certain elements and modifies others. This occurs also in
the nave of Strasbourg. These modifications often respond to design elements
introduced in other monuments in Paris, such as the work on the west towers,
lateral chapels, and transepts of Notre-Dame, as well as the new buildings at St-
Germain-des-Prés. The chevet of Amiens and the Ste-Chapelle exploited different kinds of interior effects and tracery patterns that were then borrowed, along
with a version of the Dionysian pier, in the work on the chevet of Cologne,
begun in 1248. At the same time, the thin, flat wall surfaces of the interior of
Notre-Dame were copied in the design of Clermont-Ferrand and Tournai cathedrals.[64] Indeed, the architecture of the mid–thirteenth century develops in many
different directions at once, on the one hand exploiting the plasticity of the wall
with an abundance of small-scale shafts and on the other pressing all weight and
substance out of the wall to create an architecture made up of the superposition of
thin, brittle screens.[65] Both tendencies can be related to some extent to the
elevation of St-Denis, but this source has been combined with others to create
dramatically different kinds of interior effects. But this is the story of the evolution of Rayonnant architecture as a whole, a style in which St-Denis plays an
important introductory role.

7 ❖

Conclusion

THE REBUILDING OF ST-DENIS IN THE THIRTEENTH CENTURY CAN NOW BE SEEN
as one of the first steps in the development of the Rayonnant Gothic style.
Begun in 1231, the earliest part of the rebuilding comprised the delicate fusion of
Suger's chevet with a dramatic and innovative new design for the transept and
nave. This was not the work of two successive architects, as has hitherto been
thought, but rather of one nameless and highly original master, who, beginning
with the decision to preserve Abbot Suger's chevet, transformed the old church
into the first monumental statement of the new Rayonnant sensibility. The
design for the transept and nave was an integral part of the plans for the new
church from the very beginning of the work in the hemicycle in 1231, and indeed
every aspect of the reworked chevet can be seen as a process of subtle accommodation from the old to the new, preserving a remarkable unity in the building
as a whole.

The new church stands at a critical moment in the development of the
Gothic style. In contrast to the structural experiments of the preceding decades
and the gigantism of High Gothic, there is now a concentration upon pure design
and a new subtlety and refinement of effects. The need for concordance with the
proportions of the older building was not a limitation but rather the point of
departure for a new spaciousness of the interior—a spaciousness revealed in
every aspect of the plan and elevation, inside and out. Among the many remarkable features of this church is the reconsideration of forms that had appeared in
Early Gothic buildings of the twelfth century, most notably the return to the
compound pier. Other elements, such as the wall-passages in the aisles and the
linkage of the upper stories, suggest a broad familiarity with architectural devel-
opments in the Champagne, Burgundy, Picardy, and of course Paris itself. But
the fact remains that in spite of the range of sources in regional styles, the
architecture of St-Denis remains profoundly original and innovative.

The redating of the complete design of St-Denis to 1231 has important
implications for our knowledge of the development of the Rayonnant Gothic
style. Rather than being a program "arrived at" in the 1230s, when other experiments in the Rayonnant direction were already under way, St-Denis must be

[161]

seen as a point of departure for the new sensibility. But the serious analysis of this phase of the Gothic style has just begun, and many of the major monuments remain unstudied. Long considered a decadent phase of Gothic that departed from the classic monumentality of Chartres, Reims, and Amiens, Rayonnant Gothic has rarely received more than cursory attention. Only in the last twenty years, inspired in part by the publication of Robert Branner's *Saint Louis and the Court Style in Gothic Architecture,* have scholars of medieval architecture begun to study this phase of the Gothic style in depth and in detail. Not enough has been done to date to permit a synthetic analysis of the style in all its ramifications, but the recent redating of the campaigns at Beauvais and St-Nicaise at Reims as well as studies of Meaux, Cologne, Clermond-Ferrand, and the facade of Amiens has begun to clarify the historical and archaeological situation.[1]

It is perhaps premature, therefore, to expound at great length on the place of St-Denis in the evolution of Rayonnant Gothic. But this study does permit a few conclusions. Dating the design of St-Denis to 1231 reveals the new church as a radical and early departure from High Gothic principles—a much more dramatic break than the elevation of St-Nicaise in Reims, often considered the Rayonnant Gothic monument par excellence. St-Nicaise, after all, maintains the *pilier cantonné* of Chartres, Reims, and Amiens cathedrals, and the linkage of the upper two stories reflects the disposition of the nave of Amiens.[2] The facade of St-Nicaise, now redated to the 1240s, is seen to display the increasingly fragile and mannerist characteristics emerging elsewhere in the transept facades and tower galleries at Notre-Dame, the interior of the Ste-Chapelle, and the upper stories of Troyes.[3] At St-Denis the large-scale, High Gothic forms that persisted in the nave of St-Nicaise are broken down into a multiplicity of small parts, and the particularly striking clustering of elements in the triforium seems to initiate one of the major tendencies of Rayonnant Gothic architecture: the proliferation of slender shafts and moldings to create a new kind of delicacy and plasticity of architectural form, beautifully exemplified in the passage to the chapel at St-Germer-de-Fly and in the chevet of Cambronne, both in the Oise.[4] At the same time, there is an alternative taste for flat, pressed surfaces, such as those of Clermont-Ferrand Cathedral and other southern buildings, which surely derive from the nave of Notre-Dame in Paris and perhaps from the destroyed abbey church of Royaumont.[5]

Rayonnant Gothic may thus be seen to develop in two different directions. These are in many respects diametrically opposed to one another, yet both are rooted in the architecture of Paris and its environs. The style does not consist of one single dominant esthetic but rather of a series of themes and variations derived from widely contrasting sources. The one consistent element in the Rayonnant style is the tendency toward a great delicacy of effect, subtle relationships between the parts, and the frequent use of wall-passages to create thin, superimposed screens of wall.

It is difficult to sustain Branner's concept of a French "Court Style" and his association of mid-thirteenth-century architecture with Louis IX. One can, however, clearly identify the new style with Paris and its environs—including, of course, St-Denis—and indeed its success had much to do with the prestige of the king and his court. The receptivity of the capital to artistic currents in the provinces, particularly Burgundy, the Champagne, and Normandy, gave a new vigor to Gothic design. This paralleled the expansion of the kingdom of France itself, which under Philip Augustus and his successors had established its authority over large, new territories while at the same time emphasizing more and more the importance of Paris as the center.[6] The political expansion is paralleled in the spread of Rayonnant Gothic to the provinces, as at Carcassonne.

The importance of Paris notwithstanding, the direct association that has been created between King Louis IX and the new architectural style is misleading in many ways, and a few more words might be said here about the Court Style. Aside from Royaumont and the Ste-Chapelle, no two churches are more closely associated with Louis IX than St-Denis and the palace chapel at St-Germain-en-Laye.[7] Surely if any buildings are to be connected with the king and court, it must be these.[8] The difficulty lies in the fact that aside from St-Denis and St-Germain-en-Laye, which resemble one another closely, each royal program differs profoundly from the others.[9] Royaumont can perhaps be dismissed as a Cistercian foundation subject to the architectural rigors and homogeneity of that order, but the very different style of St-Denis and the Ste-Chapelle suggest that royal taste, insofar as it can be defined, adjusted itself to the context and requirements of each separate building program as well as to the individual styles of different architects. All of these royal buildings, including Royaumont, influenced the architecture of the following decades, but none of them *defined* it. The churches identified by Branner as Court Style take their inspiration as much from Parisian monuments unrelated to king and court as from those the king erected there and elsewhere. The continuing work on the west facade, nave chapels, buttresses, and transept terminals of Notre-Dame, the refectory of St-Martin-des Champs, the chapel and refectory erected at St-Germain-des-Prés (plate 74), and the narthex of the Temple[10] were only the most outstanding of a series of architectural monuments erected in midcentury Paris.[11] A number of mendicant churches, now destroyed, provided an austere alternative to these more luxurious structures.[12] The Court Style as it has been identified is actually the reflection of the wonderfully eclectic, inventive, and delicate architecture erected during these decades in Paris and in its environs, most prominently outside the city in the reconstruction of the chevet and transept of Meaux and the additions to the church at St-Sulpice-de-Favières. In its refinement and sophistication, it is the most dramatic and tangible expression of the emergence of Paris as the cultural and artistic center of the kingdom. The edifices identified as full-blown Court Style[13] monuments have in fact no formal connection with the king and court, nor even with the king's buildings erected between 1227 and 1254.[14] The source is rather the artistic milieu of Paris as a whole.

A further argument could be made that as Louis IX grew older, and especially after his return from his first crusade, his increasing piety and asceticism lessened his interest in building programs. He continued to make pious foundations, but no indications whatsoever survive to show that he was in-

Plate 74. St-Germain-des-Prés, fragments of the portal to the Virgin Chapel.

terested in the architecture of these establishments. After 1254 the greater number of the new foundations were mendicant houses, the architecture of which was in any case usually restrained, and there is evidence that the king himself wished to join one of those orders.[15]

But Paris was the center of the kingdom, and the work on the great monuments of Notre-Dame, St-Germain-des-Prés, and, in the near vicinity, St-Denis, established the character of the new style even as the king turned to more austere and restrained establishments. The former provided a number of up-to-date prototypes in much the same way that Chartres had served as a model thirty years earlier. The diversity of architectural solutions provided by these models, from the delicate plasticity of St-Denis and the Ste-Chapelle to the brittle and flat surfaces of the chapel at St-Germain-des-Prés (plates 64 and 74) and the transept facades at Notre-Dame, meant that the architectural monuments that followed were also diverse. The traditional designation of the style as Rayonnant Gothic, which leaves aside the personality and predilections of Louis IX, is ultimately far more satisfactory.

As is well known, the importance and prestige of St-Denis lay in part in its role as the necropolis of the kings of France. No other church or abbey in Europe could claim as long a tradition of royal burial. And to my knowledge, no other church has a comparable expansion of the transept, which with its de-tached towers gives a monumentality and prominence to the exterior equal to the great swelling of the space on the interior. The function of the abbey church as a royal necropolis, emphasized by the funereal connotations of the transept towers, led to an unprecedented grandeur in this part of the church.

But not only the originality of the plan is important. The elevation, adjusted to create a harmonious and fluid relationship between the older and newer parts of the church, also introduces a new approach to glass and stone. No longer is the wall penetrated by windows, but rather light and masonry now interact in a series of subtle and changing relationships on all levels of the eleva-tion. If it is indeed true that the glazed triforium appears first at St-Denis as an integral part of a monumental elevation, it is tempting to suggest that this was particularly appropriate, for the writings of Dionysius the Pseudo-Areopagite were still of paramount importance, as attested by the writings of Grosseteste, Thomas Aquinas, and Albertus Magnus. Suger had indicated that the meta-physics of Dionysius were the inspiration for his twelfth-century church, and it is likely that they were also in the thoughts of Eudes Clément and his architect. For at the same time that the new church preserved as much of Suger's building as possible, it fulfilled in every sense his words and its uniquely Dionysian heritage:

> Once the new rear part is joined to the part in front,
> The church shines with its middle part brightened.
> For bright is that which is brightly coupled with the bright,
> And bright is the noble edifice pervaded by the new light.

Appendix 1
THE RECONSTRUCTION OF TROYES AND ST-DENIS

The chevet of Troyes is closely related to St-Denis, and the precedence of one monument over the other has long been under discussion.[1] In recent years, Robert Branner has stated firmly that the upper stories of the chevet at Troyes preceded the elevation of St-Denis, and that the same architect, the "St-Denis Master," was responsible for both buildings.[2] The first part of Branner's thesis has been seconded (with some hesitation) in the last few years by Norbert Bongartz in his monograph on the chevet of Troyes, although this author rejects the attribution of both buildings to the same man.[3] A careful analysis of the monuments, however, sustains neither Branner's nor Bongartz's hypotheses, and I suggest that after the hurricane of 1228 the reconstruction and completion of the upper two stories of the chevet of Troyes were delayed and that they are in fact a modified and slightly modernized copy of the elevation of St-Denis (plates 17 and 72).[4]

The chronology of Troyes is complicated; this, if nothing else, is certain. The conspicuous variation in the types of capitals and bases suggests that some parts of the triforium antedate others and may have been either prepared or in place before the storm of 1228. Bongartz has thus been led to conclude that the original, prehurricane program for the upper stories and the final structure may have closely resembled each other, including some modern elements of the design, such as linkage of the triforium and clerestory and the glazing of the back wall.[5] His comparison of certain details at Troyes with what remains of the triforium at the destroyed abbey church of Royaumont is telling,[6] especially in view of the existence of a glazed triforium in the west wall of the south transept arm and in the west facade of the abbey church.[7] But Royaumont was founded only in 1228, the very year in which the terrible damage at Troyes took place, and the relative chronology of the program of the upper stories at Troyes, the design of Royaumont, and the revised program subsequently adopted at Troyes are now difficult, if not impossible, to unravel, especially given the fragmentary state of the evidence.

The surviving parts of the first triforium at Troyes are the lower beds of

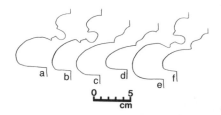

Figure 34. Base profiles, chevet triforium of Troyes Cathedral.

the responds that rise to the departure of the main vaults and the attached shafts of the triforium arcading. The base profiles and capital styles are more archaic (fig. 34a,b,e). The newer elements of the triforium, with flattened bases (fig. 34c,d,f) and the more modern capitals with "detached" leaves (plates 75 and 76) appear only *within* the bay. The most striking elements of the design within the bay—the continuation of the mullions of the clerestory, the inverted trilobes, and the glazing of the back wall—were therefore not necessarily anticipated in the original design prior to 1228; indeed, a similar handling of the shafts in the remains of Royaumont existed for a program that contained neither linkage nor (with the exception of one wall) glazing.[8]

The relation of the elevation of Troyes as it exists today to St-Denis can, however, be established by an examination of certain details. At Troyes, both the abaci and the plinths in the triforium arcade are set at an angle, a modification in design that appears at St-Denis only in the east wall of the south transept arm, which can be dated to the last years of the 1230s or circa 1240.[9] The same is true of the clerestory abaci, which at Troyes are consistently set at an angle, while at St-Denis the rounded abacus is retained throughout the work of the 1230s as far as the east wall of the south transept arm (plate 59).[10] The central groupings of shafts within the bay are cut in one long *en délit* piece, a detail that at St-Denis begins only in the last bay prior to the crossing on the south side of the chevet (plate 57). The glazed openings in the back wall of the triforium are conceived as a unit at Troyes, with the spandrels between the lancets and oculi glazed, a disposition adopted at St-Denis in the last campaign of construction (beginning in 1258) that completed the five western bays on either side of the nave. This much reduces the flat, plate-tracery effect of this part of the wall at St-Denis. The relieving arches beneath the glazed openings of the back wall of the triforium, which exist only in the bays erected above Suger's ambulatory (plate 20), make no appearance at Troyes, although the glazed openings are set as high in the wall of the cathedral as they are in the chevet of the abbey church.

Two further details are also telling. In the triforium of Troyes, the trilobes are reversed, with the wider part of the pattern on top (plate 72). The

Plate 75. Troyes, Cathedral of St-Pierre, triforium capitals in the chevet.

Plate 76. Troyes, Cathedral of St-Pierre, triforium capitals in the chevet.

effect is to dilate the openings, apparently diminishing the weight of the wall as the enclosing arches are stilted to contain the reversed trilobes (plates 17 and 71). At St-Denis, on the other hand, the position of the trilobe, with its narrowest part uppermost, corresponds with the form of the arch that encloses it. Troyes would seem to reflect a certain "mannerist" taste for dilated openings that appears in the architecture of the late 1230s and 1240s, for example, in the towers of Notre-Dame, which also have reversed trilobes (plate 73) or in the transept facades of that same cathedral, where quatrefoils set within pointed arches now carry that sensibility even further. And finally, at Troyes, the forms in both the triforium and the clerestory are elongated. As Bongartz has pointed out, the proportions of the lancets and rosettes in the straight and turning bays of the chevet are consistent throughout, whereas the lancets in the turning bays at St-Denis are much taller than those elsewhere (plate 1). But this has to do with the wide spacing of the hemicycle piers at Troyes as opposed to the narrow, small-scale positioning of Suger's hemicycle supports, which meant that above in the clerestory each bay was still very narrow. The retention of the lower parts of Suger's chevet therefore did not permit the continuation of the four-light tracery pattern in the turning bays of the chevet (plate 13); in the reduced pattern of two lancets and a rosette, the lancets inevitably had to be taller.[11] In any case, the elongated proportions of the tracery at Troyes, later adopted in the nave of St-Denis in the work after 1250 (plate 63), reflect the taste for increasingly attenuated forms characteristic of Rayonnant Gothic design in the late 1230s and the 1240s.

The architectural and stylistic evidence can leave no further uncertainty. No architect would introduce more archaic forms in a second version of a design; nor does the appearance of the same tracery patterns signify the work of the same man. The relation of these two monuments to each other brings to mind Satan's words in book IX of *Paradise Lost,* where he compares earth to heaven as "built / With second thoughts, reforming what was old! /For what God, after better, worse would build?" Troyes is surely "built with second thoughts," a slightly modified version of the new elevation of St-Denis that incorporates various improvements worked into the design of the abbey church as work proceeded, and the renewal of construction of the upper stories of the cathedral should therefore be dated to circa 1235 at the very earliest. The attribution of both programs to the same architect thus becomes even more improbable. Rather, it seems likely that transmission of the design took place in the form of drawings or sketches made at the abbey and influenced, perhaps, by certain ideas derived from the ongoing construction at Notre-Dame in the handling of details which were carried to Troyes and used in the reconstruction of the half-finished chevet. Troyes thus becomes a somewhat provincial reflection of the architectural innovations of Paris and its immediate environs, one of the earliest examples of the exportation of Parisian Gothic well outside the confines of the Ile-de-France. The elevation of St-Denis, as we have seen, was conceived as a system involving a subtle relation of all three stories of the elevation to the new proportions and dimensions of the older church *and* the new plan, an interpretation of space in which all aspects of the design are interlocked. No similar unity of conception applies to the chevet of Troyes; it too is magnificent, but as an accumulation of ideas rather than as the expression of a single, unified vision.

Appendix 2

PIERRE DE MONTREUIL

The name of Pierre de Montreuil has exerted a magnetic attraction on historians of the Middle Ages; indeed, virtually every building erected in Paris and its environs between about 1230 and his death in 1267 has at one time or another been attributed to him.[1] All that survives of this architect's presence at the abbey of St-Denis is a document of 1247 that mentions Pierre de Montreuil as "cementarius de Sancto Dyonisio."[2] The only other works securely attributed to him are the south transept arm of Notre-Dame in Paris and the refectory and Virgin Chapel at St-Germain-des-Prés. Only small fragments of either structure survive at St-Germain.

Pierre de Montreuil's role at the abbey of St-Denis is difficult to define with precision, however. Robert Branner suggested that he was simply a master mason there, inasmuch as the document does not contain the words or title "Magister operum."[3] This has been convincingly refuted by Louis Grodecki, who has pointed out that this title was never used to refer to the architect in any of the surviving documents of the abbey, and there are a considerable number of these for the late thirteenth century and parts of the fourteenth.[4] A comparison of what survives of his work at St-Germain-des-Prés with St-Denis suggests two very different sensibilities in operation: the plasticity and bundling of forms as well as the amplitude of the volumes at St-Denis are profoundly different from the thin, attenuated, isolated shafts of the refectory or Virgin Chapel at St-Germain-des-Prés (plates 1 and 64). The tracery of the surviving window of the refectory, now embedded in a wall of a recently constructed apartment house, resembles that of St-Denis only superficially, in the disposition of a four-light window crowned with three rosettes. The handling of the shafts, the proportions of the forms, the absence of capitals, and the flattened bases without a scotia are all profoundly different from the meticulously punctuated handling of the forms in the eastern parts of St-Denis. Moreover, the Virgin Chapel at St-Germain-des-Prés, with its brittle, linear shafts and moldings that have no hint of mass or weight (plate 64), its delicate leaf ornament above the arches and on the portal now at Cluny (plate 74), and its pointed trilobes inscribed in pointed arches, are very different from the preference for rounded and more solid forms penetrated by lateral arches at the abbey church of St-Denis.

Yet the differences between what we know of Pierre de Montreuil's work and St-Denis do not necessarily mean that this famous architect was *not* at St-Denis—there is no reason to contest the document or demote the architect, surely by then a well known, important master. What is most probable is that the elevation had been determined long before he came on the scene sometime in the 1240s, and that he simply continued a program already established. Given that the document is dated to 1247, it seems likely that he was at St-Denis during the construction of the south transept arm, begun circa 1240 but perhaps not vaulted until the late 1250s.[5] However, as the south transept portal is significantly more archaic in style than his portal of the Virgin Chapel at St-Germain-des-Prés (plates 46, 47, and 74), it can probably be assumed that the design and construction of the portal at St-Denis predate his arrival. Indeed, if this portal does date to the early 1240s, then the relationship between the sculpture and the architecture of St-Denis and that of St-Germain-des-Prés is analogous, with the taste for rounded, plastic forms at the former transformed to the thin, delicate, and brittle effects of the latter.

If Pierre de Montreuil left his mark anywhere at St-Denis, it may have been in the adoption of new proportions in the clerestory windows in the eastern bays on the south side of the nave (plate 2), perhaps erected in the last years of the abbacy of Guillaume de Massouris in 1252–54. Certainly the longer and more attenuated forms seem consistent with the proportions of the Virgin Chapel, erected between 1245 and 1250/55. But these new proportions, the linkage of the stories, and the thinner, more brittle forms were already being used in Paris in the chapels erected along the north side of the nave at Notre-Dame.[6]

It is my inclination to leave these questions open for the present. The names of architects that begin to appear occasionally in the thirteenth century have often tended to obscure and confuse rather than clarify our understanding of the buildings, and there is rarely enough material to permit the identification of an architect's style. We must be content for the present to pursue the study of Gothic architecture as a "Kunstgeschichte ohne Namen" rather than to invent personalities ("the Saint-Denis Master") or try to unravel the mysteries of an individual's way of doing things when all we have is a name. As so often in the realm of medieval architecture, Jean Bony has the last word on the subject: "But . . . why worry about names, which convey little more than does complete anonymity, in the face of the finished work, so very much more revealing and more instructive than any text?"[7]

ABBREVIATIONS AND SHORT TITLES

AA: Annales archéologiques

AB: The Art Bulletin

AIBLM: Académie des inscriptions et belles-lettres, mémoires

AN: Paris, Archives Nationales

BEC: Bibliothèque de l'école des chartes

BM: Bulletin monumental

BN: Paris, Bibliothèque Nationale

CA: Congrès archéologique

Conway: W. Martin Conway, "The Abbey of Saint-Denis and its Ancient Treasures," *Archaeologia*, 2d. ser., 66 (1915):103–58.

Crosby (1942): Sumner McKnight Crosby, *The Abbey of St-Denis, 475–1122*, vol. 1 (New Haven: Yale University Press, 1942)

Crosby (1953): Sumner McKnight Crosby, *L'Abbaye royale de Saint-Denis* (Paris: P. Hartmann, 1953)

Crosby (forthcoming): Sumner McKnight Crosby, *The Royal Abbey of Saint-Denis from Its Beginnings to the Death of Suger* (New Haven, Yale University Press)

Doublet: J. Doublet, *Histoire de l'abbaye de S.Denys en France* (Paris: Jean de Heuqueville, 1625)

Erlande-Brandenbourg, *Le Roi:* Alain Erlande-Brandenbourg, *Le Roi est mort:* *Étude sur les funérailles, les sépultures, et les tombeaux des rois de France jusqu'à la fin du XIIIème siècle* (Paris: Arts et métiers graphiques, 1975)

Félibien: Dom Michel Félibien, *Histoire de l'abbaye royale de Saint-Denys en France* (Paris: F. Leonard, 1706)

GBA: Gazette des Beaux-Arts, Paris

GC: Gallia christiana in provincias ecclesiasticas distributa . . .

JSAH: Journal of the Society of Architectural Historians, Philadelphia

JWCI: Journal of the Warburg and Courtauld Institutes, London

MA: Le moyen-âge, revue d'histoire et de philologie, Paris

MH: Paris, les Archives de la Commission des Monuments Historiques

SNAFM: La société nationale des antiquaires de France, mémoires, Paris

Spiegel, *The Chronicle Tradition:* Gabrielle Spiegel, *The Chronicle Tradition of Saint-Denis: A Survey* (Brookline, Mass., and Leyden, 1978)

Viollet-le-Duc, *Dictionnaire:* Eugène Emmanuel Viollet-le-Duc, *Dictionnaire raisonné de l'architecture français du XIè au XVIè siècle.* 10 volumes (Paris: Bance, 1854–68)

Notes

INTRODUCTION

1. *St-Denis* will refer to the abbey, *Saint Denis* to the man, and *St. Denis* to the town. All names are given in French except in cases where a common English equivalent exists (such as Philip Augustus for Philippe Auguste).

2. The identification of Saint Denis as the Apostle of the Gauls is due to Abbot Hilduin in the ninth century. This forms part of the expansion of the legend of Saint Denis that confuses him with a disciple of Saint Paul, thus giving him a first-century date. See below, n. 6, and M. Buchner, *Das Vizepapstum des Abtes von St. Denis* (Paderborn: F. Schöningh, 1928).

3. In *GC* the historians of St-Maur refer to the abbey of St-Denis as *Omniusque facile totius Galliae, et forsam Europae abbatiarum princeps* (vol. 7, p. 332). The bibliography on the abbey and its history is too long to include here. However, on the history of the monastery to c. 1700 the most complete source is still Félibien. More recent historical and archaeological sources are: Crosby (1942); Crosby (1953); Crosby (forthcoming); and Spiegel, *The Chronicle Tradition*.

4. See Suger's own references to the older church, published in *Abbot Suger on the Abbey Church of St.-Denis and its Art Treasures,* 2d ed., trans. and ed. Erwin Panofsky (Princeton: Princeton University Press, 1979), p. 101. Indeed, the desire to preserve significant portions of earlier structures also operated in the Carolingian reconstruction of the Merovingian church (see Crosby [forthcoming], part I, chap. 3).

5. Ibid. One can point to the crypts of St-Germain at Auxerre and St-Sernin at Toulouse as other examples of older crypts preserved and incorporated into later churches. On the latter, see Marcel Durliat, "Les Cryptes de Saint-Sernin de Toulouse; bilan des recherches récentes," *Les Monuments historiques de la France* 17 (1971):25–40.

6. On the conflation and confusion of Saint Denis of Paris with Dionysius, see Crosby (1942), pp. 24ff., and more recently Crosby (forthcoming), part I, introduction. Also P. G. Théry, "Contribution à l'histoire de l'Aréopagitisme au IXᵉ siècle," *MA* 2ème sér., 25 (1923):111–53; Robert Bossuat, "Traditions populaires relatives au martyre et à la sépulture de Saint Denis," *MA* 4ème sér., 11 (1956):479–509; and Otto von Simson, *The Gothic Cathedral: Origins of Gothic Architecture and the Medieval Concept of Order,* Bollingen Series, vol. 48 (New York: Pantheon, 1956), pp. 103–05.

7. Only the briefest summary of the succession of churches is given here as a prelude to the discussion of the thirteenth-century church. The reader is directed to Crosby's volumes on the earlier churches.

8. Crosby (forthcoming), part I, introduction.

9. Little is known of the plan or disposition of this early church. There has also been considerable doubt as to its original location. See Crosby (1942), pp. 65–73, and more recently Crosby (forthcoming), part I, chap. 1, as well as Spiegel, *The Chronicle Tradition,* pp. 14–15.

10. Gregory of Tours in the sixth century speaks of *custodes* at the site, presumably guardians of the cult of Saint Denis (Gabrielle Spiegel, "The Cult of Saint Denis and Capetian Kingship," *Journal of Medieval History* 1 [1975]:51; Spiegel, *The Chronicle Tradition,* pp. 15–17; Léon Levillain, "Etudes sur l'abbaye de Saint-Denis à l'époque mérovingienne," *BEC* 76 [1925]:60–64; and Crosby [forthcoming], part I, chap. 1).

11. Panofsky, *Abbot Suger,* pp. 59, 71, 87, 224–25.

12. The legend does not appear in written sources until the eleventh century and is mentioned as an impediment to both Suger's and Eudes' rebuilding. Both abbots believed the Carolingian church to have been Dagobert's structure. See Charles J. Liebman, "La Consécration légendaire de Saint-Denis," *MA,* 3d ser., 45 (1935):252–64, esp. 255. The cult of this consecration was perpetuated in the fifth chapel on the north side of the nave, referred to by Doublet as the chapel of Saint Ladre (Doublet, p. 326). Interestingly, the Benedictine abbey of Westminster, rebuilt by Henry III beginning in 1245, was, according to legend, consecrated by Saint Peter, its patron saint.

13. For an extended discussion, see Crosby (1942), pp. 87–164, and the more recent revised analysis in Crosby (forthcoming), part I, chap. 3.

14. Crosby (1942), pp. 95–112; and Richard Krautheimer, "The Carolingian Revival of Early Christian Architecture," in *Studies in Early Christian, Medieval and Renaissance Art,* ed. J. Ackerman et al. (New York: NYU Press, 1969), pp. 206–07.

15. Crosby (forthcoming), part I, chap. 3. The annular crypt and its *confessio* survived until the restorations of Viollet-le-Duc in the 1860s.

16. Three centuries later, there is a vivid description of such crowding in Panofsky, *Abbot Suger,* pp. 87–89. See also Jean Hubert, *L'Art pré-roman* (Paris: Editions d'art et d'histoire, 1938), pp. 53–65, on the general subject of crypts. Hilduin's crypt contained the relics of the Passion. The arrangement of the two crypts and their relics was described by Haimon in the eleventh century, a text quoted in Crosby (forthcoming), part I, chap. 4, note 14.

17. Spiegel, "The Cult of Saint Denis," pp. 43–70, esp. 46–53.

18. Crosby (1942), pp. 32–33; and Crosby (forthcoming), part I, chap. 4.

19. See above, n. 6. While a monk at St-Denis, Abelard discovered that these saints were different individuals. See Félibien, pp. 147–48. The confusion persisted until this century.

20. As Spiegel has pointed out, the identification of Saint Denis of Paris with Dionysius the Areopagite mentioned by Luke thus gave an apostolic date for the saint and also therefore for the origin of the abbey of St-Denis ("The Cult of Saint Denis," p. 48).

21. See Panofsky's introduction to *Abbot Suger,* pp. 18–21 and 36–37, and von Simson, *The Gothic Cathedral,* pp. 52–53, 103–07.

22. Panofsky, *Abbot Suger,* pp. 43, 87, 89, 101.

23. The symbolism of the facade has been discussed by a number of authors: Crosby (forthcoming), part II, chap. 3; von Simson, *The Gothic Cathedral,* 109–15; and P. Gerson, "The West Facade of St.-Denis: An Iconographic Study" (Ph.D. diss., Columbia University, 1970).

24. Abbot Suger was never able to bring his work on the nave to completion. Crosby (forthcoming), part II, chap. 6.

25. See, for example, Louis Grodecki, "Les Vitraux allégoriques de Saint-Denis," *Art de France* 1 (1961):24.

26. The writings of Dionysius the Pseudo-Areopagite became increasingly important in the later twelfth and thirteenth

centuries, culminating in a translation and commentaries by Robert Grosseteste (in 1239–43) and commentaries by Albertus Magnus (c. 1248) and Thomas Aquinas (1256–59). The *Dictionnaire de spiritualité*, vol. 3, col. 343, states, "Au 13ᵉ siècle naît et se développe un courant spirituel appelé dionysien. . . ." Grosseteste probably became familiar with the works of Dionysius the Pseudo-Areopagite while a student in Paris between 1209 and 1214. See further the summaries in the *Dictionnaire d'histoire et de géographie ecclésiastiques*, vol. 14, cols. 290–95, and the *Dictionnaire de spiritualité*, vol. 3, cols. 318–58.

27. Dom Simon Germain Millet, *Le Trésor sacré, ou inventaire des sainctes reliques et autres précieux joyaux qui se voyent en l'église et au trésor de l'abbaye royale de S. Denys en France*, 4th ed. (Paris: Billaine, 1645), p. 30.

28. According to Suger, his predecessor, Abbot Adam, neglected the old church to such an extent that there were great fissures in the walls. See Suger's description in Panofsky, *Abbot Suger*, pp. 43, 95.

29. Ibid., p. 53.

30. That the church was not completed may have been the result of the sequence of short abbacies following that of Suger.

31. Félibien, pp. 192–99.

32. Ibid., and see also Spiegel, *The Chronicle Tradition*, p. 53.

33. The Valois Portal has recently been the object of a session at the Eighteenth International Congress of Medieval Studies in Kalamazoo, Michigan, May 1983. It is variously dated between 1160 and 1175, and recent scholarship tends to support a date in the early 1160s. See Crosby (1953), pp. 48, 57–58; Willibald Sauerländer, "Die Marienkrönungsportale von Senlis and Mantes," *Wallraf-Richartz Jahrbuch* 20 (1958):115–62, esp. 149ff.; Louis Grodecki, "La 'Première sculpture gothique': Wilhem Vöge et l'état actuel des problèmes," *BM* 117 (1959):265–89, esp. 284–86; and Jean Bony, "La Collégiale de Mantes," *CA* (Paris-Mantes) 104 (1946): 147ff.

34. Félibien, p. 198.

35. The controversy over the relics of Saint Denis is in part derived from different versions of the legend, one of which suggests that the cranium of Saint Denis was separated from the rest of his head by a bungling executioner (see Spiegel, "The Cult of Saint Denis," pp. 48–50). The controversy continued for many centuries: see H. François Delaborde, "Le Procès du chef de Saint Denis en 1410," *Extrait des mémoires de la Société de l'histoire de Paris et de l'Ile-de-France*, (Paris, 1884), pp. 297–409. The Cistercian abbey of Longpont in the Aisne also claimed to have the head of Saint Denis, given to the abbey by Bishop Nivelon de Chérisy in 1205. There is no record of the response of the monks of St-Denis to this donation. The relic of Saint Denis at Notre-Dame was found during the construction of the new cathedral.

36. During this time a number of miracles occurred, usually considered proof of the legitimacy of relics. (Jonathan Sumption, in *Pilgrimage, An Image of Medieval Religion* [London: Faber and Faber, 1975], p. 214, points out also that this exhibition of the relics of Saint Denis coincided with the departure of Philip Augustus on crusade and associates the exhibition of relics with periods of national crisis.)

37. In 625 Clothair described Saint Denis as *peculiaris patronis* of the throne (see Spiegel, *The Chronicle Tradition*, p. 20; Crosby [forthcoming], part I, introduction; von Simson, *The Gothic Cathedral*, p. 70; and P. E. Schramm, *Der König von Frankreich* [Weimar: Hermann Böhlaus Nachfolger, 1960], vol. 1, pp. 131–44, esp. 135–37). As Gabrielle Spiegel has pointed out, this role as protector of the realm included the unique function of recording the official history of the French monarchy. The summary of the history in the following pages is derived primarily from Félibien, pp. 190–253. When other sources are used, this is indicated in a footnote.

38. Crosby (forthcoming), part I, chap. 3, points out that Charles Martel may have patronized St-Denis as a means of proclaiming his own legitimacy.

39. On the tenth-century reforms, see Crosby (1942), pp. 79, 82–83.

40. A. Lecoy de la Marche, *Oeuvres complètes de Suger* (Paris: Renouard, 1867), pp. 161f., 442.

41. See Crosby (1942), pp. 50–52.

42. Panofsky, *Abbot Suger,* pp. 101–03. See also Bossuat, "Traditions populaires," pp. 480–81; and Crosby (forthcoming), part II, introduction.

43. Although the king contributed gems for the decoration of the tomb of the saint, Suger leaves no record of his financial contributions toward the building itself. It is possible, therefore, that the construction of the church was paid for largely by the abbey.

44. On the regalia, see Schramm, *Der König,* pp. 132, 204–15; Crosby (1953), pp. 8–9; and Spiegel, *The Chronicle Tradition,* pp. 31–33.

45. On the abbey as the burial church of kings, there are a number of extensive studies: Erlande-Brandenbourg, *Le Roi;* Crosby (1953), pp. 8–9; Spiegel, *The Chronicle Tradition,* pp. 13, 19–21; and Georgia Sommers Wright, "A Royal Tomb Program in the Reign of St. Louis," *AB* 56 (1974):224–43. See also the forthcoming articles by Elizabeth A. R. Brown, cited below, n. 61, and in chap. 5.

46. The first royal tomb is that of Queen Arnegonde, who died c. 565–70. In 580 the son of Chilperic was also buried at the abbey. See Erlande-Brandenbourg, *Le Roi,* pp. 68–69.

47. Charlemagne founded a school at St-Denis, later attended by Suger and Louis VI. See Spiegel, *The Chronicle Tradition,* pp. 20–22; and Panofsky's introduction in *Abbot Suger,* pp. 2–3.

48. English translation quoted from Sumption, *Pilgrimage,* p. 131. See Lecoy de la Marche, *Oeuvres complètes de Suger,* pp. 148–49.

49. In 1108 Philip I was interred at St-Benoît-sur-Loire, and in 1180 Louis VII was buried at the Cistercian abbey of Barbeau. Suger commented that the burial of Philip I away from St-Denis was against *jus naturalis* (Crosby [forthcoming], part I, introduction, note 55).

50. On the donations of Charles the Bald, see Panofsky, *Abbot Suger,* pp. 67–71, 129–31, as well as Blaise de Montesquiou-Fezensac and D. Gaborit-Chopin, *Le Trésor de Saint-Denis* (Paris: Picard, 1973), vol. 1, p. 7.

51. The necrology of the abbey was published by Félibien, pp. ccvii–ccxix.

52. See ibid., pp. 215–16, on these relics, and Montesquiou-Fezensac and Gaborit-Chopin, *Le Trésor,* vol. 1, p. 9.

53. Félibien, pp. 222–23.

54. On Eudes Clément du Mez, see the references in the recent article by Louis Grodecki, "Les Problèmes de la peinture gothique et le 'Maître de Saint Chéron' de la cathédrale de Chartres," *Revue de l'art,* no. 40–41 (1978):43–64, esp. 58; and P. Anselme, *Histoire généalogique et chronologique de la maison royale de France, des grandes officiers de la Couronne et de la Maison du Roy . . .* (Paris: La Compagnie des Libraires, 1726–33), vol. 6, pp. 618ff. Also Yves Delaporte, *Les Vitraux de la cathédrale de Chartres* (Chartres: Houvet, 1926), pp. 439–41, and Élie Berger, *Histoire de Blanche de Castille, reine de France,* Bibliothèque des écoles françaises d'Athènes et de Rome, vol. 70 (Paris: Thorin et fils, 1895), pp. 57–68, 297–98. Jean Clément, the brother of Eudes, is represented in one of the windows of the south transept of Chartres Cathedral receiving the Oriflamme from Saint Denis.

55. AN, LL 1157, pp. 227–29.

56. Guillaume de Nangis, *Chronique latine,* Société de l'histoire de France (Paris: J. Renouard, 1843), vol. 1, p. 183. The text is the basis for a longer statement in the *Grandes Chroniques de France,* ed. J. Viard, 7:61. Charles Liebman has pointed out the continued importance of this legend in the thirteenth century, with its inclusion in the *Speculum historiale* of Vincent of Beauvais, and the illuminated life of Saint Denis produced at

the abbey in the second quarter of the thirteenth century ("La Consécration légendaire," pp. 352–56).

57. AN, LL 1157, p. 85. This document and the ones that follow are discussed in greater length in chapter 5. The text in the *Grandes Chroniques,* cited above, adds that the vaults of the old structure were collapsing.

58. Ed. É. Berger, *BEC* 40 (1879):281. Although Félibien and *GC* date the beginning of Clément's abbacy to 1229, both versions of the *Chronicon* state that it began in 1228.

59. On the first regency of Blanche de Castille, see Berger, *Blanche de Castille,* pp. 46–224.

60. Bossuat, in "Traditions populaires," p. 481, has also pointed out the possibility that the threats to the young king in the early years of his reign were one of the reasons for the active exploitation of the cult of Saint Denis and his relationship to the throne. This was expressed not only in the reconstruction of the church and the installation of an elaborate program of royal tombs, but also with the compilation of a life of Saint Denis in 1233. The consciousness of St-Denis as a symbol of the monarchy, as representing the core of the kingdom, had been especially cultivated by Suger a hundred years earlier (see von Simson, *The Gothic Cathedral,* pp. 82–89). It took place on any number of levels, not only in the role of the abbey as the official historiographers of the monarchy, but also as the focus of the kingdom in the popular imagination through the *chansons de geste,* and received additional impetus during the reign of Louis IX. See also Spiegel, "The Cult of Saint Denis," pp. 60–65.

61. Elizabeth A. R. Brown, "The Prince is the Father of the King: The Character of Philip the Fair of France," forthcoming, and Wright, "A Royal Tomb Program," p. 224. Indeed, Guillaume de Nangis states that Louis actually participated in the rearrangement of the tombs (*Chronique latine* vol. 1, pp. 232–33).

62. Louis is said to have considered becoming a mendicant friar himself (Brown, "The Prince," p. 29, and W. C. Jordan, *Louis IX and the Challenge of the Crusade* [Princeton: Princeton University Press, 1979], p. 130) and is listed as a tertiary in the Franciscan Order (G. Kaftal, *Iconography of the Saints in Tuscan Painting* [Florence: Sansoni, 1952], p. 640). Louis was also a great patron of the Cistercians (on this, see Anselme Dimier, *Saint Louis et Cîteaux* [Paris: Letouzey et Ané, 1954]).

63. Brown, "The Prince," p. 29, and Le Nain de Tillemont, *Vie de Saint Louis,* 6 vols. (Paris: S. Renouard, 1847–51), 4:256 and 5:357.

64. The implications of this gesture are discussed in Spiegel, "The Cult of Saint Denis," pp. 60–61.

65. Félibien, p. 227, says: "Aussi voit-on presque par tout dans le choeur et dans la croisée et jusques sur le marchepied de quelques autels du chevet les armes de Castille jointes à celles de France." See also Doublet, p. 287. These are still visible on the south transept arm portal. These insignia are prominent on the north transept rose at Chartres, a window donated by Blanche de Castille and Louis IX.

66. Against this, see Robert Branner, *St. Louis and the Court Style in Gothic Architecture* (London: Zwemmer, 1965), pp. 46–47, who tends to detach Louis from the reconstruction of the church, and Wright, "A Royal Tomb Program," who likewise removes the king from active involvement in the church and the carving of the new series of royal tombs. But as has been pointed out above, it was Louis's dying wish that St-Denis be the exclusive burial place of kings, and his lifelong devotion to the abbey and its patron saint indicates that this is not an example of deathbed piety.

67. This will be discussed in greater detail in chapter 6.

CHAPTER 2. THE RESTORATION

1. The long and complicated history of the restoration is especially well summarized by Crosby (1942), pp. 7–12, and Louis Grodecki, *Les Vitraux de Saint-Denis: étude sur le vitrail au XIIème siècle* (Paris: CNRS, 1976), pp. 39–60; see also Baron François de Guilhermy, *Monographie de l'église royale de Saint-Denis* (Paris: Didron, 1848), pp. 52–208, for a contemporary account.

2. See Viollet-le-Duc's scathing observations on his predecessor's work in his article, "L'Église impériale de Saint-Denis," *Revue archéologique* 3 (1861):304–08.

3. Crosby (1942), pp. 99–108.

4. On the restoration of Notre-Dame, see Viollet-le-Duc's and Lassus's remarks in *Projet de restauration de Notre-Dame de Paris, rapport adressé à M. le Ministre de la justice et des cultes, annexé au projet de restauration, remis le 31 janvier, 1843* (Paris: Mme de Lacombe, 1843), pp. 3–4; also in Viollet-le-Duc, *Dictionnaire*, 2:288, n. 3; Viollet-le-Duc and Guilhermy, *Description de Notre-Dame, cathédrale de Paris* (Paris: Bance, 1856); and the catalogue of the recent exhibition "Viollet-le-Duc," Grand Palais, Paris, 1980, pp. 72–81.

5. See the notes taken by the Baron de Guilhermy on the restoration, preserved in the BN, Nouvelles acquisitions fr. 6121 and 6122: "Notes archéologiques," pp. 2–10; as well as the chronicle of Ferdinand Gautier, "Recueil d'anecdotes et autres objets curieux relatifs à l'histoire de l'abbaye de St.-Denys en France," BN, MS Français 11681, especially p. 103. Gautier was the organist at the abbey and witnessed much of the destruction that took place during the Revolution. He conceived his notes as the continuation of Félibien's *Histoire* of 1706.

6. See Debret's notes, "Notes historiques sur la fondation de l'église royale de St-Denis, sa dévastation, et sa restauration," AN, F(21) 1451, pp. 13–14, 16.

7. Ibid., p. 17.

8. Ibid., p. 39.

9. AN, F13 1296, folder 1831–34; also AN, F(21) 1451.

10. Debret's designs for this ornament can still be seen in his papers, conserved in MH, as well as in papers and drawings on the restoration of St-Denis conserved in a private collection in Strasbourg. The last of this decoration was removed in 1956–57 by Formigé but can still be seen, for example, in plates 77 and 79 of Crosby (1953).

11. See Louis Réau, *Les Monuments détruits de l'art français*, 2 vols. (Paris: Hachette, 1959), esp. 2:11–132.

12. Leaving aside the article by Viollet-le-Duc, cited above in n. 2, the reader should see Guilhermy's remarks on the restoration in his *Monographie*, pp. 52–208; Didron in the early issues of the *Annales archéologiques;* and most recently, Grodecki, *Les Vitraux*, pp. 39–60.

13. This interest emerged with the early issues of the *Annales archéologiques* and other architectural and archaeological reviews in the 1840s, such as César Daly's *Revue générale de l'architecture*.

14. Robin Middleton and David Watkin, *Neoclassical and Nineteenth-Century Architecture* (New York: Abrams, 1980), p. 340, date the beginning of the Gothic Revival in France to 1840. See also the recent catalogue of the exhibition *Le Gothique retrouvé* at the Hôtel de Sully, Paris, 1979–80. A distinct interest in the Gothic style persisted, however, among antiquarians and architectural theorists going back to the sixteenth century. See R. D. Middleton, "The Abbé de Cordemoy and the Graeco-Gothic Ideal," *JWCI* 25 (1962):278–320; and 26 (1963): 90–123.

15. See G. Germann, *Gothic Revival in Europe and Britain: Sources, Influences, and Ideas* (Cambridge: MIT Press, 1973); and Marcel Aubert, "Le Romantisme et le Moyen-Age," in *Le Romantisme et l'art*, ed. E. Herriot (Paris: Laurens, 1928), pp. 23–48, esp. 29–33.

16. Cellerier: 1742–1814; Percier: 1764–

1853; Fontaine: 1762–1853; and Debret: 1777–1850; whereas Viollet-le-Duc: 1814–79; Lassus: 1807–57; Didron: 1806–67; Daly 1811–93; and Guilhermy: 1801–78.

17. See, for example, Didron's admonitions in the early issues of the *Annales archéologiques*, vols. 1–4.

18. See, for example, Thomas Lyman on the restoration of St. Sernin at Toulouse: "Saint-Sernin de Toulouse: que faire du XIX siècle?" *BM* 139 (1981): 4–67. Also, Viollet-le-Duc, "Restauration," *Dictionnaire*, 8:15–34.

19. These chapels have never been the object of serious study, and no documents concerning their construction have yet been found. The style of the tracery indicates a date early in the fourteenth century.

20. The entire north wall of the nave on the aisle level is thus nineteenth-century restoration by Viollet-le-Duc, with the exception of the responds and the vaults. This is also true on the south side, as will be seen below (see fig. 2). On the north side in particular, the responds and their capitals in the western bays are still coated with a heavy layer of whitewash.

21. On this chapel, see the forthcoming article by Elizabeth A. R. Brown, "The Chapels and Cult of Saint Louis at Saint-Denis."

22. Ibid.

23. See Félibien's plan, plate 3. Thin walls were added to close this chapel off from the eastern aisle of the south transept arm, which gave access to the stairway leading to the monks' dormitory, some vestiges of which can still be seen. On the larger problem of the vestries at St-Denis, see below, chapter 5.

24. Crosby (1942), p. 5. The enlargement of this chapel was connected with Charles V's decision to be buried in this location (he died in 1380). See also P. Vitry and G. Brière, *L'Église abbatiale de Saint-Denis et ses tombeaux,*

notice historique et archéologique (Paris: D. A. Longuet, 1908), p. 68.

25. There is, to date, no serious study of the Valois Chapel. For a few general observations, see Anthony Blunt, *Art and Architecture in France: 1500–1700* (London and Baltimore: Penguin Books, 1970), pp. 95–98.

26. "Lettres patentes sur arrest pour la démolition de la chapelle des Valois, données à Paris le 24 Mars, 1719," in the BN, MS Latin 12, 668: "Nous avons ordonné et ordonnons que les tombeaux d'Henry II, de Catherine de Medici, et des Princes et Princesses leurs enfants seront transportés dans la grande église et placcz dans la croisée du Septentrion . . . ainsi que pour faire la démolition des murs, voûtes, et comble de ladite Chapelle des Valois, et les reparations aux murs de l'église." These *réparations* seem to have been minimal, however, as A. P. M. Gilbert, in *Description historique de l'église royale de Saint-Denys* (Paris: Plancher, 1815), p. 43, mentions a blocked-up doorway in this location.

27. A lithograph of the north transept arm by Chapuy dated to 1822 shows no evidence of the door that formerly occupied this location. A plan by Legrand dated to 1806 in a private collection in Strasbourg shows this doorway still in place at the beginning of the restorations, however. Debret's "Notes Historiques" in the AN indicate that he was working in this part of the church between 1813 and 1820, though there do not seem to be any specific references to work on this wall.

28. See below, chapter 3, for an extended discussion of this painting.

29. Félibien's plan, plate 3, and below, chapter 5.

30. Gilbert, *Description,* p. 75; and Guilhermy, *Monographie,* pp. 50–51. See also Félibien, pp. 513–14.

31. Gautier, "Recueil d'anecdotes," p. 102. For the restoration, see the "Attachements" in the MH, "Maçonnerie, 1807–1818," for 1807 and also the letters of Legrand in the AN, F^{13} 1296, report of July 1806.

32. MH, "Attachements, 1825" and Guilhermy, "Notes archéologiques," p. 188.

33. Guilhermy, "Notes archéologiques," pp. 208, 310.

34. On the rebuilding of the monastic buildings, see the unpublished thesis by Jannie Mayer-Long, "L'Abbaye de Saint-Denis au XVIIIe siècle," in the library of the MH. A number of plans and other drawings are preserved in the BN, Estampes, and in the AN. Extensive proposals were also made in the eighteenth century for the renewal of the pavement and the removal of the royal tombs in the church: see J. J. Guiffrey, *Un Chapitre inédit de l'histoire des tombes royales* (Paris: Menu, 1876).

35. Crosby (1942), pp. 7–10.

36. The treasury was demolished to make room for the parish church added to the south aisle. This was later transformed into a "chapelle d'hiver." See the discussion of this chapel in the following pages.

37. Gautier, in his "Recueil d'anecdotes," gives a detailed account of the repairs and changes that took place in the church in the eighteenth century. These were for the most part superficial and did not affect the structure of the medieval church apart from the destruction of the west portals.

38. Crosby (1942), pp. 7–10; and Guilhermy, "Notes archéologiques," passim, for accounts of the damage to the earlier parts of the church.

39. Gautier has left us a vivid description of this, "Recueil d'anecdotes," pp. 98–106. See also Louis-Victor Flamand-Grétry, *Itinéraire historique, géographique, topographique, statistique, pittoresque, et biographique de la Vallée de Montmorency* (Paris: Bertrand, 1840), pp. 105–46; and Guilhermy, "Notes archéologiques," pp. 2ff.

40. Grodecki, *Les Vitraux*, pp. 39–46. Part of the roof was subsequently covered with tile, but this work was suspended in 1797, and the remainder of the vaults were left exposed (Flamand-Grétry, *Itinéraire*, p. 109). Alexandre Lenoir also took most of the dado

arcading to decorate the walls of his Musée des Monuments Français (illustrated in *Le Gothique retrouvé*, p. 76, plate 160). There are documents on this in the AN, F^{13} 1293, a letter of Legrand on the 25th Floreal, an 13 (1805).

41. Vitry and Brière, *L'Église abbatiale*, p. 28.

42. Ibid.

43. On the proposals to transform the church into a market, see ibid., p. 29, and the documents in the AN, F^{13} 1293: years 1801–02. A letter of the 11th of Messidor, an 10 (1802), on this subject exemplified the ambivalence that characterized this decision: "L'un des prédécesseurs du ministre après avoir rendu compte des beautés que presente . . . l'église abbatiale de St-Denis, a decidé . . . que cet édifice doit être conservé, mais que pour le rendre utile, il y sera établi une halle fermée."

44. Quoted by Vitry and Brière, *L'Église abbatiale*, p. 29.

45. Ibid., p. 30.

46. Guilhermy, "Notes archéologiques," p. 14. Also, Viollet-le-Duc, "L'Église impériale," p. 305. This was officially proclaimed in the imperial decree of February 20, 1806 (cf. Vitry and Brière, *L'Église abbatiale*, p. 31).

47. Ibid. For a description of the state of the church in 1807, see the "Coup-d'oeil historique," in *Recueil polytechnique des ponts et chaussées*, vol. 2 (1807), pp. 145–55. I would like to thank Hélène Lipstadt for bringing this to my attention.

48. Debret, "Notes historiques," pp. 6–7, and Gilbert's description of the interior circa 1810–15, *Description*, pp. 49–56. Also, documents in AN, F^{13} 1296; especially a letter of Legrand to the minister dated to the 6th Frimaire, an 14 (1806).

49. Ibid. This is still evident in the north side of the nave in the elevation of the north flank of the abbey done by Debret (plate 11).

50. Guilhermy, "Notes archéologi-

ques," p. 13; and Vitry and Brière, *L'Église abbatiale*, p. 31. This decree is dated to February 20, 1806.

51. AN, F^{13} 1293, documents of November 1807. Cellerier was instructed to follow Legrand's projects without modification (letter to Cellerier of March 10, 1809).

52. Guilhermy, "Notes archéologiques," p. 29. See AN, F^{13} 1296, 1818–19 for the correspondence concerning this chapel, and the plan by Cellerier made in 1809 in the AN, F^{13} 1293. In 1842 work was still in progress on the decoration of the chapel (Guilhermy, p. 41).

53. Ibid., pp. 14–15.

54. Vitry and Brière, *L'Église abbatiale*, p. 33.

55. See Viollet-le-Duc's notes on the restoration in "L'Église impériale," pp. 308 ff., and his brief comments in the *Dictionnaire*, 8:22–23. The dado arcading had been used by Lenoir in his Musée des Monuments Français, (see n. 40). It was also used in the fabrication of the tomb of Abelard and Eloise and now is in the Père Lachaise Cemetery in Paris.

56. Guilhermy, "Restauration de l'église royale de Saint-Denis," *AA* 5 (1846):202, 210. Also, AN, F^{13} 1295, documents of 1811–12, especially the "Etats des travaux" of 1812.

57. Debret, "Notes historiques," p. 10; and Vitry and Brière, *L'Église abbatiale*, p. 33. Cellerier had essentially been "kicked upstairs" and appointed a member of the Conseil des bâtiments civils. His teacher, Charles Percier, had made a number of sketches in the 1790s of the interior of St-Denis before the restoration was begun. These were later used by Viollet-le-Duc in his restoration of the monument, and are used by scholars today. Two of these are reproduced here as plates 14 and 15. See Georges Huard, "Percier et l'abbaye de Saint-Denis," *Les Monuments historiques de la France*, no. 3 (1936):134–44; no. 4 (1936):173–82.

58. Debret, "Notes historiques," p. 30. In spite of the clear indications that the construction of the parish chapel was causing severe problems in the stability of the church, Debret never seems to have considered removing it and returning the church to its original disposition. See also Vitry and Brière, *L'Église abbatiale*, p. 35, for details of the funding of the restoration. The instability of the south side seems to have been pointed out first in September 1819, before the chapel was complete (AN, F^{13} 1296).

59. See Debret's "Notes historiques," pp. 30–40. Also Didron, "St-Denis, restauration de l'église royale," *AA* 1 (1844):230–36.

60. Most of these documents are in MH. There are also a significant number of restoration drawings in the collection of Doctor Stemmer in Strasbourg. It is not known how or when these drawings found their way to Strasbourg; they were found by Doctor Stemmer in a pile of garbage awaiting collection.

61. Didron also pointed out the consequences of the new disposition of the roofs on the exterior appearance of the buttresses: "La substitution de terrasses dallées aux anciens combles en charpente est venue aussi changer complètement la physionomie de cette partie de l'édifice. Les contreforts se trouvent ainsi déchaussés jusqu'à leur base, et produisent à l'oeil l'effet d'un homme ivre, qui vacille en cherchant un point d'appui qui lui manque. Un système de terrasses développé, comme on l'a fait à Saint-Denys, répugne à l'architecture gothique du nord; s'il en existe quelques exemples, ce sont de rares exceptions" ("St-Denis," p. 234). (On the original disposition of these roofs, see below, chapter 3, as well as the engraving of the north flank of the church by Marot, plate 4.)

62. Didron, "St-Denis," p. 236, describes this vestry as having "tout l'apparence d'un de ces établissements qu'on cherche à rendre inodores."

63. Grodecki, *Les Vitraux*, pp. 47–48.

64. An engraving of this organ is reproduced in the catalogue of the exhibition *Le Gothique retrouvé*, plate 330. A painting in the sacristy by E. B. Garnier of the funeral of Dagobert shows, in a somewhat exaggerated

view, the juncture of the nave with the western bays prior to the insertion of the organ.

65. Didron has summarized the story of the reconstruction of the tower in "La Flèche de Saint Denis," *AA* 4 (1845):175–85. See also Vitry and Brière, *L'Église abbatiale*, pp. 35–36.

66. AN, F¹³ 1296, correspondence of November 1833.

67. Debret's position at this date seems to have remained quite secure. See his lecture, "Notice sur les diverses constructions et restaurations de l'église St-Denis," in *Séance publique des cinq académies* (1842), pp. 9–28. Also, Vitry and Brière, *L'Église abbatiale,* pp. 35–36; and Didron, "St-Denis," p. 231.

68. Apparently the transfer of the tombs from the Musée des Monuments Français back to St-Denis was accomplished with great carelessness. Guilhermy described the process:

L'ordonnance de 1816 avait un côté moral; la décence publique réclamait le rétablissement des tombeaux profanés pendant la révolution. Mais, comme toujours, les exécuteurs subalternes allèrent au delà des volontés du maître. On mit un acharnement incroyable à effacer jusqu'à la dernière trace du musée des monuments français. Pour faire la place libre à la nouvelle école des beaux-arts, on precipita pêle-mêle dans les cours les tombeaux et les statues; depuis 1793 pareille chose n'était pas arrivée; les jeunes gens qui venaient en ce lieu étudier les principes de l'art avaient ainsi, sous les yeux, l'exemple du vandalisme le plus brutal et du mépris le plus effronté pour les oeuvres des grands artistes français. . . . Je me souviens d'avoir ramassé aux Petits-Augustins, dans mon enfance, des fragments de dais peints, dorés et incrustés de verroteries dont l'aspect élégant réjouissait déjà mes yeux; à travers les intervalles des palissades de planches, j'apercevais, au milieu de hautes herbes, de graves figures revêtues de longs manteaux fleurdelisés; je me rappelle encore l'émotion que produisait en moi ce triste

spectacle, auquel se montraient complètement indifférents architectes et professeurs (*Monographie,* pp. 103–04).

On the removal of the tombs to St-Denis, see the documents in the AN, F¹³ 1295, folder II, letters of 1817. Debret proposed the construction of a cloister made from fragments from the Musée des Monuments Français to be placed in the area north of the church.

69. For a list of the origins of the various figures included in the collection of sculpture at St-Denis, see Guilhermy, *Monographie,* p. 107. The closing off of the winter chapel was due to complaints from the chapter about the cold. AN, F¹³ 1295, documents of 1819.

70. Guilhermy, *Monographie,* p. 105.

71. Didron, "La Flèche," pp. 175–85, esp. 179.

72. Guilhermy, *Monographie,* p. 10. See also his article "Restauration," p. 212.

73. Viollet-le-Duc, "L'Église impériale," pp. 305–06.

74. Ibid.

75. Gilbert, *Description,* p. 49.

76. Ibid., p. 28.

77. Flamand-Grétry, *Itinéraire,* p. 150.

78. Gilbert, *Description,* p. 58.

79. Ibid., p. 49, and Flamand-Grétry, *Itinéraire,* p. 96.

80. Didron, "Introduction," *AA* 1 (1844).

81. Idem, "Saint-Denis," pp. 230–36.

82. Vitry and Brière, *L'Église abbatiale,* pp. 40–42.

83. Ibid.

84. Ibid., p. 38. As Viollet-le-Duc put it, "Quand le mal fut bien constaté, quand on put mettre un peu d'ordre au milieu du désordre historique qui s'était glissé dans toutes les parties de l'édifice, l'argent manquait" ("L'Église impériale," p. 308).

85. Viollet-le-Duc, "Rapport sur l'état

des constructions au 15 Décembre, 1846," in the *Dossier de l'administration,* MH, 1841–76.

86. This plan, dated to 1860, is in the collection of documents on the restoration of St-Denis in the Palais de Chaillot, n. 1190. It is reproduced in the catalogue of the exhibition "Viollet-le-Duc" at the Grand Palais, 1980, p. 185.

87. Guilhermy, "Notes archéologiques," pp. 212ff., esp. 212, 222. The dado arcading in the church today is entirely new; none of the surviving fragments seem to have been used in the restoration. Some of these can be seen in the Musée Lapidaire at the abbey. See also Viollet-le-Duc, "Étaiement pour la reprise en sous-oeuvre des piles de l'église impériale de Saint-Denis," *Gazette des architectes et du bâtiment* (1867), pp. 33–36.

88. Branner, *St. Louis,* pp. 143–44, discusses this portal as an example of thirteenth-century portal design. Viollet-le-Duc's drawings for it are in the Palais de Chaillot. The absence of any previous doorway at this location is evident from Félibien's plan, plate 3, as well as from other documents.

89. MH, file 1235. The following information is from MH, files 1235, 1236, and 1237 covering the years 1887 through 1958.

90. MH, file 1235 dossier 4.

91. See the article by André Chastel, "Quel est le sens des bouleversements annoncés pour la basilique de Saint-Denis?" *Le Monde,* February 13, 1953, and MH, file 1236.

CHAPTER 3. THE NEW CHURCH

1. Erwin Panofsky, *Gothic Architecture and Scholasticism* (Latrobe, Indiana: Saint Vincent Archabbey Press, 1951), pp. 43–52, 84–88.

2. For this reason, the precise role of Pierre de Montreuil is difficult to determine. For an extended discussion of the problem, see Appendix 2.

3. On the earlier buildings at the site, see the forthcoming volume by Sumner McK. Crosby, as well as Crosby (1942) and (1953).

4. Crosby (1953), p. 61, made the astute observation that the double aisles create a centralized space around the crossing that specifically reflects the function of this part of the church as a *nécropole dynastique.* The expansion of the transept had inevitable consequences for the conventual buildings that abut it to the south, as will be seen below, especially in chapter 5.

5. The standard thirteenth-century Gothic plan usually has four straight bays between the crossing and the hemicycle and double aisles in the chevet (for example, Chartres and Amiens).

6. The paired aisles to the east and west give the transept a particular character that will be examined in the following pages. I shall henceforth refer to the transept as having double aisles, i.e., two to the east and two to the west.

7. The last five bays of the nave at St-Denis had therefore relatively little explicit function other than the accommodation of crowds and processions on great occasions.

8. The location of some of these screens is visible in the Félibien plan of 1706 (plate 3; also plates 7, 15, 16). Some vague suggestions of the location of these screens can be derived from the "Fragments de l'enquête à Saint-Denis en 1282 en vue de la canonisation de Saint Louis," *Mémoires de la Société de l'histoire de Paris et de l'Ile-de-France* 23 (1896):1–71.

9. Crosby (forthcoming), part II, chap. 6.

10. Ibid.

11. Ibid.

12. Ibid., and therefore what survived of these earlier conventual buildings could be

preserved. There is evidence of some twelfth-century work on the cloister, however, as attested by a surviving statue column in the Metropolitan Museum in New York and several capitals in the Louvre.

13. This is one of the many indications that Suger accomplished his professed desire for concordance and unity between the old and new churches. See Suger's own remarks to this effect in Panofsky, *Abbot Suger,* p. 101.

14. The change in levels is the result of nineteenth-century restoration. See above, chapter 2, and Crosby (1942), p. 9.

15. The present organ and its support were designed by Cellerier and Debret and inaugurated in 1841.

16. The shorter bay at Chartres has been used as evidence to support the arguments for the construction of the cathedral from east to west. Although this has now been rejected for Chartres, at St-Denis construction did indeed proceed in this manner, as will become evident in the following chapters.

17. The angle of the walls in the first bay east of the crossing adjusts the width of the nave from that intended in Suger's church to the new, wider proportions of the thirteenth-century nave.

18. For a more extensive discussion of these towers and their role in supporting the main vaults, see below, chapter 4. Louis Grodecki, in conversation with me, argued that these towers are unfinished. Their lightness of structure, particularly that of the northeast tower (which also has no stair), suggests rather that they were never intended to rise above their present level in line with the tops of the transept roses. There are no indications that spires were intended. Only the southwest transept tower seems to have risen slightly higher than the others, in order to support a set of bells (this detail will become important in the discussion of the dating of the phases of construction in chapter 5). See below, chapter 6, and plates 9, 11. Branner, *St. Louis,* p. 48, also states that the towers were unfinished.

19. See below, chapter 6; and in general, the article by Pierre Héliot, "Sur les tours de transept dans l'architecture du Moyen-Age," *Revue archéologique* 1 (1965):169–200; 2 (1965):57–95.

20. In other monuments the separate character of the transept facades and the west facade is less marked, resting primarily on the relative scale and proportions of the portals.

21. At Chartres and at Reims, on the other hand, the location of the towers adjoining the extremities of the transept blocks the windows and makes this part of the church slightly dark.

22. Crosby (forthcoming), Album plate 2.

23. The *confessio* was destroyed when Viollet-le-Duc created a *caveau impérial* inside the foundations of the Carolingian apse. See above, chapter 2, n. 3, and Crosby (1942), pp. 100–01. A similar continuity existed at St-Sernin at Toulouse (chapter 1, n. 5).

24. Wright, "A Royal Tomb Program," p. 231, and Erlande-Brandenbourg, *Le Roi,* p. 81. See also Crosby (1953), p. 61. Suger was, however, very conscious of the importance of burial near the relics and makes this point in his biography of Louis VI, as seen above.

25. For Suger's own words, see Panofsky, *Abbot Suger,* pp. 43, 87–91. There is a long series of double-aisled naves in the eleventh and early twelfth centuries. In Paris itself, the Merovingian church of St-Etienne had double aisles.

26. Indeed, given the efforts on the part of the monks of the abbey to increase the fame and prominence of St-Denis, perhaps the design of the unique plan was also motivated by self-promotion. See Spiegel, "The Cult of Saint Denis," pp. 53–61.

27. Wright, "A Royal Tomb Program," p. 229.

28. Erwin Panofsky, *Tomb Sculpture* (New York: Abrams, 1962), p. 51.

29. As William Clark has pointed out, this development seems to take place shortly after 1150 at St-Germain-des-Prés. See his article "Spatial Innovations in the Chevet

of Saint-Germain-des-Prés," *JSAH* 38 (1970):360, n. 36. A good view of the evolution of medieval tomb design can be seen in the drawings of Gaignières: Jean Adhémar and Gertrude Dordor, *Les Tombeaux de la collection Gaignières: dessins d'archéologie du XVIIᵉ siècle* (from *GBA* [July–Sept. 1974]). On the growing interest in genealogy, see Georges Duby, "Remarques sur la littérature généalogique en France au XIᵉ et XIIᵉ siècles," in *Hommes et structures du Moyen Age; recueil d'articles* (Paris: Mouton 1973), pp. 287–98, and Spiegel, *The Chronicle Tradition,* pp. 73ff.

30. It was common practice in medieval construction to preserve some part of the church for liturgical services. See, for example, the provisions for assuring the continuity of the liturgy at Westminster, recorded in the *Building Accounts of King Henry III,* ed. H. M. Colvin (Oxford: Clarendon Press, 1971), p. 197.

31. The painting is discussed in William M. Hinkle, "The Iconography of the Four Panels by the Master of Saint Giles," *JWCI* 28 (1965):110ff. See also Conway, pp. 105–12. The two descriptions in question are the "Description de Paris par Thomas Platter le Jeune de Bâle," ed. L. Seiber, *Mémoires de la Société de l'histoire de Paris et de l'Ile-de-France* 23 (1896):167–224, esp. 216; and A. Vidier, "Les Abbayes de Saint-Denis, Saint-Crépin-le-Grand, Sainte-Geneviève, et Saint-Père de Melun au XVIᵉ siècle," *Bulletin de la Société de l'histoire de Paris et de l'Ile-de-France* 25 (1898):3–16, esp. p. 5. Both descriptions date to the sixteenth century: that of Thomas Platter to 1599 and that published by Vidier to 1517.

32. The location of the altar and staircase was modified at this date to the disposition shown in Charles Percier's view of the crossing and chevet, plate 15. For the changes made in 1610, see Conway, "The Abbey of Saint-Denis," pp. 112–13.

33. Ibid.

34. Vidier, "Les Abbayes," p. 6.

35. Illustrated and discussed by Erwin Panofsky, *Early Netherlandish Painting* (New York: Harper and Row, 1971), pp. 298, 301.

A similar arrangement appears in *The Raising of Lazarus* by Albert van Outwater: cf. Panofsky, pp. 320–23, 327.

36. On Canterbury, see Francis Woodman, *The Architectural History of Canterbury Cathedral* (London: Routledge and Kegan Paul, 1981); pp. 119ff. deal with the Trinity Chapel.

37. A raised hemicycle is visible also in the Romanesque church of St-Benoît-sur-Loire, although here the relics of Saint Benedict continued to be kept in the crypt, except on feast days. There seems to have been a general tendency in the thirteenth century to translate relics from a crypt to an upper sanctuary, as happened also at St-Sernin in Toulouse in 1258. See Durliat, "Les Cryptes."

38. See Jules Formigé, *L'Abbaye royale de Saint-Denis: recherches nouvelles* (Paris: Presses Universitaires, 1960), pp. 101–02.

39. For these accounts, see Félicie d'Ayzac, *Histoire de l'abbaye de Saint-Denis en France* (Paris: Imprimeries impériales, 1861), vol. 2, pp. 520–21.

40. The stalls presently at St-Denis are from the chapel of the château of Gaillon.

41. The only flat areas are the spandrels of the arcade, which contrast emphatically with the strongly modeled forms of moldings and shafts above, below, and to either side (plate 2). This flat surface is especially pronounced in the hemicycle between the top of the arcade and the base of the triforium, as the arcade here preserves the height of Suger's twelfth-century ambulatory (plate 13).

42. In this context it should be pointed out that the differences between the chevet and the rest of the church have generally been accounted for by attributing the early stages of the reconstruction in the thirteenth century to two different architects. I am convinced that there was only one. See below, chapter 4, esp. notes.

43. See above, chapter 2, on the restoration and fig. 2. Both sides were returned to something approximating their original de-

sign by Viollet-le-Duc later in the century, a restoration based on the drawings of Charles Percier (plate 14). On these see also Huard, "Percier et l'abbaye de Saint-Denis." The Percier drawings are mentioned by Viollet-le-Duc in the *Dictionnaire*: 2:40–48, 262–63; 5:14–16; 6:404; and 9:32–35, 447–48. The original drawings are in the Bibliothèque Municipale of Compiègne.

44. The surviving fragments of the dado arcading cannot, of course, be attributed to specific parts of the church and are therefore of little interest in establishing the chronology of construction. One of Percier's drawings, plate 14, suggests that in some bays, at least in the north transept arm, the dado arcading may have been supported by corbels, possibly because an altar was placed against the wall in this location (the altar of St. Hyppolitus—see below, chapter 5). If these corbelled supports were indeed part of the original program, they would seem to indicate especially strong ties to Burgundy, specifically to such monuments as the cathedrals of Auxerre and Nevers.

45. Such arcading also appears in Normandy in the sacristy of Bayeux Cathedral.

46. The trilobes in the spandrels of the triforium passage on the transept terminal walls also existed in the outer wall, where they are glazed (plate 25). Jane Hayward has recently discovered fragments of stained glass from these trilobes.

47. The thirteenth-century buttresses in the chevet are planted at an angle differing from that of the twelfth-century buttresses between the chapels beneath them. The reason for this twisting lies in the particular character of the twelfth-century plan, which made the disalignment between the twelfth- and thirteenth-century parts inevitable. See Crosby (forthcoming), part II, chap. 3.

48. The raised roof is confirmed in other views of the south flank of the church. The presence of bells in the southwest transept tower is important for the chronology of construction, as noted below, chapter 5.

49. Murray, "The Choir of St. Pierre," pp. 548–49, and Peter Kurmann, *La Cathédrale Saint-Etienne de Meaux: étude architecturale*, Bibliothèque de la Société française d'archéologie (Geneva: Droz; and Paris: Arts et métiers graphiques, 1971), p. 75 and esp. n. 325.

50. See chapters 4 and 5.

51. Octagonal pinnacles of this type are typical of the Parisian area after about 1250 as well as of monuments in other areas constructed under the influence of Parisian monuments. See Kurmann, *La Cathédrale de Meaux*, p. 75. At St-Denis, those on the north are slightly simpler than those on the south: on the north side of the nave, there are simple oculi above the gables in the decorative arcading, while on the south these are filled with trefoils. Both sides were completely restored in the nineteenth century.

52. See Branner, *St. Louis*, p. 63.

53. The repetition of trilobes in the rose windows repeats the motif of trilobed arcading in the dado and triforium.

54. Branner, *St. Louis*, pp. 26–28.

55. Ibid., pp. 51–55, and below, chapter 4.

56. This treatment of the rose windows in the transepts is to some extent anticipated in the rectangular frame enclosing the trefoil arches of the dado arcade, at St-Denis also conceived as a screen placed in front of the wall.

57. On this group of buildings, see Marcel Aubert, *Notre-Dame de Paris, sa place dans l'histoire de l'architecture du XIIᵉ au XIVᵉ siècle* (Paris: Laurens, 1920), pp. 177–216.

58. Branner, *St. Louis*, pp. 37, 100.

59. Ibid., pp. 138–40.

60. On St-Germain-des-Prés, see Hélène Verlet, "Les Bâtiments monastiques de l'abbaye de Saint-Germain-des-Prés," *Paris et l'Ile-de-France* 9 (1957–58):9–68, esp. 20ff., 40ff.

61. Jean-Pierre Ravaux, "La Cathédrale

gothique de Châlons-sur-Marne," *Mémoires de la Société d'agriculture, commerce, sciences, et arts du departement de la Marne* 91 (1976):171–227, esp. 205; and Kurmann, *La Cathédrale de Meaux*, pp. 59–84.

62. And as far afield as San Lorenzo Maggiore in Naples, built by French architects brought by Charles d'Anjou.

63. See Branner, *St. Louis*, pp. 93–96, 102–03, 106–08. On St-Germer-de-Fly, there is also the classic study by A. Besnard, *L'Église de Saint-Germer-de-Fly* (Paris: Lechevalier, 1913), pp. 92–116, and Louis Regnier, "St-Germer-de-Fly," *CA* 68 (1905):85–87.

64. There is also of course the contrast between the abaci of the hemicycle and those of the first compound piers, which comprises a special problem. See chapter 4. Changes in the abaci of the aisle windows are not reliable because these have all been rebuilt, often long after the destruction of the originals. Some fragments survive in the Cluny Museum, Paris.

65. On the dating of St-Germain-en-Laye, see J. de Terline, "La Tête de Saint Louis à Saint-Germain-en-Laye," *Monuments et mémoires, Fondation E. Piot*, AIBLM 45 (1951):123–40. This chapel is discussed at greater length in chapter 4. At Reims the rounded abaci appear in the radiating chapels of the chevet, dated 1210–20. See Francis Salet, "Chronologie de la cathédrale," *BM* 125 (1967):347–94; and Jean-Pierre Ravaux, "Les Campagnes de construction de la cathédrale de Reims au XIIIᵉ siècle," *BM* 137 (1979):7–66.

66. This portal is the subject of a forthcoming article by Alain Erlande-Brandenbourg and Jacques Moulin.

67. Whether a tympanum once existed is difficult to determine: the inside of the arch is a simple flat surface. The angels in the first row of archivolts turn toward the center, however, suggesting that there may once have been something there. One hopes that these questions will be resolved in the forthcoming article cited above. Formigé's restoration in *L'Abbaye royale*, plate 92, seems largely imaginary.

68. See below, chapter 4, for a longer discussion of this chapel.

69. See below, chapter 5, for the dating of the south transept arm.

70. The Virgin Chapel was begun in 1245, and the Porte Rouge, according to Sauerländer, dates to c. 1260 (W. Sauerländer, *Gotische Skulptur in Frankreich 1140–1270* [Munich: Hirmer Verlag, 1970], p. 170). Sauerländer, on p. 152 of the same book, dates the south transept portal at St-Denis to c. 1240–45 on stylistic grounds.

71. Ravaux, "Les Campagnes de construction," p. 18. See also Kurmann, *La Cathédrale de Meaux*, pp. 78–80.

72. These are similar, for example, to those at Royaumont, dated roughly to 1228–36. See C. Bruzelius, "Cistercian High Gothic: The Abbey Church of Longpont and the Architecture of the Cistercians in the Early Thirteenth Century," *Analecta cisterciensia* 35 (1979):3–204, esp. pp. 90–110.

73. In chapter 4 and appendix 1, there is an extended discussion of these two monuments and their attribution to the same architect.

74. This disposition was recorded in a painting in the sacristy of St-Denis representing the funeral of Dagobert by E. B. Garnier. The painting in question is one of a series commissioned by Debret to decorate the new sacristy erected in the 1820s and 30s.

75. On the royal foot, see A. Machabey, *Histoire des poids et mesures en France depuis le treizième siècle* (Paris: Revue de métrologie pratique et légale, 1962), pp. 37–40. Also S. Murray, "An Expertise at Beauvais Cathedral," *Journal of the British Archaeological Association* 130 (1977):133–44, esp. 135. Crosby (1953), p. 61, also identified the rod at St-Denis as the "royal foot," that is, .325 meters.

76. The same unit is also used for the width of the smaller blind arches in the lower part of the south transept terminal wall. On

the north, these dimensions were modified to incorporate the older Valois Portal.

77. Measurements are made wall to wall across the nave, not counting the dado arcad-

ing that projects as a screen in front of the wall.

78. Crosby (1953), p. 61.

CHAPTER 4. CONSTRUCTION

1. Both versions of the *Chronicon Sancti Dionysii ad cyclos paschales* state that work was begun in the chevet in 1231 (*BEC* 11 [1879]:262–95). Nonetheless, E. Medding-Alp in an article on the beginning of the reconstruction of the church dates the commencement of the work on stylistic grounds to circa 1200 ("Zur Baugeschichte des Abteikirche von Saint-Denis," *Zeitschrift für Kunstgeschichte* 5 (1936):246–50). This is repeated by Paul Frankl in *Gothic Architecture* (Baltimore: Penguin Books, 1962), p. 98. In his discussion of the thirteenth-century church in *L'Abbaye royale* (1953), Crosby tends to delay the conception and design of the upper stories of the chevet and the remainder of the thirteenth-century church to the early 1240s, as Pierre de Montreuil is thought to have been at St-Denis in 1247 (pp. 59–60). Both of these propositions will be discussed in the pages that follow as well as in the next chapter and appendix II, devoted to Pierre de Montreuil.

2. There is no twelfth-century masonry in the chevet arcade above the level of the abaci except for fragments of the twelfth-century elevation hidden on the exterior face of the triforium wall, visible from the crawl spaces over the twelfth-century vaults.

3. See Crosby (forthcoming), part II, chap. 6, for the work done on the transept in the twelfth century.

4. "In reparatione ecclesie nostre tam utili quam necessaria cum ruinam minaretur. . . ." AN, LL 1157, p. 85, L 836, and LL 1159, 54b–56b. The text of the document is published also in Félibien, p. 236. See also Medding-Alp, "Zur Baugeschichte," p. 247; and Kenneth John Conant, "Observations on the Vaulting Problems of the Period 1088–1211," *GBA* series 6, 26 (1944):131. See also Crosby's discussions of Suger's chevet, Crosby (forthcoming), part II, chap. 5.

5. Suger's chevet would have been smaller in scale and probably considerably lighter in structure. See Crosby's reconstruction in ibid., fig. 118.

6. See Panofsky, *Abbot Suger,* p. 43, for a description of the state of the old church prior to Suger's repairs and rebuilding.

7. See *Abbot Suger,* p. 109, and Erwin Panofsky's lucid discussion of this controversial text on pp. 242–44.

8. Viard, *Grandes Chroniques,* vol. 6, pp. 61–62: "Si estoient les voltes si viez et si corrompues qu'il estoient aussi comme au trebuschier, ne li abbés n'i osoit rienz renouveler pour ce qu'il avoit esté dedié presentement et en apert par Notre Signeur Jhesu Crist."

9. *Chronique latine,* vol. 1, p. 183.

10. That elevation, however, seems to have been somewhat like that of Sens, with a false triforium in the second story opening onto the area underneath the ambulatory roof. See Crosby's reconstruction (forthcoming), fig. 118.

11. Crosby has estimated that Suger's vaults may have been approximately 20 meters high, as opposed to 27 meters for the thirteenth-century church.

12. On the use of monoliths in hemicycles, see Kurmann, *La Cathédrale de Meaux,* p. 66, esp. n. 258.

13. Ibid., p. 69, and Charles Seymour, *Notre-Dame of Noyon in the Twelfth Century,* (New Haven: Yale University Press, 1939), pp. 77, 108.

14. The abaci range between 34 and 37 cm. in height, and 104 to 109 cm. in length on each side, between the chamfered edges (cut later). In contrast, the abaci of the ambulatory supports are generally about 31 cm. tall and

range from 95 to 100 cm. on each side (there are no chamfered edges here). Abaci such as those in the chevet arcade are not improbable for the thirteenth century, as similar examples of abaci that are rectangular in profile and have chamfered edges can be found in a number of smaller churches in the area of Paris, such as the nave of Beaumont-sur-Oise (plate 54).

15. Crosby (1953), p. 59; Robert Branner, "Paris and the Origins of Rayonnant Gothic Architecture down to 1240," *AB* 44 (1962):44, n. 24, and Formigé, *L'Abbaye royale,* p. 107.

16. Kurmann, *La Cathédrale de Meaux,* p. 70, points out that the thirteenth-century reconstruction of the chevet of Meaux is perhaps the most ambitious project of this type. However, smaller-scaled reconstructions *en sous-oeuvre* can be seen in any number of other monuments, for example, in the nave of Rouen, in occasional supports in the chevet of Notre-Dame in Paris, and in the chevet of Noyon (fifteenth century).

17. Suger's crypt supports are approximately 88 cm. in diameter, whereas those erected in the thirteenth century have a diameter of 94 cm.; the attached shaft has a diameter of 47 cm.

18. On these chapels, see Dieter Kimpel, *Die Querhausarme von Notre-Dame zu Paris und ihre Skulpturen* (Bonn: Rheinischen Friedrich-Wilhems Universität, 1971), pp. 33–43; Monique Lasalle, "Les Fenêtres des chapelles de la nef de Notre-Dame de Paris," *L'Information de l'histoire de l'art* 17 (1972):28–32; and Branner, *St. Louis,* p. 47, who describes the reworking of the hemicycle supports as having been done by a "master from Notre-Dame." This forms part of a larger argument by Branner and others that the early work at St-Denis was done by two different architects. See below for my thoughts about this theory.

19. The clumsy recutting of the abaci to create the continuation of the shafts suggests that the masons were working under somewhat trying circumstances. Furthermore, the upper beds of the masonry and arcade arches would have been put into place as soon as possible after the reconstruction of the column below in order to stabilize the twelfth-century vaults behind.

20. This narrow band of masonry continues across the shafts over the first compound pier and is interrupted only after it reaches the last arch of the arcade on the north side of the chevet, which is raised much higher than its predecessors (plate 19).

21. The diameters of Suger's ambulatory supports average about 45 cm. However, all but one of the supports is covered with a layer of plaster about one centimeter thick. On the one exposed column, the surface is badly abraded.

22. Medding-Alp, "Zur Baugeschichte," has associated these capitals with those on the cylindrical piers in the nave of the cathedral of Châlons-sur-Marne and believes the latter can be dated to c. 1200. Recent scholarship has, however, generally given the piers in the nave of Châlons a later date: about 1230 at the earliest and perhaps as late as 1250–60. See Ravaux, "La Cathédrale de Châlons-sur-Marne," pp. 171–227, esp. 207–08. See also Robert Branner, "La Cathédrale de Châlons-sur-Marne et l'architecture gothique en Champagne au XIIIᵉ siècle," *Mémoires de la Société d'agriculture, commerce, sciences, et arts du département de la Marne* 80 (1965):113–20. In any case, the capitals at St-Denis do not seem particularly close to those at the cathedral of Châlons, except for the later campaigns at the abbey church. Conversely, they *do* relate closely in style and conception to those in the ruins of the abbey of Royaumont, of the 1230s, and those at Mantes and Beaumont-sur-Oise (plate 54).

23. This type runs counter to the lighter floral decoration that had become popular at Reims and was adopted in the western bays of the nave of Notre-Dame in Paris. See Denise Jalabert, *La Flore sculptée* (Paris: A. and J. Picard, 1965), pp. 99–103.

24. Medding-Alp, "Zur Baugeschichte," p. 246.

25. On the dating of these two programs, see the more detailed discussion in chapter 6 below.

26. This raises the question of defining the point of transition from the space of the chevet to that of the transept. The fact that the easternmost aisle of the transept is on the same level as the chevet (the walls widen to the dimensions of the crossing only after this point) would seem to indicate that the first pair of compound piers was seen as marking the entrance to the sanctuary space of the chevet. The chapels placed in the east walls of the north and south transept arms would thus have formed part of the constellation of chapels radiating around the chevet.

27. This argument was perhaps first suggested by the Baron de Guilhermy, *Monographie*, p. 15, where he speaks of the cylindrical supports of the chevet as having been erected by an architect "un peu different." See also Branner, "Paris and the Origins of Rayonnant Gothic," p. 44; idem, *St. Louis*, pp. 46–53, esp. 49; Crosby (1953), p. 59; and Formigé, *L'Abbaye royale*, p. 107: "On se trouve évidemment en présence d'une direction nouvelle. . . ."

28. See, for example, Formigé's somewhat telegraphic account of the rebuilding of this part of the church in *L'Abbaye royale*, pp. 107–10.

29. At Canterbury, the supports undergo a complex sequence of types from the single columns in the choir to paired columns around the Trinity Chapel, to which the remains of Thomas Becket were translated in 1220. The transition is punctuated by single and paired columns with Purbeck marble shafts, similar to the eastern nave supports in the nave of Laon Cathedral. The paired columns of the chevet of Canterbury recall, of course, those of Sens.

30. There is, it seems to me, a particular appropriateness in the use of columns in the hemicycle around the altar and relics. Probably originating in Early Christian baldachins, this use of columns appears frequently in Gothic churches even when the remainder of the piers are compound, as in Clermont-Ferrand Cathedral. For similar examples in Romanesque Rome, see R. Krautheimer, *Rome: Profile of a City 312–1308* (Princeton: Princeton University Press, 1980), pp. 161–73.

31. On the setting-out of the twelfth-century plan, see Crosby (forthcoming), part II, chap. 3, section 3.

32. The height of the twelfth-century arcade must have been close to that of its thirteenth-century replacement in the turning bays of the hemicycle (plate 13).

33. Whereas the arcade to the base of the triforium measures 8.91 meters in the axial bay, in the transept and nave it measures 12.15–12.20 meters. This difference is mostly the result of the 2.52 meter change in floor level from the apse to the transept. In the hemicycle the top of the arcade is separated from the base of the triforium by an expanse of flat wall (plate 20), absorbed by the increasing height of the arcade arches in the western bays of the chevet.

34. There is considerable evidence of nineteenth-century recutting and restoration here, however, as the (now destroyed) screen in front of the sanctuary passed between these supports.

35. Here, however, the floor level has been raised in the eastern aisle of the bay that gives access to the St-Louis Chapel and the nineteenth-century sacristy. Where the lower level is preserved, the plinths of the responds measure 80–81 cm. This corresponds to the height of the plinths in the north transept arm at 7N(1), 7N(2), 8N(1), 8N(2), through 10N.

36. Illogical though this may seem, there were in fact cogent and convincing reasons for the delay on the south side, which is confirmed in any number of details.

37. This is suggested by Branner, *St. Louis*, pp. 49–50.

38. Branner, "Paris and the Origins of Rayonnant Gothic," p. 44, n. 24.

39. These seams in the masonry appear above piers 1S and 2S (in the lower beds of the eastern spandrels), above 3S in the second bed beneath the narrow strip of masonry that represents the floor level of the triforium, and on both sides of 4S and 5S up to the same level. The bedding of the masonry on the north side is more consistent, and irregularities seem to appear only in the lower beds, at the juncture

of the arcade arches with the shafts of the responds.

40. On the north the irregularities presumably occurred because the preservation of parts of the earlier church caused difficulties in the layout of the new plan.

41. The plinths in the triforium arcade of the chevet usually measure 14.5 × 14.5 and are about 22 cm. high. In bay 3S–4S, a plinth 13 × 13 and 24 cm. high is introduced. In bay 4S–5S, a plinth of these latter dimensions is planted diagonally. Other plinths in bay 4S–5S measure 16 × 17 by 20.5 cm. in height, and then, in bay 6S–7S, 18 × 18 × 13.

42. This disjuncture in the planting of abacus and plinth occurs when diagonally planted elements are first introduced in the late 1220s and early 1230s. Previously, abaci in this context had been set parallel to the axis of the nave. The circular abaci used in the clerestory windows are typical of the third and fourth decades of the thirteenth century; they reappear, for example, in the ambulatory and radiating chapels of the chevet of Beauvais.

43. This mixture appears especially in the eastern bays on the south side of the nave at the triforium level, where a significant interruption in construction of the abbey church seems to have occurred.

44. The southeast crossing pier was probably constructed as part of the work on the upper stories of the north side of the chevet. There is a pronounced seam between the wall of the arcade and the crossing pier (plate 57).

45. It is most improbable that construction of the fliers supporting the upper wall would have been delayed, as they performed an important function in strengthening the wall after construction of the roof but prior to erection of the interior vaults. See John Fitchen, *The Construction of Gothic Cathedrals* (Chicago and London: University of Chicago Press, 1961), pp. 77–78. Fitchen also points out that the Gothic architect was always concerned with an economy of means (pp. 87ff.). It would have been illogical to support the upper walls and roof with a substantial wooden scaffolding when the flying buttresses supported by the transept towers would eventually perform that task in any case. Fitchen points out, however, that on occasion the upper buttress supporting the upper wall may have been constructed before the lower, supporting the vaults (pp. 77ff.).

46. As pointed out above, the size of the buttresses here is determined by the spurs of wall on which they sit.

47. Specifically, this appears in the wall just to the west of the responds at 9N(2). On the exterior, breaks in the masonry occur on either side of the wall buttress at this point. These are the first indications of an interruption in the horizontal bedding of the first level of the church. If such evidence once existed on the eastern side of the north transept arm, the insertion of a door to the Valois Chapel and the reconstruction of these walls during the nineteenth-century restorations have completely obliterated the original masonry. We can only assume that the masonry here was continuous, as it is on the arcade, triforium, and clerestory levels from the north wall of the chevet through the north transept terminal wall.

48. John James, *The Contractors of Chartres* (Dooralong, Australia: Mandorla Press, 1979), has pointed out the importance of stairways in the sequence of construction, pp. 54–55, 67.

49. The consistency in the handling of details militates against the assumption of any significant interruption in this part of the church.

50. There is a break in the bonding of the masonry along the back wall of the triforium in the west wall of the north transept. Here again, this seems to be a question of the upper stories "catching up" with the lower.

51. For the state of the land to the north, see Panofsky in the notes to *Abbot Suger,* pp. 154–57. Aside from the short-lived tower erected by William the Conqueror, there seem to have been a variety of small-scale memorial structures at one time or another in this location, including perhaps some sort of tomb or mausoleum for Saint Denis (pp. 156–57).

52. We know virtually nothing of the conventual buildings at the site prior to the beginning of the reconstruction in 1231, as they were largely rebuilt in the thirteenth-century and again in the eighteenth. The dormitory would have been placed next to the south transept arm because of the night offices, and remnants of the thirteenth-century stair leading to it can still be seen in the east aisle of the south transept arm.

53. See Michael Davis, "The Choir of the Cathedral of Clermont-Ferrand: The Beginning of Construction and the Work of Jean Deschamps," *JSAH* 40 (1981):197. See also below, chapter 5.

54. And this is not, as has been suggested, a "search" for those thirteenth-century proportions (Branner, *St. Louis,* p. 49).

55. The passage would have been used as access for the workmen during construction and would have protected the lower walls.

56. Elimination of these bases was probably not an oversight but rather an attempt to resolve the problem of the higher plinths in the shafts attached to the main responds, which occurs throughout the triforium arcades in the north and south transepts as well as elsewhere in the nave.

57. See chapter 3, on the proportions.

58. Aubert, *Notre-Dame,* pp. 128–32, and Branner, *St. Louis,* pp. 27, 50.

59. Indeed, the design of the north transept rose seems closer in date to the north transept rose of Notre-Dame, generally dated to c. 1250, than to the west facade rose at Notre-Dame of about twenty-five years before.

60. This evidence is interesting but highly problematic and involves the heights of the plinths in the north transept arm, in three eastern bays of the nave, and in the corresponding parts of the church on the south; these last seem to follow certain patterns. All these bases and plinths were rebuilt in Viollet-le-Duc's restoration of the original floor level, and it is now impossible to determine to what extent, if at all, the reconstruction reproduced the heights of the original plinths. Keeping

the problematic nature of this evidence in mind, we can nonetheless establish the following groupings:

a. plinths between 75 and 85 cm. in height: 8N–10N, except for the responds in the west corner of the north transept arm (10N[1]; 10N[2]; and 11N[1], all of which measure between 89 and 91 cm.). This first group corresponds to 6S; 6S(1); and 6S(2) as well as those at 8S(2) and 9S(2).

b. the taller plinths of c. 90 cm. in the northwest corner of the north transept arm correspond to those in the west side of the south transept arm 8S; 8S(1); 9S; 9S(1); 10S; and 11S.

61. On St-Germain-en-Laye, see the study by J. de Terline, "La Tête de Saint Louis," pp. 123–49. See also Branner, *St. Louis,* pp. 51–55.

62. Branner, *St. Louis,* pp. 51–55.

63. Ibid.

64. The attribution of both buildings to the same architect raises the interesting question of the modus operandi of the individual in question. In his study on Meaux, Peter Kurmann has pointed out the arrangements of Gautier de Varinfroy, who was employed at two building sites at the same time, his contract stipulating that he spend a certain period of time each year at Meaux (Kurmann, *La Cathédrale de Meaux,* pp. 59–60). See also, D. Kurmann and Dethard von Winterfeld, "Gautier de Varinfroy, ein Denkmalpfleger im 13 Jahrhundert," *Festschrift für Otto von Simson* (Propyläen Verlag, 1977), pp. 101–59. See appendix 2 below for further reflections on this type of arrangement.

65. This seam appears on the interior just to the east of the juncture of the south and west walls of the south transept, behind the responds above the dado passage. There are, however, a number of difficulties with the masonry of the walls in this part of the building, as they have been restored and reworked on a number of occasions.

66. Here again, the reworking of the walls presents insuperable difficulties. My

conclusions are based on an analysis of the capitals and the bonding of the masonry in the spandrels of the arcade. As noted in chapter 2, none of the outer walls of the south side of the nave at aisle level survives; all that remains of the original structure are the aisle responds and the arcade and its upper stories (fig. 2).

67. However, the design at St-Denis is expanded to conform to the much larger dimensions of the rose. This was accomplished by adding trilobes around the circumference of the window, each placed with the single lobe on the upper side pointing outward. As Branner has pointed out, the design of the south rose is derived from those in the transepts of Reims, dated after 1236 (*St. Louis*, p. 51, n. 37).

68. It is, however, dangerous to generalize about the carving of capitals, as this varied widely from building to building and often depended on the scale of the elements on which they were placed. Although general types can be observed and described, the confusion in the dating of campaigns at the cathedral of Reims, for example, should demonstrate the dangers of this procedure. On St-Denis, see Robert Branner, *St. Louis*, p. 145: "There are no parts in the church that can be irrefutably assigned to the 1240s or even to the early or mid-1250s, for that matter. Although the forms may look the same, various details such as the capital style indicate that the triforium and clerestory of the south wall of the nave and of the last five bays on the north (west of the monks' choir) were not erected until about 1260 or later." As is noted in these pages, there are indeed stylistic changes in the types of capitals; these, combined with breaks in the masonry, permit a separation of the work on the south side of the church into three campaigns.

69. The old Carolingian nave, which was set inside the piers of the thirteenth-century church, may still have been in place and have remained in use while work proceeded on the south transept arm and the eastern bays on the south side of the nave (fig. 31).

70. See Branner, *St. Louis*, chap. 5. As Branner defines it, the Court Style begins

only in the 1250s. See my remarks on this subject in the conclusion to this book.

71. The Virgin Chapel was begun in 1245. See Branner, *St. Louis*, pp. 69–70, and Verlet, "Les Bâtiments Monastiques," p. 24.

72. Aubert, *Notre-Dame*, plan.

73. This work included the new vault in the eastern of Suger's western entrance bays on the south side. That on the north was rebuilt in a later campaign as part of the construction of the arcade on the north. Until the completion of the south aisle to join Suger's narthex, the old nave must have been used as the primary access to the new church. This also occurred at Bourges; see R. Branner, *La Cathédrale de Bourges* (Bourges: Tardy, 1962), p. 31.

74. Polygonal abaci and plinths seem always to have existed in the dado arcade at St-Denis, as is indicated by the fragments that survive in the Orangerie at the abbey. See also the remarks by Viollet-le-Duc, *Dictionnaire*, 1:95. On the problem of polygonal abaci in general, see ibid., pp. 2–3. While the abaci in the dado arcade and triforium at Amiens and the dado arcade alone at the Ste-Chapelle were polygonal, both buildings had rounded abaci in the clerestory. The transition to diagonally planted abaci in the east wall of the south transept arm at St-Denis is therefore a significant departure from the standard practice. As noted above in the text, there were rounded abaci in the windows of the chapel at St-Germain-en Laye.

75. Pointed trilobes, which are characteristic of Rayonnant Gothic architecture, must be seen as an elaboration of the rounded type that appeared in the triforium of St-Denis. A similar process takes place between the dado arcading in the nave and that in the chevet of Amiens; it becomes pointed in the eastern parts of the church.

76. After 1250, gables become a standard element in the design of arcading, as in the chevets of Amiens and Evreux, the latter begun about 1254 by Gautier de Varinfroy. See Kurmann, *La Cathédrale de Meaux*, pp. 71ff.,

and Kurmann and von Winterfeld, "Gautier de Varinfroy."

77. These repeat the forms of the pinnacles on either side of the transept terminals. Kurmann, *La Cathédrale de Meaux*, p. 75, sees these forms as typically Parisian, and indeed they do seem to be one of the dominant characteristics of exterior ornament in buildings erected in the second half of the thirteenth century.

78. Ibid.

79. There is some question about the date of the inception of the work here. See Branner, *St. Louis,* p. 93; Besnard, *L'Église de Saint-Germer-de-Fly,* pp. 92–116.

80. This repeats many of the forms of the Ste-Chapelle built by Saint Louis in Paris. Branner, *St. Louis,* pp. 93–97.

81. There were already many close similarities in the design of the transept roses, as has been seen above, as well as in the articulation of the lower half of the terminal wall. This has been noted by Branner, *St. Louis,* pp. 76–80, and by Aubert, *Notre-Dame,* pp. 151–55. There are also a number of connections with the arcading in the upper stories of the west facade.

82. Murray, "The Choir of St. Pierre," pp. 547–49.

83. These windows are dated by Branner, *St. Louis,* p. 121, to the 1270s, but work certainly continued on them until the end of the century. See especially Aubert, *Notre-Dame,* pp. 137–76.

CHAPTER 5. DATING AND CHRONOLOGY

1. See below, n. 77.

2. Élie Berger has published the *Chronicon* as the *Annales de Saint-Denis, BEC* 40 (1879):261–95.

3. The first version was probably written year by year, in a hand that, according to Berger, ceases in 1264. The second version seems to have been begun in the early 1260s and involved expansion of the original entries. The first hand in which entries are made in the second version ceases in 1264 as well. See Berger, *Annales,* p. 270, and Branner, *St. Louis,* p. 47, n. 30.

4. Berger, *Annales,* p. 290.

5. Crosby (1953), p. 60, infers that the *chorum* described in the text means the chevet. However, this is inconsistent with the medieval use of the term, in which the *chorum* is the area containing the stalls of the monks or canons and is sometimes distinct from the chevet. Although the term *choir* is often used to denote the entire area east of the transept, whether or not that area contains choir stalls, the term as used in the Middle Ages refers specifically to the liturgical choir used by monks or canons. For examples of medieval texts in which distinctions are made between the choir and the apse or chevet, see Victor Mortet and Paul Deschamps, *Recueil de textes relatifs à l'histoire de l'architecture, XI–XII siècles* (Paris: Editions Auguste Picard, 1929): on Notre-Dame in Cambrai, p. 68; on Coutances, p. 72; on Auxerre, p. 94; on Saint-Trond, p. 169. Gervaise of Canterbury also consistently makes these distinctions (ibid., pp. 208–17). See also Panofsky, *Abbot Suger,* pp. 199, 210–11.

6. The syntax also suggests two separate locations. Charles du Fresne, Sieur du Cange, *Glossarium ad scriptores mediae et infimae latinitatis* (Paris: Librairie des sciences et des arts, 1938), vol. 8, p. 175, mentions this text from the *Chronicon* and also suggests that the terms refer to the same thing: "Ubi revestiarium et vestiarium idem sonant. . . ."

7. Ordinarily, the vestry would have been attached to the chevet or to the eastern side of the transept, normally on the south. As the chapel added to the south transept arm in honor of Saint Louis was soon reconverted into a vestry, a vestry may have originally

occupied that location, placed conveniently next to the apse and beside the stairs rising to the monks' dormitory. It is also possible that a vestry was located to the south of the south transept arm and was destroyed when the conventual buildings were reconstructed in the eighteenth century. Unfortunately, descriptions of the church are not helpful on this point. For remarks on the chapel of Saint Louis, see the article by Brown, "The Chapels and Cult of Saint Louis," forthcoming.

8. In his description of the entry into the new choir at Canterbury in 1180, Gervaise refers to the inspection of the relics in the *vestiarium* of the cathedral (Robert Willis, *The Architectural History of Canterbury Cathedral* [London: Pickering and Bell, 1845], p. 53).

9. Vidier, "Les Abbayes," p. 143.

10. See Du Cange, *Glossarium,* vol. 8, pp. 175, 292. Viollet-le-Duc mentions the frequency of double vestries, one of which often served as a treasury (*Dictionnaire,* 8:69–72). See also Mortet and Deschamps, *Recueil de textes,* vol. 1, p. 42, n. 4, on the reference to a *revestiarium* at St-Benigne in Dijon.

11. Michel Germain, *Monasticon gallicanum,* ed. Achille Peigné-Delacourt (Paris: Delisle, 1871). This is confirmed in an engraving of the south side of the church by Chastillon as well as the engraved plate used as the frontispiece for Félibien's *Histoire* illustrating the funeral of Louis IX.

12. There were apparently bells in the east end of the Carolingian church in a tower above the crossing: see Panofsky, *Abbot Suger,* pp. 159–60, n. 2. Doublet, p. 355, mentions "la cloche qui est proche du couvent," which suggests a bell tower on the south side of the church.

13. Reference to the bells in the crossing of St-Denis is also made by George H. Forsyth, "St-Martin's at Angers and the Evolution of Early Medieval Church Towers," *AB* 32 (1950):315, n. 8.

14. This is the point at which a change in the design of the clerestory takes place, and

there is a distinct seam up the west side of the southwestern crossing pier. See chapter 4.

15. *Perfecit,* of course, normally does mean finished or completed. The late (or simply progressive?) design of the north transept rose might suggest, however, that it was added later (in the 1240s) and if so, the term *perfecit* in the *Chronicon* might have been loosely used to mean completion of the full height of the walls. It should be remembered that the second version, which summarizes the work done by Eudes Clément, was written after the fact, in the early 1260s, and probably represents a recollection of the state of the work in 1245.

16. Berger, *Annales,* p. 281. The relics were acquired by Fulrad in 763 (Félibien, p. 53). For an extended discussion of these relics, see Panofsky, *Abbot Suger,* pp. 152ff. In 1209 a chaplaincy was founded for the altar of Saint Hyppolytus (Félibien, p. 217). Prior to the translation of these relics in 1236 they were located in *media navi ecclesie.*

17. "Sinistra parte novi operis. . . ." The plan by LeBlond in Félibien's *Histoire* places this altar in the center of the eastern aisle of the western part of the north transept (plate 3). See Panofsky, *Abbot Suger,* pp. 152–53, on the use of this term by Suger and on the original location of the relics of Saint Hyppolytus; and Sumner Crosby, "The Inside of St-Denis' West Façade," in *Gedenkschrift Ernst Gall* ed. M. Kühn and L. Grodecki (Munich, Berlin: Deutschen Kunstverlag, 1965), pp. 66–69.

18. Montesquiou-Fezenzac and Gaborit-Chopin, *Le Trésor,* vol. 2, p. 438.

19. The year in which the relics were transferred to their new location and the chapel and altar were put into use.

20. Panofsky, *Abbot Suger,* p. 105.

21. Though it was probably far from complete in 1236. Bruzelius, "Cistercian High Gothic," pp. 90–91; and Branner, *St. Louis,* pp. 31–33.

22. At Westminster Abbey, 600–800 men worked on the rebuilding at a time. See

Peter Brieger, *English Art 1216–1307* (Oxford: Clarendon, 1957) pp. 107–08.

23. These charters are in the cartulary of the abbey in the AN, LL 1157, pp. 85–87, 91–93; and LL 1158, pp. 1–2. The third of these, charter CLXX, has been published by Félibien and in *GC* in the *Instrumenta* cols. 103–04.

24. The relics of Saint Eustache are mentioned in the *Comptes de la Grande Commanderie*, AN, LL 1240, fol iv. for 1229–30. The matutinal altar served the monks' choir and was therefore placed in the first bay west of the crossing (see Panofsky, *Abbot Suger*, p. 194). Panofsky (ibid., pp. 155, 157–58) deduces that in the twelfth century the altar of Saint Eustache was located on the south side, and during a procession the monks passed through this chapel on their way out of the church. Its inclusion in the charters of 1241 would seem to suggest that it had to be moved from its location on the south side (then under construction) and installed in the completed north transept. The Carolingian nave may well have remained intact and perhaps continued to be used well after 1241, as noted above in chapter 4.

25. The liturgy instituted by Abbot Eudes therefore has nothing to do with the "disappearance" of the architect posited by Branner (*St. Louis*, pp. 53, 145–46).

26. The inscriptions recording the dedications are published by Félibien, pp. 531–32, 535–36. The altar of Saint Hilaire (the last radiating chapel to the south) was dedicated in 1247; that of Saint Osmanna (the last radiating chapel on the north) in 1243; that of Saint Cucuphas (the first to the right of the axial chapel), in 1244, though on p. 531 Félibien contradicts himself and states that this altar was dedicated in 1248; that of Saint Maurice (the second chapel from the axial on the north side) in 1245; and the Virgin Chapel (the axial chapel) in 1253. There is some disagreement over the dedication of the chapel of Saint Peregrin (the first to the left of the axial chapel) in 1230. On these dedications, see also Branner, *St. Louis*, p. 144, n. 9. As the dedications of the chapels remained unchanged from

Suger's, it may be assumed that the rededications resulted from the refurbishing of the chapels.

27. AN, LL 1157, p. 85.

28. Ibid.

29. Colvin, *Building Accounts of King Henry III*, pp. 203–87, esp. 219, on Westminster Abbey. For Suger's expenditures, see von Simson, *The Gothic Cathedral,* p. 91.

30. The gifts of Philip Augustus are recorded in Félibien, p. 215. Usually such patronage stimulated other pious donations on the part of the nobility. In 1219 Pope Innocent III gave St-Denis further relics of Saint Denis brought back from Constantinople (see above, chapter 1). In his will, Philip Augustus left St-Denis all his jewels and gold crosses to be sold in order to purchase land to support twenty additional monks (ibid., p. 222). Guillaume de Nangis (*Chronique latine,* vol. 1, p. 170) records that Louis VIII brought these back for 12,000 *livres,* a sum equivalent to the expenses for the first years of construction on the church as recorded by Eudes Clément in the document of 1241. Hence Philip Augustus is considered one of the principal benefactors of the abbey.

31. See above, chapter 1.

32. AN, LL 1157, p. 670.

33. AN, LL 1157, pp. 84, 642, and LL 1170, pp. 55–56.

34. As the *Comptes de la Grande Commanderie,* which list income and expenditures at the abbey, are missing for the years during which the church was under construction, there is no known surviving record of royal donations.

35. Matthew Paris, *English History,* trans. from the Latin by the Rev. J. A. Giles (London: H. G. Bohn, 1852–54), vol. 2, p. 231.

36. Félibien, p. ccxi.

37. This has received a most interesting confirmation in the studies of Anne Walters; in a recent doctoral thesis at Yale University (1984). In her thesis, "Music and Liturgy at

the Abbey of Saint-Denis, 567–1567: A Survey of the Primary Sources," she has found an ordinary that can be dated between 1241 and 1259 (B.N. 976) and that includes a greatly expanded number of processions, including services at the altar of Saint Firmin (the first chapel on the north side of the chevet from the west), which do not appear in a slightly earlier ordinary (Maz 526) of 1234–36. I would like to thank Anne Walters for communicating this information to me.

38. The episode is recounted in great detail in Félibien, pp. 228–32.

39. The death of Philip Hurepel is recorded in the *Chronicon*. The location of his tomb is given in Félibien's plan and is confirmed by various descriptions (see plate 3).

40. See Félibien, pp. 237–38.

41. See above, chapter 3, for a broader discussion of this painting and n. 31 there for bibliography.

42. Eudes Clément's appointment as archbishop was contested by the chapter at Rouen, and although Eudes was appointed in March 1245, the matter was not settled until the following month. Abbot William was elected before Eudes departed, as he is named as abbot in charters of March 1245. See Félibien, p. 238.

43. This suggestion has already been made by Branner, (*St. Louis*, p. 145), although it is incorrect to assume that work stopped altogether in 1248. See, for example, n. 55 below on a donation to the fabric in 1250. Chronicles also indicate that poor weather, frost, and famine prevailed between 1251 and 1256, which would have had considerable effect on the revenues of the abbey. See the *Recueil des historiens de Gaule et de la France,* vol. 21 (1855), pp. 83–84.

44. On the financial aspects of the administration of Guillaume de Massouris, see J. Cordey, "Guillaume de Massouris, abbé de Saint-Denis," *Troisièmes Mélanges d'histoire du Moyen-Age* (Université de Paris: Bibliothèque de la Faculté des Lettres), vol. 18 (1904), pp. 187–256.

45. Félibien, p. 238.

46. Ibid., p. 239.

47. Ibid., p. 240. See also Cordey, "Guillaume de Massouris," pp. 187–256.

48. See Élie Berger, *Louis IX et Innocent IV, étude sur les rapports de la France et du Saint-Siège* (Paris: Thorin et fils, 1893), pp. 172–97. See also Ernest Lavisse, *Histoire de la France* (Boston: D. C. Heath, 1923), vol. 3, part 2, pp. 64–70; and Jordan, *Louis IX,* pp. 79–80. The tithes imposed in 1245 lasted until 1252.

49. Félibien, p. 240.

50. Ibid. This action parallels that of Suger one hundred years before. See Crosby (forthcoming), part II, introduction.

51. Félibien, p. 240.

52. See above, n. 27.

53. The inscriptions are given by Félibien, pp. 531–32, 535–36.

54. Ibid.

55. AN, LL 1157, p. 114. F. F. Niermeyer, *Mediae Latinitatis Lexicon Minus* (Leiden: E. J. Brill, 1976), p. 402, defines *fabrica* as the building operations, the erection and repair of the building of a church, or the building of the edifice itself. It is, of course, possible that an office of the fabric could have existed even though work might have been temporarily suspended.

56. Ibid., p. 117. The text is published by Henri Stein, "Pierre de Montereau, architecte de l'église de Saint-Denis," *SNAFM* 61 (1902):81–82.

57. Branner believed that Pierre de Montreuil played no significant role in the construction of St-Denis (*St. Louis,* p. 144) and went to some lengths to prove that no actual construction took place between 1241 and 1259—an interruption of eighteen years. See also appendix 2, and R. Branner, "A Note on Pierre de Montreuil and Saint-Denis," *AB* 45 (1963):355–57.

58. Félibien, p. 242. There is no mention of Henri Mallet in the necrology of the abbey.

Dom A. Wilmart, "Les Anniversaires célé-brés à St-Denis au milieu du XIV siècle," *Revue Mabillon* 15 (1924):29.

59. Ibid. Henri Mallet was appointed prevost of the priory of Berneval.

60. Branner, "Rectification," *SNAFM* (1965):84. Jordan, in *Louis IX*, p. 123, points out the dismal economic circumstances in France on Louis IX's return in 1254.

61. This is suggested also by Branner, al-though he believed that the interruption had begun in 1241 (*St. Louis*, p. 144).

62. See chapter 4.

63. For the construction and dating of these chapels, see Branner, "Paris and the Or-igins of Rayonnant Gothic," pp. 43–44; Kimpel, *Die Querhausarme von Notre-Dame*, pp. 40–43; Henry Kraus, "New Documents for Notre-Dame's Early Chapels," *GBA* 74 (1969):121–34; and Aubert, *Notre-Dame*, pp. 138–40.

64. No serious work has been done on the upper parts of the west facade of Notre-Dame. Branner (*St. Louis*, p. 27) suggests in passing that it was completed immediately after 1225, but Aubert (*Notre-Dame*, p. 35) suggests a date of 1245 for the completion of the towers. I concur with the latter, as the forms of the trilobed arcade seem significantly later in date than 1225.

65. See appendix 1 on Troyes. Le Mans has been dated by Branner, *St. Louis*, pp. 80–83, to c. 1248–54, when the chevet was conse-crated. See also Joel Herschman, "The Nor-man Ambulatory of Le Mans Cathedral and the Chevet of the Cathedral of Coutances," *Gesta* 20 (1981):323–32.

66. The windows on the east wall of the chevet in the small church of Angicourt in the Oise must, therefore, be dated to between 1240 and 1250.

67. On Amiens, see Branner, *St. Louis*, pp. 138–40, and Alain Erlande-Branden-bourg, "La Façade de la cathédrale d'Amiens," *BM* 135 (1977):254–96. The monograph by Georges Durand, *Monographie* *de l'église Notre-Dame, cathédrale d'Amiens* (Paris: Picard, 1901–03), is still the fundamen-tal source for the monument.

68. This concept of internal unity was important in the construction of the earlier parts of the church, where new forms were introduced only after a new part of the church (such as the south transept arm) had been reached.

69. See Branner, *St. Louis*, pp. 68–71; Verlet, "Les Bâtiments monastiques," pp. 20–21; and Dom Brouillart, *Histoire de l'ab-baye royale de St. Germain-des-Prés* (Paris: Du-pois, 1724). I do not wish to suggest, howev-er, that there are any other than general stylistic similarities between the two.

70. In the elongation of the lancets and in the reduction in size of the rosettes (plate 62).

71. Branner, "Rectification," p. 84.

72. On the dating of the tombs, see Wright, "A Royal Tomb Program," pp. 231–40.

73. *Chronique latine*, vol. 1, p. 269.

74. *Les Grandes Chroniques de France*, 8:129.

75. Félibien, pp. 241–53.

76. Ibid., p. 241.

77. D. Yonge gives the following trans-lation in *The Flowers of History* (London: H. G. Bohn, 1953), vol. 2, p. 365:

About the same period of this year a la-mentable disaster took place in the coun-try of France, one above all others ever-lastingly to be bewailed by the men of the religious order. In the church of St. Denis (*sic*), the apostle of the French, there was a certain new erection, raised on high, sup-ported by a great many wooden beams joined and fastened together. And when, one day, several men of the convent, with several also of the secular clergy, were walking under it, examining what had been done, lo! a great and fearful clap of thunder came, which violently shook the scaffolding of beams, and loosening the fastenings, entirely threw it down, and dashed to the ground and slew a great many both of the monks and secular clergy. And it is affirmed, in the relation of many who visited the spot, that all the monks of that monastery except fourteen, and a vast number of the secular clergy, were killed by that one calamity, on which account a great lamentation arose (and no wonder) throughout all France, when life was changed into death, and joy converted into mourning.

78. Henry III spent one month at St-Denis in 1259, and it was perhaps because of the presence of the king and his English retainers at the abbey that the report of this disaster is recorded only in an English source. For Henry's stay at St-Denis, see Félibien, p. 243, and Le Nain de Tillemont, *Vie de Saint Louis*, 4:175.

79. Fitchen, *The Construction of Gothic Cathedrals*, pp. 168–74.

80. On the use of numbers, see Alexander Murray, *Reason and Society in the Middle Ages* (Oxford: Clarendon Press, 1978), pp. 78–79.

81. As was the case during the construction of Cologne, during which the lower story was used while work proceeded on the upper. See Arnold Wolff, "Chronologie der ersten Bauzeit des Kölner Domes, 1248–1277," *Kölner Domblatt* 28–29 (1968):226.

82. Berger, *Annales*, p. 291, and Wright, "A Royal Tomb Program," p. 231. See also Erlande-Brandenbourg, *Le Roi*, pp. 81–82.

83. There is some question about the date when the royal tombs were installed; not all the sources are in agreement. While the *Chronicon* states that they were placed in the transepts in 1264 (pp. 292ff.), Guillaume de Nangis places the translation in 1267 (*Chronique latine*, vol. 1, pp. 232–33). It seems highly probable that the earlier date is correct, and it is this date that is generally used (as in Branner, *St. Louis*, p. 145; Wright, "A Royal Tomb Program," p. 237; and Erlande-Brandenbourg, *Le Roi*, p. 128).

84. See above, chapter 3.

85. Ibid.

86. AN, LL 1159, pp. 124–25.

87. See chapter 4.

88. Berger, *Annales*, p. 293.

89. Panofsky, *Abbot Suger*, p. 53.

90. See Jean Favier, "Les Finances de Saint Louis," *Septième centenaire de la mort de Saint Louis* (Paris: Les Belles Lettres, 1976), pp. 138–39.

91. See Palmer A. Throop, *Criticism of the Crusades: A Study of Public Opinion and Crusade Propaganda* (Amsterdam: Swets and Zeitlinger, 1940), pp. 73–74; and Lavisse, *Histoire de la France*, vol. 2, part 2, pp. 65–70.

92. Berger, *Louis IX et Innocent IV*, pp. 194–97.

93. See, for example, the recent article on the construction of Clermont-Ferrand by Michael Davis, "The Choir of the Cathedral of Clermont-Ferrand," *JSAH* 40 (1981):181–202. On taxation, see Jordan, *Louis IX*, p. 215.

94. Matthew Paris in his *English History* includes a decree on this subject issued by the papal legate to England (vol. 1, pp. 75–76):

Moreover, as we have seen ourselves, and have heard from many, that such a wholesome service (consecration) is despised, or at least, neglected by some, since we find that many churches, and even cathedrals, which have been built of old, have not yet been consecrated with the oil of sanctification; we therefore wishing to put a stop to this negligence, decree and enjoin that all cathedral, conventual, and parochial churches, which have been built and completed, shall within the space of two years, be consecrated by the diocesan bishops in whose jurisdiction they are, or by some other persons under authority from them; and in this manner within the same period, it shall be done with all churches to be rebuilt anew. And in order that this wholesome decree may not fall into contempt, we decree that, if any churches shall not have been dedicated within two years from the time of their completion, they shall be interdicted from the performance of mass till they are consecrated, unless any reasonable excuse can be alleged. In addition to this, we by the present decree strictly forbid abbots and rectors of churches to presume to destroy the old consecrated churches under pretense of building more beautiful or larger ones, without permission of the diocesan bishop; and the diocesan should carefully consider whether it would be expedient to give or refuse permission; if he give permission, he must give attention and use his endeavours to have the work com-

pleted as soon as possible; which condition we decree shall be extended to those already begun.

On delayed consecrations, see also René Crozet, "Étude sur les consecrations pontificales," BM 104 (1946):5–46, and Francis Salet, "Cluny III," BM 126 (1968):239–247.

95. Brown, "The Chapels and Cult of Saint Louis," forthcoming. See also above, chapter 1.

96. These visits are mentioned by Félibien as well as by Le Nain de Tillemont in *Vie de Saint Louis.*

97. Brown, "The Prince is the Father of the King," forthcoming.

CHAPTER 6. SOURCES AND INFLUENCES

1. The style is perhaps best described and defined in Hans Jantzen's *High Gothic* (New York: Random House, 1962).

2. This is exemplified in the confusion in the dating of Reims. In smaller buildings where more often than not there are no documents, dating is determined on a stylistic basis, frequently a precarious enterprise.

3. Branner, for example, states that the "Saint-Denis Master" came from Burgundy and worked on the cathedrals of Notre-Dame in Paris and Troyes prior to coming to St-Denis. On this, see the Appendices, in which I discuss the dating of the upper stories of the chevet of Troyes and the question of Pierre de Montreuil (see also Branner, *St. Louis,* pp. 39–55, 143–46).

4. Indeed, Villard de Honnecourt draws an ideal plan that results from a conversation he had with Pierre de Corbie. (Francois Bucher, *Architector: The Lodge Books and Sketchbooks of Medieval Architects* [New York: Abaris Books, 1979]). Whether Villard himself was or was not an architect is another question. See Carl F. Barnes, Jr., *Villard de Honnecourt, The Artist and His Drawings* (Boston: G. K. Hall, 1982), introduction.

5. For example, Saint-Vincent at Laon. This phenomenon has been described by Jean Bony in "Resistance to Chartres in Early Thirteenth-Century Architecture," *British Archaeological Journal,* 3d series, 19–21 (1956–58):40–41. A document recently discovered by Madeleine Caviness of Tufts University places Saint-Yved at Braine at the beginning of this group of churches.

6. It is a mistake, however, to conclude that Chartres was the only source of this disposition. There are certain indications that Soissons also was begun in the early 1190s and is not, therefore, a "copy" of Chartres (see the forthcoming work of Carl F. Barnes on Soissons). The traditional view on these matters has ignored the local context out of which the elevation of Soissons was derived. The recent publication by Richard Pestell, "The Design Sources for the Cathedrals of Chartres and Soissons," *Art History* 4 (1981):1–13, although correct in its assertion that Chartres and Soissons are contemporary, discusses the architectural context of the Aisne only superficially.

7. On St-Germain-des-Prés, see Clark, "Spatial Innovations in Saint-Germain-des-Prés," pp. 348–65.

8. Indeed, the A : B : A elevation of Chartres and Soissons is copied only at Reims and later in the nave of Strasbourg.

9. Branner, in *La Cathédrale de Bourges,* does not explore this aspect of its influence.

10. To these differences can be added Amiens' dramatically different approach to the design of the triforium arcade, to the tracery of the clerestory (which with its elongated lancets is more "modern" than that of St-Denis), and to the carving and positioning of the abaci, plinths, capitals, and other decorative and structural elements. There is, however, a strong similarity between Amiens and St-Denis in the handling of the abaci of the nave and aisle responds. In both churches, the abacus of the central respond under the main vaults is planted on the diagonal (plates 63 and 66), while in the aisles the central respond is parallel with the axis of the church (plate 18). At Strasbourg, the diagonal planting of the central abacus is rejected in both the nave and the aisles.

11. Branner has suggested that the interruption of wall-rib shafts at the base of the triforium reflects Burgundian influence or even, at St-Denis, a Burgundian architect (*St. Louis,* p. 40; and "Remarques sur la nef de la cathédrale de Strasbourg," *BM* 122 [1964]:261–68, esp. 261). However, in the major Burgundian examples, such as Auxerre Cathedral and Notre-Dame in Dijon, the shafts stop at the base of the clerestory. Only at Chalon-sur-Saône do they descend to the base of the triforium, and this church dates only to the 1230s (Branner, *Burgundian Gothic* [London: Zwemmer, 1964], pp. 124–25). The elimination of a Burgundian source renews the strong affinities between Strasbourg and St-Denis, which have tended to be deemphasized in the literature.

12. On Fécamp, see Jean Vallery-Radot, "Fécamp," *CA* 89 (1926):405–58; and ibid., *L'Église de la Trinité de Fécamp* (Paris: Petites monographies des grands edifices, 1928). On Lisieux, see William W. Clark, "The Nave of Saint Pierre at Lisieux: Romanesque Structure in a Gothic Guise," *Gesta* 16 (1977):29–38; and Alain Erlande-Brandenbourg, "La Ca-

thédrale de Lisieux et les campagnes de construction," *CA* (Le Bessin et le Pays d'Auge) 132 (1974):138–72.

13. See Clark, "Lisieux," p. 34 and n. 44.

14. Linkage is discussed in a number of studies on twelfth- and thirteenth-century Gothic; see, for example, the study by Anne Prache, *Saint-Remi de Reims: l'ouevre de Pierre de Celle et sa place dans l'architecture gothique* Bibliothèque de la Société française d'archéologie (Geneva: Droz, and Paris: Arts et métiers graphiques, 1978), pp. 95–97. On Essomes and Orbais, see Pierre Héliot, "Deux églises champenoises," *Mémoires de la Société d'agriculture, commerce, sciences, et arts du département de la Marne* 70 (1965):102–25; and more recently, on Orbais, Alain Villes, "L'Ancienne abbatiale Saint-Pierre d'Orbais," *CA* (Champagne) 135 (1977):549–89. See also Branner, "Remarques sur la nef de la cathédrale de Strasbourg," p. 264. In the chevet of Reims Cathedral, the clerestory and triforium are linked by the central mullion. Here, however, the shaft that links these two stories is corbeled out from the wall at the base of the triforium, so that the wall plane behind remains the same.

15. Shortly before St-Denis, linkage also appeared in the triforium and windows in the ambulatory of Beauvais: see Murray, "The Choir of St. Pierre," pp. 533–51, esp. 540–44.

16. Also, of course, the chevet of St-Martin-des-Champs in Paris and other examples in the Beauvaisis, including St-Etienne in Beauvais itself, La Villetertre, and Cambronne. The compound pier was also revived sometime after 1210 as the alternating supports in the chevet of Auxerre.

17. Amiens, for all its relative thinness and lightness of structure, adheres closely to the High Gothic tradition and has very little to do with the design of St-Denis. The same can be said of the chevet of Beauvais; neither the first program in the transept nor the second in the eastern parts of the ambulatory and the radiating chapels has any connection with St-Denis.

18. Murray, "The Choir of St. Pierre," p. 547.

19. The churches at Les Andelys are presently the subject of a Ph.D. dissertation being readied by Nelda Lewis of the University of California at Berkeley.

20. Branner, *St. Louis*, p. 49, n. 39, has pointed out that cylindrical piers with three engaged shafts exist in the twelfth-century nave of Bury.

21. The existence of this passage has been one of the reasons for the attribution of thirteenth-century St-Denis to a Burgundian or Champenois master. On wall-passages in general, see, for example, Prache, *Saint-Remi de Reims,* pp. 118–19. There are also a number of publications by Pierre Héliot on this subject; for example, "Les Églises de Cuis, Rieux, et les passages muraux dans l'architecture gothique de Champagne," *Mémoires de la Société d'agriculture, commerce, sciences, et arts du départment de la Marne* 82 (1967):128–43.

22. Branner, *Burgundian Gothic,* pp. 42–43, 50–53; see also Bony, "Resistance to Chartres," pp. 42–44.

23. Seymour, *Notre-Dame of Noyon,* pp. 127–33.

24. Prache, *Saint-Remi de Reims,* pp. 118–19.

25. Branner, *Burgundian Gothic,* pp. 38–62. At Auxerre and Clamecy there is a flat expanse of wall beneath the windows, an element adopted at St-Germain-en-Laye, where the passage passes also in front of the windows in the interior.

26. But there is, of course, the startling passage inserted at the top of the facade of Mantes.

27. For example, at Auxerre and Notre-Dame in Dijon.

28. Fécamp is close to Reims also in the relationship of the transverse wall and its arch to the responds in front (plates 67 and 68).

29. The chevet of Montiérender is usually dated between c. 1200 and 1230. See P. Arnoult, "L'Église abbatiale de Montier-en-Der," *CA* 113 (1955):270; M. Aubert, "A propos du choeur de Montier-en-Der," ibid., pp. 277–81, esp. 277.

30. This, to my knowledge, is the first time that the window tracery continues above the wall-rib in the outer plane of the wall, aside from the treatment of the rose window in the north transept arm at St-Denis. At the abbey church, however, the tracery is blind, whereas at St-Germain-en-Laye it is glazed. The same technique is later adopted at St-Urbain and becomes one of the characteristic features of Rayonnant Gothic.

31. As exemplified particularly in the axial chapel of the cathedral of Auxerre. Furthermore, as mentioned in n. 25, the flat panel of wall beneath the windows at St-Germain-en-Laye also suggests Burgundian sources.

32. See appendix 1.

33. Bruzelius, "Cistercian High Gothic," pp. 105–06; also Norbert Bongartz, *Die frühen Bauteile der Kathedrale in Troyes, Architekturgeschichtliche Monographie* (Stuttgart: Hochschulverlag, 1979), pp. 228, 236–37.

34. This grouping appeared also in the last quarter of the twelfth century in the chevet of Arras, now destroyed.

35. For the new date of the facade, see Erlande-Brandenbourg, "La Façade de la cathédrale d'Amiens," pp. 284–85.

36. There are a number of discussions on the glazing of the triforium. Branner, *St. Louis,* pp. 22–23, states that this glazing originates in the area of Paris in the 1220s and mentions the triforium of the ambulatory of Beauvais and that of Chelles, Vaudoy-en-Brie, Gonesse, and St-Leu-d'Esserent. See also Viollet-le-Duc, *Dictionnaire,* 1:205–06, and 9:294–96. It is my belief that it goes back to slightly earlier monuments, such as the small church of Mello in the Oise (plate 70), which can probably be dated c. 1200–10, and that the continuation of the glazed passage from a facade, as at Brie-Comte-Robert and Royaumont, or from a transept terminal wall (St-Germer-de-Fly) was an easy matter. On the phenomenon of the glazed triforium, see also

Bongartz, *Die frühen Bauteile der Kathedrale in Troyes*, pp. 226–28, and R. Branner, "Le Maître de Beauvais," *Art de France* 2 (1962):78–92.

37. For example, at St-Julien-le-Pauvre in Paris, as is indicated by surviving fragments of the thirteenth-century west facade still *in situ*, as well as at buildings such as Brie-Comte-Robert, dated by Branner to between 1225 and 1235 (*St. Louis*, p. 34).

38. Branner, "Beauvais," pp. 78–92.

39. This system of aisle roofing created severe drainage problems at St-Denis, ultimately solved by the radical change in the roofing in the nineteenth century.

40. See Branner, "Paris and the Origins of Rayonnant Gothic," pp. 49–50. This pattern occurs in the south aisle of Beauvais. See Murray, "The Choir of St. Pierre," in which he dates the aisles to c. 1225–32. On Amiens, see Erlande-Brandenbourg, "La Façade de la cathédrale d'Amiens," pp. 253ff.

41. The double aisles in the transept also create a centralized space in the interior. See the extensive discussion of transept towers by Pierre Héliot, "Sur les tours de transept dans l'architecture du Moyen-Age," *Revue archéologique*, no vol. (1965):57–95, 169–200.

42. The reconstruction of the chevet at Meaux began in 1253 (Kurmann, *La Cathédrale de Meaux*, pp. 59–62; Murray, "The Choir of St. Pierre," pp. 547–58).

43. For example, in the choir of Vendôme, begun in 1306.

44. *St. Louis*, pp. 39–45. See appendix 1 for a more complete discussion of Troyes.

45. Bongartz, *Die frühen Bauteile der Kathedrale in Troyes*, pp. 236–38.

46. Ibid.

47. See Hans Reinhardt, "La Nef de la cathédrale de Strasbourg," *Bulletin de la Société des Amis de la cathédrale de Strasbourg*, 4 (1937):3–28. Branner, in his "Remarques sur la nef de la cathédrale de Strasbourg,"pp.

261ff., downgrades the dependence of Strasbourg on St-Denis. See also Louis Grodecki, "Les Arcs-boutants de la cathédrale de Strasbourg et leur origine," *Gesta* 15 (1976): 43–51; and Anne Prache, "La nef de la cathédrale de Strasbourg et l'architecture Rayonnante en Champagne," *Bulletin de la cathédrale de Strasbourg: Hommage à Hans Reinhardt*, 15 (1982):99–103.

48. The relationship is especially visible on the north side, dated to c. 1250. Indeed, Grodecki cites Notre-Dame as the source for the flier design at Strasbourg ("Les Arcs-boutants," pp. 45–49). The transformation of shafts to flattened surfaces takes place in a number of monuments from the 1230s on, as in the south aisle windows in the chevet of Troyes and the aisles of St-Martin-aux-Bois and St-Sulpice-de-Favières.

49. See Branner, "Paris and the Origins of Rayonnant Gothic," pp. 43–44. This motif may derive from the Ste-Chapelle.

50. This is not the case at St-Denis, where the tracery in the clerestory consists of twice as many units as the pattern below the aisles.

51. For example, at Auxerre Cathedral and at Fécamp. Branner, as a result, believes that the master of Strasbourg could have worked on Auxerre, Dijon (Notre-Dame), and Chalon-sur-Saône before coming to work at Strasbourg ("Remarques sur la nef de la cathédrale de Strasbourg," p. 262). This seems most improbable.

52. These can be dated to the third quarter of the thirteenth century. See Jalabert, *La Flore Sculptée*, pp. 102–03.

53. On their date and design, see Kimpel, *Die Querhausarme*, passim.

54. Indeed, at Evreux, where this appears as part of the work of Gautier de Varinfroy, the shafts underneath the wall-rib are also interrupted at the base of the triforium, as at St-Denis, so that the upper two stories are set back in depth, though here on a steep *glacis*.

55. This work dates to the third quarter of the thirteenth century. There are also strik-

ing similarities between Freiburg-im-Breisgau and St-Denis in the design of the piers and the carving of the capitals.

56. On St-Sulpice, see Yves Sjöberg, "Saint-Sulpice de Favières," *CA* 103 (1944):246–64, and Kurmann, *La Cathédrale de Meaux,* pp. 73–75. Also, Branner, *St. Louis,* p. 76.

57. Kurmann, *La Cathédrale de Meaux,* p. 75, leans toward a date of c. 1270 for St-Sulpice, basing his argument in part on elements established in the Rayonnant reworking of Meaux. Branner's date in the 1240s is altogether too early.

58. Bony himself expresses some uncertainty as to the date of these rebuilt supports. See "La Collégiale de Mantes," pp. 184–86.

59. Bruzelius, "Cistercian High Gothic," p. 125.

60. Ibid., pp. 121–22. On Gonesse, see Daniel Bontemps, "La Nef de l'église Saint-Pierre-de-Gonesse et ses rapports avec l'abbatiale de Saint-Denis," *BM* 139 (1981):111–28.

61. Also, for example, at Cormeilles-en-Vexin and Cuiry-House in the Aisne.

62. On these see M. Aubert and M. Minost, "La Fenêtre occidentale du réfectoire de Saint-Germain-des-Prés, oeuvre de Pierre de Montreuil," *BM* 112 (1954):275–80; and Verlet, "Les Bâtiments monastiques," pp. 20–21, 40.

63. Branner, in "Remarques sur la nef de la cathédrale de Strasbourg," suggests that here, too, Burgundian architecture plays an important role (p. 262).

64. See Davis, "The Choir of the Cathedral of Clermont-Ferrand," pp. 181–202.

65. The former, for example, at Cambronne and Chambly in the Oise. See also the thirteenth-century chapel and its corridor at St-Germer-de-Fly. This multiplication of shafts appears also in English monuments of the mid to late thirteenth century, as in the angel choir at Lincoln. I would like to thank Mary Dean for bringing this to my attention in a lecture given in San Francisco in 1980.

CHAPTER 7. CONCLUSION

1. These studies have all been cited previously in the text.

2. Maryse Bideaut and Claudine Lautier, "Saint Nicaise de Reims: Chronologie et nouvelles remarques sur l'architecture," *BM* 135 (1977):297–330, have established that the facade was not begun, as had been previously thought, in 1231 but rather at least a decade later. The nave elevation, however, is exactly contemporary with that of St-Denis.

3. Indeed, the facade of St-Nicaise seems to exemplify this tendency, with the continuous screen of arches and gables that stretches across the lower part of the facade and conceals the buttresses behind.

4. The chevet of Cambronne was dedicated in 1239 (Branner, *St. Louis,* p. 18).

5. Davis, "The Choir of the Cathedral of Clermont-Ferrand," pp. 181–202.

6. See von Simson, *The Gothic Cathedral,* pp. 62–64.

7. Indeed, St-Germain-en-Laye has a supposed portrait of the young king on one of the keystones; Terline, "La Tête de Saint Louis à Saint-Germain-en-Laye."

8. But by Branner's definition, the style begins only with the late 1240s. See *St. Louis,* pp. 64–111. The discussion here deals with monuments that have only a remote connection—if any at all—to the king and court.

9. Ibid., pp. 39–55, on Branner's view of St-Denis and St-Germain-en-Laye.

10. Ibid., pp. 72–73.

11. Unfortunately, most other monuments have been destroyed. See Yvan Christ, *Eglises parisiennes actuelles et disparues* (Paris: Editions, "Tel," 1947), and Branner, *St. Louis,* pp. 86–90.

12. For example, the churches of the Dominicans and Franciscans as well as the Carthusians, the Mathurins, the hospice of Quinze-Vingts for the blind, and the abbeys of St-Catherine at Val-des-Ecoliers and Notre-Dame-des-Blancs-Manteaux. See both Christ, *Eglises parisiennes,* and Branner, *St. Louis,* pp. 86ff.

13. Such as St-Urbain at Troyes or the chapel at St-Germer-de-Fly.

14. Certainly the ongoing work in the cathedral of Paris, at St-Germain-des-Prés, and at other lost buildings in Paris exerted as much influence as the royal monuments.

15. Branner, *St. Louis,* pp. 86–90, also points out the simplicity and austerity of these foundations after 1254. See also above, chapter 1, n. 62, on Louis's desire to become a friar, and Jordan, *Louis IX,* p. 130.

APPENDIX 1

1. See Bongartz, *Die frühen Bauteile der Kathedrale in Troyes,* pp. 234–35, for a summary of the positions taken on the relative dating of the upper stories of Troyes relative to the abbey church of St-Denis. The confusion in the dating of Troyes is perhaps exemplified by Robert Branner, "Les Débuts de la cathédrale de Troyes," *BM* 118 (1960):111–22, who states that Troyes is later than St-Denis and then contradicts this chronology in *St. Louis,* pp. 39–50.

2. Branner, *St. Louis,* pp. 39–50.

3. Bongartz, *Die frühen Bauteile der Kathedrale in Troyes,* pp. 241–43.

4. I would like to emphasize that I had anticipated the reverse when I went to Troyes: my conclusions are not the result of a Dionysian chauvinism.

5. Bongartz, *Die frühen Bauteile der Kathedrale in Troyes,* pp. 236–37. See in his text figure 20 and plates 73 and 74.

6. Ibid.

7. Bruzelius, "Cistercian High Gothic," pp. 106–07. This glazing is not noted by Bongartz, and enhances further the similarities between the triforium of Royaumont and the chevet of Troyes.

8. Ibid., and Bongartz, *Die frühen Bauteile der Kathedrale in Troyes,* pp. 236–37.

9. See above, chapter 4.

10. Ibid. In churches where the original clerestory of St-Denis is copied, as at St-Martin-aux-Bois in the Oise, or in the same area the chevet windows of the small parish church of Angicourt, the abaci are rounded, in spite of more modern features in other aspects of the "copies."

11. Bongartz, *Die frühen Bauteile der Kathedrale in Troyes,* pp. 238ff. Bongartz argues that the retention of a consistent height to the lancets throughout the chevet of Troyes is further evidence of the precedence of Troyes, and that it represents a more fully resolved design.

APPENDIX 2

1. See Louis Grodecki, "Pierre, Eudes, et Raoul de Montreuil à l'abbatiale de Saint-Denis," *BM* 122 (1964):269–74, for a complete bibliography and discussion of the question; see also Stein, "Pierre de Montereau," pp. 79–104; and Marcel Aubert, "Pierre de Montreuil," *Festschrift Karl M. Swoboda* (Vienna: R. M. Rohrer, 1959), pp. 19–21. The most recent contributions have been the lucid article by Anne Prache, "Pierre de Montreuil," *Histoire et Archéologie, Dossiers* 47 (1980):26–38; and J. Moulin and P. Ponsot, "La Chap-

elle de la Vierge à l'abbaye de Saint-Germain-des-Prés," *Archaeologia* 140 (1980):49–55.

2. AN, LL 1157 pièce 117.

3. Branner, "A Note on Pierre de Montreuil," pp. 355–57.

4. Grodecki, "Pierre, Eudes, et Raoul de Montreuil."

5. See above, chapters 4 and 5.

6. This linkage was being used in the chapels on the north side of the nave of Notre-Dame beginning with the fifth from the west (5N); these are dated by Kimpel, *Die Querhausarme* (p. 42), to c. 1245, though by others to the 1230s (for example, Lasalle, "Les Fenètres de Notre-Dame de Paris," pp. 28–32). The dates given by Lasalle are problematic, however, as she bases her arguments on Branner's dating of the construction of St-Denis.

7. Jean Bony, *French Cathedrals*, (Boston: Houghton, 1951), p. 10.

Selected Bibliography

I have excluded from this list sources cited only once or twice and sources that are peripheral to my main topic.

I. PRIMARY SOURCES AND DOCUMENTS

A. Archives Nationales de France

1. L836: Listes des fondations, 1231–1771

2. LL1157 and LL1158: Les Grandes Cartulaires Blancs

3. LL1159: Cartulaire de l'Office des Charités

4. LL1165: Cartulaire de l'Office du Grand Prieur

5. LL1167: Cartulaire de Rueil

6. LL1174, LL1175, and LL1176: Cartulaire de l'Aumône

7. LL1240 and LL1241: Comptes de la grande commanderie, 1229–1343

8. F(21) 1451: François Debret, "Notes historiques sur la fondation de l'église royale de St-Denis, sa dévastation et sa restauration" (c. 1832)

9. F^{13}1293–1296: Restoration documents, 1806–1835

10. F^{13}1397: Restoration documents, 1811–1825

B. Archives de la Commission des Monuments Historiques

1. Registres des attachements de ser-rurerie, de menserie, de marbrerie, de plomberie, de sculpture

2. Correspondance administrative, St.-Denis, 1836–1851

3. Dossier Viollet-le-Duc, 1841–1876

4. Album Debret

C. Bibliothèque Nationale, Paris

1. Nouv. acq. fr.6121 and 6122: Baron de Guilhermy, "Notes archéologiques, St.-Denis," 2 vols.

2. Fr. 11681: Alfred Gautier, "Recueil d'anecdotes et autres objets curieux relatifs à l'histoire de St.-Denys en France"

3. Lat. 5415: Fragments du Cartulaire Blanc

4. Lat. 17111: Collection Gagnières. Copie des privilèges accordés par les rois.

5. Lat. 12668: Monasticon benedictinum

II. SECONDARY SOURCES

Anfray, Marcel. L'Architecture normande, son influence dans le nord de la France au XIe et XIIe siècles. Paris, 1939.

Aubert, Marcel. Notre-Dame de Paris, sa place dans l'histoire de l'architecture du XIIe au XIVe siècle. Paris, 1920.

———. "Le Romantisme et le Moyen-Age." In Le Romantisme et l'art, edited by E. Herriot, pp. 23–48. Paris, 1928.

———. "Pierre de Montreuil." *Bulletin de la société nationale des antiquaires de France* (1943–44), pp. 115–118.

———, and M. Minost. "La Fenêtre occidentale du réfectoire de Saint-Germain-des-Prés, oeuvre de Pierre de Montreuil." *Bulletin monumental* 112 (1954): 275–89.

———. "Pierre de Montreuil." *Festschrift für Karl M. Swoboda,* pp. 19–21. Vienna, 1959.

Ayzac, Félicie de. *Histoire de l'abbaye de Saint-Denis en France.* 2 vols. Paris, 1860–61.

Bandmann, Günther. *Mittelalterliche Architektur als Bedeutungsträger.* Berlin, 1951.

Barbieri, Franco. "Vincenzo Scamozzi, studioso ed artista." *Critica d'Arte* 8 (1949)222ff.

Berger, Élie. *"Annales de St.-Denis, généralment connue sous le titre de Chronicon Sancti Dionysii ad cyclos paschales."* XI (1879), pp. 261–295.

———. *Louis IX et Innocent IV, étude sur les rapports de la France et du Saint-Siège.* Paris, 1893.

———. *Histoire de Blanche de Castille.* Paris, 1895.

Bober, Harry. "A Reappraisal of Rayonnant Architecture." In *The Forward Movement of the Fourteenth Century,* edited by F. L. Utley, pp. 9–30. Columbus, Ohio, 1961.

Bongartz, Norbert. *Die frühen Bauteile der Kathedrale in Troyes, Architekturgeschichtliche Monographie.* Stuttgart, 1979.

Bony, Jean. "La Collégiale de Mantes." *Congrès archéologique* 104 (1946):163–220.

———. *French Cathedrals.* Boston, 1951.

———. "The Resistance to Chartres in Early Thirteenth Century Architecture." *Journal of the British Archaeological Association* 20–21 (1957–1958): 35–52.

———. *The English Decorated Style.* Ithaca, 1979.

———. *French Gothic Architecture of the Twelfth and Thirteenth Centuries.* Berkeley, California, 1983.

Branner, Robert. "Paris and the Origins of Rayonnant Gothic Architecture down to 1240." *The Art Bulletin* 44 (1962):39–51.

———. "A Note on Pierre de Montreuil." *The Art Bulletin* 45 (1963):355–57.

———. "Remarques sur la nef de la cathédrale de Strasbourg." *Bulletin monumental* 122 (1964):261–68.

———. "Rectification de la chronologie de l'église abbatiale de Saint-Denis." *Bulletin de la société nationale des antiquaires de France* (1965), pp. 84–85.

———. "La Cathédrale de Châlons-sur-Marne et l'architecture gothique en Champagne au XIIIᵉ siècle." *Mémoires de la Société d'agriculture, commerce, sciences, et arts du département de la Marne* 80 (1965):113–120.

———. *St. Louis and the Court Style in Gothic Architecture.* London, 1965.

———. "La Place du 'Style de Cour' de Saint Louis dans l'architecture du XIIIe siècle." In *Le Siècle de Saint Louis,* edited by R. Pernoud and A. Chamson, pp. 133–39. Paris, 1970.

Brière, Gaston, and Paul Vitry. *L'Abbaye de Saint-Denis.* Petites Monographies des Grands Edifices de la France. Paris, 1948.

Brown, Elizabeth A. R. "The Chapels and Cult of Saint Louis at Saint-Denis." Forthcoming.

———. "The Prince is the Father of the King: The Character of Philip the Fair of France." Forthcoming.

Bruzelius, C. "Cistercian High Gothic: The Abbey Church of Longpont and the Architecture of the Cistercians in the Early Thirteenth Century." *Analecta cisterciensia* 35 (1979):3–204.

Christ, Yvan. *Eglises parisiennes actuelles et disparues.* Paris, 1947.

Colvin, H. M., ed. *The Building Accounts of King Henry III.* Oxford, 1971.

Conway, Sir William Martin. "The Abbey of Saint-Denis and its Ancient Treasures." *Archaeologia, or Miscellaneous Tracts Relating to Antiquity,* 2d series, 66 (1915):103–58.

Cordey, J. "Guillaume de Massouris, abbé de Saint-Denis (1245–1254)." In *Troisièmes Mélanges d'histoire du Moyen-Age,* pp. 187–262. Paris, 1904.

Crosby, Sumner McKnight. *The Abbey of St.-*

Denis 475–1122. Volume I. New Haven, 1942.

—. *L'Abbaye royale de Saint-Denis*. Paris, 1953.

—. "Crypt and Choir Plans at Saint-Denis." *Gesta* 5 (1966):4–8.

Debret, François. "Notice sur les diverses constructions et restaurations de l'église St-Denis." In *Séance publique des cinq académies*, pp. 9–28. Paris, 1842.

Delaborde, H. François. "Notice sur les ouvrages et sur la vie de Rigord." *Bibliothèque de l'Ecole des Chartes* 45 (1884):584–614.

—. "Fragments de l'enquête faite à St-Denis en 1282 en vue de la canonisation de Saint Louis." *Mémoires de la société de l'histoire de Paris et de l'Ile de France* 23 (1896):1–71.

Didron, Alphonse, and François Baron de Guilhermy. "St-Denis, restauration de l'église royale." *Annales archéologiques* 1 (1844–1845):230–36; 2:245–46; 3:245–46; 4:175–85.

—. "Achevement des restaurations de Saint-Denis." *Annales archéologiques* 5 (1846):107–13.

—. "Démolition de la flèche de Saint Denis." *Annales archéologiques* 5 (1846): 62–68.

Doublet, Dom Jacques. *Histoire de l'abbaye de S.Denys en France*. Paris, 1625.

Erlande-Brandenbourg, Alain. "La Priorale Saint Louis de Poissy." *Bulletin monumental* 129 (1971):85–112.

—. *Le Roi est mort. Étude sur les funérailles, les sépultures, et les tombeaux des rois de France jusqu'à la fin du XIIIème siècle*. Bibliothèque de la Société française d'archéologie, 7. Paris, 1975.

—. *L'Eglise abbatiale de Saint-Denis, I: Historique et visite*. Paris, 1976.

Eydoux, Henri-Paul. *Saint Louis et son temps*. Paris, 1971.

Fawtier, Robert. *The Capetian Kings of France*. New York, 1960.

Félibien, Dom Michel. *Histoire de l'abbaye royale de Saint-Denys en France*. Paris, 1706.

Fitchen, John. *The Construction of Gothic Cathedrals: A Study of Medieval Vault Erection*. Chicago, 1961.

Flamand-Grétry, Louis-Victor. *Itinéraire historique, géographique, topographique, statistique, pittoresque, et biographique de la Vallée de Montmorency*. Paris, 1840.

Formigé, Jules. "Travaux de mise en valeur à l'église abbatiale de Saint-Denis." *Les Monuments Historiques de la France*, nouv. série, 1 (1955):106ff.

—. "Les Travaux récents de la basilique de Saint-Denis." *Académie des Beaux-Arts* (1956–57), pp. 77ff.

—. "L'Eglise de l'abbaye royale de Saint-Denis en France." In *Revue de Touring Club de France*, no. 706 (1960):328–55.

—. *L'Abbaye royale de Saint-Denis: Recherches nouvelles*. Paris, 1960.

Frankl, Paul. *Gothic Architecture*. Baltimore, 1962.

Germann, G. *Gothic Revival in Europe and Britain: Sources, Influences, and Ideas*. Cambridge, 1973.

Gilbert, A. P. M. *Description historique de l'église royale de Saint-Denys*. Paris, 1815.

Le Gothique retrouvé. Paris, 1980.

Grodecki, Louis. *The Stained Glass of French Churches*. Translated by Rosemary Edmunds and A. D. B. Sylvester. London, 1948.

—. "Le Vitrail et l'architecture aux XIIe et XIIIe siècles." *Gazette des Beaux-Arts*, 6th ser., 36 (1949):5–24.

—. "Pierre, Eudes, et Raoul de Montreuil à l'abbatiale de Saint-Denis." *Bulletin monumental* 122 (1964):269–74.

—. *Les Vitraux de Saint-Denis: Étude sur le vitrail au XIIème siècle*. Volume 1. Paris, 1976.

Guiffrey, J. J. *Un Chapitre inédit de l'histoire des tombes royales*. Paris, 1876.

Guilhermy, François, Baron de. "Restauration de l'église royale de Saint-Denis." *Annales archéologiques* 5 (1846):212–14.

—. *Monographie de l'église royale de Saint-Denis: Tombeaux et figures historiques*. Paris, 1848.

Héliot, Pierre. "Sur les tours de transept dans l'architecture du Moyen-Age." *Revue archéologique* 1 (1965):169–200; 2 (1965):57–95.

Hinkle, William M. "The Iconography of the Four Panels by the Master of Saint Giles." *Journal of the Warburg and Courtauld Institutes* 28 (1965):110ff.

Huard, Georges. "Percier et l'abbaye de Saint-Denis." *Les Monuments historiques de la France*, no. 3 (1936):134–44; no. 4 (1936):173–82.

Hubert, Jean. *L'Art pré-roman*. Paris, 1938.

Jordan, William Chester. *Louis IX and the Challenge of the Crusade*. Princeton, 1979.

Kimpel, Dieter. *Die Querhausarme von Notre-Dame zu Paris und ihre Skulpturen*. Bonn, 1971.

Kraus, Henry. "New Documents for Notre-Dame's Early Chapels." *Gazette des Beaux-Arts* 74 (1969):121–34.

Kurmann, Peter. *La Cathédrale Saint-Etienne de Meaux: étude architecturale*. Bibliothèque de la Société française d'archéologie, 1. Paris, 1971.

Kurmann, Dieter, and Dethard von Winterfeld. "Gautier de Varinfroy, ein 'Denkmalpfleger' im 13 Jahrhundert." In *Festschrift für Otto von Simson*, pp. 101–59. Frankfurt am Main, Berlin, Vienna, 1977.

Lasalle, Monique. "Les Fenêtres des chapelles de la nef de Notre-Dame de Paris." *L'Information d'histoire de l'art* 17 (1972):28–32.

Le Nain de Tillemont. *Vie de Saint Louis*. Paris, 1847–51.

Lecoy de la Marche, A. *Oeuvres complètes de Suger*. Société de l'Histoire de France, no. 139. Paris, 1867.

———. *La France sous Saint Louis et Philippe le Hardi*. Paris, 1893.

Liebman, Charles J. "La Consécration légendaire de la basilique de Saint-Denis." *Le Moyen-Age*, 3d ser., 45 (1935):252–64.

Loomis, Laura Hibbard. "The Oriflamme of France and the WarCry Monjoie in the Twelfth Century." In *Studies in Art and Literature for Belle da Costa Greene*, pp. 67ff. Princeton, 1954.

Mayer-Long, Jannie. "L'Abbaye de Saint-Denis au XVIIIe siècle." M.A. thesis. Paris, 1978.

Medding-Alp, Emma. "Zur Baugeschichte des Abteikirche von Saint-Denis." *Zeitschrift für Kunstgeschichte* 5 (1936):246–50.

Middleton, Robin, and David Watkin. *Neoclassical and Nineteenth-Century Architecture*. New York, 1980.

Millet, Dom Germain. *Le Trésor sacré, ou inventaire des sainctes reliques et autres précieux joyaux du Trésor de l'abbaye royale de Saint-Denys en France*. 2d ed. Paris, 1638.

Montesquiou-Fezenzac, Blaise Comte de, and Danielle Gaborit-Chopin. *Le Trésor de Saint-Denis*. 3 volumes. Paris, 1973–77.

Montesquiou-Fezenzac, Blaise de. "Le Tombeau des corps saints à l'abbaye de Saint-Denis." *Cahiers archéologiques* 23 (1974):81–95.

Mortet, Victor, and Paul Deschamps. *Recueil de textes relatifs à l'histoire de l'architecture, XIIe–XIIIe siècles*. Paris, 1929.

Murray, Stephen. "The Choir of the Church of St. Pierre, Cathedral of Beauvais: A Study of Gothic Architectural Planning and Constructional Chronology in its Historical Context." *The Art Bulletin* 62 (1980):533–51.

Nangis, Guillaume de. *Chronicon guillelmi de Nangiaco ab anno 1112 ad annum 1301*. Recueil des historiens des Gaules et de la France, 20, pp. 312–463.

Panofsky, Erwin. *Gothic Architecture and Scholasticism*. 2d ed. New York, 1957.

———. *Tomb Sculpture*. New York, 1964.

———, ed. *Abbot Suger on the Abbey Church of St.-Denis and its Art Treasures*. 2d ed. edited by Gerda Panofsky-Soergel. Princeton, 1979.

Prache, Anne. *Saint-Remi de Reims: l'oeuvre de Pierre de Celle et sa place dans l'architecture gothique*. Bibliothèque de la Société française d'archéologie, 8. Paris, 1978.

———. "Pierre de Montreuil." *Histoire et Archéologie, Dossiers* 47 (1980):26–38.

Ruprich-Robert, V. *L'Architecture normande au XIème siècle et au XIIème siècle*. Paris, 1884.

Schramm, P. E. *Der König von Frankreich*. 2 volumes. Weimar, 1960.

Simson, Otto von. *The Gothic Cathedral: Origins of Gothic Architecture and the Medieval Concept of Order.* New York, 1956.

Spiegel, Gabrielle. "The Cult of Saint Denis and Capetian Kingship." *Journal of Medieval History* I (1975):43–70.

――――. *The Chronicle Tradition of Saint-Denis: A Survey.* Medieval Classics: Texts and Studies, X. Brookline, Mass., 1978.

Stein, Henri. "Pierre de Montereau, architecte de l'église de Saint-Denis." *Mémoires de la société nationale des antiquaires de France* 61 (1902):79–104.

Terline, J. de. "La Tête de Saint Louis à Saint-Germain-en-Laye." *Monuments et mémoires, Fondation E. Piot* (Académie des inscriptions et Belles-Lettres) 45 (1951):123–40.

Théry, P. G. "Contribution à l'histoire de l'Aréopagitisme au IXe siècle." *Le Moyen-Age,* 2ème série, 25 (1923): 111–53.

Viard, Jules, ed. *Les Grandes Chroniques de France.* Société de l'histoire de France. Volume 7 (1932) and Volume 8 (1934).

Vidier, A. "Les Abbayes de Saint-Denis, Saint-Crépin-le-Grand, Sainte-Geneviève, et Saint-Père de Melun au XVIe siècle." *Bulletin de la Société de l'histoire de Paris et de l'Ile-de-France* 25 (1898):3–16.

Viollet-le-Duc, E. E. *Dictionnaire raisonné de l'architecture française du XIe au XVIe siècle.* 10 vols. Paris, 1854–68.

――――. "L'Église impériale de Saint-Denis." *Revue archéologique* 3 (1861):301–20, 345–53.

――――. "Étaiement pour la reprise en sous-oeuvre des piles de l'église impériale de Saint-Denis." *Gazette des architectes et du bâtiment* (1867), pp. 33–36.

Wright, Georgia Sommers. "A Royal Tomb Program in the Reign of St. Louis." *The Art Bulletin* 56 (1974):224–43.

Index

Italicized page numbers refer to illustrations.

Aachen, 10
Abaci, 61, 62, 66, 68, 72, 82, 84–88, 91, 93, 95–96, 107–10, 120, 168; triforium, 72, 100, 107; clerestory, 72, 103, 107, 113; polygonal, 72, 118, 133; Reims, 72, 152; chevet, 77, 84–88, 91, 93, 95–96; compound piers of chevet, 77, 96, 98; twelfth-century church, 85, 120, 121; Troyes, 168
Abbots. See St-Denis, abbey
Aisles, 47; addition of chapels, 15, 47, 21–23, 25, 31, 47, 124; restoration, 31; Suger's, 34; transept, 34, 35; windows, 43; design, 47
Aisne, 139, 147
Albertus Magnus, 165
Altars, 84, 125, 127–28, 136; main altar, 10, 16, 36, 38, 127; chevet and transept, 125; matutinal, 127; Virgin, 128; donations, 128; services, 136. See also Chapels; Liturgy
Amiens, Cathedral, 6, 45, 52, 79, 81; dado arcading, 47, 62, 138, 150, 152, 157, 159, 162; transept, 58; sculptural decoration, 59, 140; capitals, 62; polygonal abaci, 118; upper stories of nave, 133, 140–43, 141, 144, 149, 159; piers, 140, 144; facade, 150; trilobed arcading, 150; tracery, 151–52, 160; roofs, 151; fliers, 152; radiating chapels, 158; glazed triforium of chevet, 159; compared to St-Denis, 160; linkage, 162
Amiens, St-Nicolas, 144
Angicourt, 160
Annales archéologiques, 15, 30
Annular crypt, 3

Arcade: raised in chevet, 45; moldings, 77, 79, 88, 93, 95, 120; distorted in chevet, 93, 95; dimensions, 105
Arcading, trilobed, 47, 59, 81, 148–49, 150. See also Dado arcade
Architect(s), 6, 12, 33, 54, 77, 81, 82, 93–94, 96, 98–99, 107, 110, 120, 138, 139, 161, 170, 173–74; nineteenth-century restoration, 14–15; Meaux, 119; Troyes, 167–71. See also Pierre de Montreuil
Arms. See Decoration
Auxerre, Cathedral: wall-passages, 147–48; tracery, 152

Bases, 75–77, 95, 96, 103; in nave destroyed, 23; restored, 31; triforium, 99–100, 106, 113, 115, 117, 118, 120; St-Germain-en-Laye, 110; Troyes, 168
Bayeux, Cathedral: tribune, 149
Beaumont-sur-Oise: columns, 90, 91
Beauvais, Cathedral, 45, 130, 160, 162; buttresses, 54, 119, 153; piers, 144; triforium, 149, 150, 156–57, 159; towers, 152; fliers, 152
Blanche of Castile, 11–12, 128
Bourges, Cathedral: proportions, 140
Brie-Comte-Robert: triforium, 156
Burgundy, 47, 139, 161, 163; wall-passages, 147–49
Burial, 1, 3, 6, 10, 12, 36–38, 165. See also Tombs
Buttresses, 54–55, 58, 153; damaged along south aisle, 23; restoration, 31, 58. See also Flying buttresses

Caen, St-Etienne, 144

Cambronne, 150, 156, 162

Canterbury, Cathedral, 41, 94

Capitals, 59–72, 91, 95, 96, 97, 100, 113; in relation to St-Germain-en-Laye, 110; in relation to building campaigns, 115, 117–18, 133

Carcassonne, St-Nazaire, 163

Catulliacum, 3

Cellerier, Jacques, architect, 21, 23, 31, 47, 124

Centering, 84

Châalis, 7

Châlons-sur-Marne, Cathedral, 66, 139–40

Châlons-sur-Marne, Notre-Dame-en-Vaux: linkage, 143

Champagne, 47, 139, 147–49, 161, 163

Champeaux, 59

Chapels: added north side of nave, 15, 47; added north transept arm, 16, 25; John the Baptist, 16; Saint Louis, 16, 97; Notre-Dame-la-Blanche, 16; Valois, 16; Saint-Eustache, 16, 25, 127–28; "Winter," 21, 23, 25, 29, 31, 47, 124; dedications changed, 23, 128; Saint Hyppolytus, 124, 127, 129; radiating chapels rededicated, 128, 132; Virgin Mary, 128, 132; Saint Cucuphas, 132; Saint Hilaire, 132; Saint Maurice, 132. See also Aisles; Altars

Charlemagne, 9, 10, 30

Charles d'Anjou, 136

Charles the Bald, 9, 11

Charles Martel, 10

Charles X, 15

Chartres, Cathedral, 52, 138, 143, 147, 149, 162, 165; west bay, 35; towers, 36, 152–53; base profiles, 75; proportions, 79, 81; rapidity of construction, 127; elevation, 139–40; piers, 143, 144, 147; triforium, 149; tracery, 152; fliers, 152; transept, 157

Chevet, 34, 35, 128; elevation, 45–47; twelfth-century upper stories dismantled, 83; thirteenth-century supports, 91; delay in construction on south, 99–103, 104–05, 107; twelfth-century chevet partly preserved, 161

Childeric, 10

Choir, liturgical, 34, 36, 38, 41, 104, 115; thirteenth-century reconstruction, 36, 38, 41; stalls, 41; left incomplete in first stage of thirteenth-century rebuilding, 113,

115, 132; completion, 118, 135–36, 137; vaults, 122; defined, 124; construction chronology, 124–25, 132; collapse of scaffolding, 135

Christophe, architect, 17

Cistercian order, 7, 61

Clamecy, St-Martin, 147, 148

Clerestory, 43, 45–47, 98, 152; abaci, 72, 103; dimensions and proportions, 80–81, 105, 152; construction interrupted, 103, 107–10; modification, 107–10, 113–15, 120, 132–33, 174; St-Germain-en-Laye, 113; west bay of nave, 120; Troyes, 153

Clermont-Ferrand, Cathedral, 105, 160, 162; piers, 158

Clothair, 9

Clovis II, 10

Cologne, Cathedral, 105, 160, 162; piers, 158

Columns with attached shafts, 41, 45, 62, 77, 82, 84–85, 88–91, 93, 95, 97, 98, 120, 144–47; influence of, 159–60. See also Piers

Commission des Monuments Historiques, 25

Confessio, 3, 36

Consecration: miraculous, 3, 4, 6, 11; of 775, 3, 9; of 1281, 4, 82, 123, 136–37

Coronations: Pepin the Short, 9; Marie de Medici, 16, 41

Cotte, Robert de, architect, 17

Court Style, 113, 162–64

Crusade: instigated by Suger, 7; of Louis VII, 10; of Louis IX, 12, 131, 132, 134, 136–37. See also Suger; Louis IX

Crypt: Carolingian, 1, 3, 4, 14; twelfth century, 1, 4; Hilduin's extension, 1, 3, 9; access to, 16, 23, 38; restoration and decoration, 25–29; imperial mausoleum created by Viollet-le-Duc, 31; plans for by Formigé, 32; thirteenth-century piers, 82, 85. See also Floor levels

Dado arcade, 46, 47, 62, 66, 150; destroyed, 23; restored, 31; fragments in the dépôt lapidaire, 41, 47; height, 81; St-Germain-en-Laye, 110; Strasbourg, Amiens, and the Sainte-Chapelle, 157; St-Sulpice de Favières, 159

Dagobert, 3, 9, 10, 11, 12

Daly, Cesar, architect, 15

Darcy, Denys, architect, 31

Debret, François, architect, 16, 23–30, 31, 47, 54, 124, 151
Decoration, 14–15; arms of Castile, 12, 14, 72; fleur-de-lys, 12, 14, 15, 72; white-washed, 21; Debret's work criticized, 25; restoration, 30, 32
Denis, Saint, 1, 3, 6; patron and protector of kings, 3, 9, 10, 11, 12; cult, 3; tomb, 3, 8; relics, 8–9. *See also* Dionysius the Pseudo-Areopagite
Didron, Adolphe-Napoléon, 15, 29, 30
Dijon, Notre-Dame, 147, 148
Dionysius the Pseudo-Areopagite, 1, 3, 4, 9, 165
Duban, Jacques Félix, architect, 30

École des Beaux-Arts, 15, 23, 25, 30
Emblems. *See* Decoration
Essomes: linkage, 143
Eudes Clément du Mez, abbot of St-Denis, 1, 3, 4, 6, 11, 123–31, 132, 137, 165; genealogy, 11
Eudes de Deuil, abbot of St-Denis, 7, 8
Eudes de Taverny, abbot of St-Denis, 8
Evreux, Cathedral, 158, 160

Fabric. *See* Financing
Falsework, 84–85
Favières, St-Sulpice, 158–59, 163
Fécamp, La Trinité, 143, 144; wall-passages, 145, 148
Financing, 10, 127–29, 131–32, 135; Suger, 7; question of Louis IX's involvement, 12; Guillaume de Massouris, 131–32. *See also* Monarchy
Fleur-de-lys. *See* Decoration
Fliers. *See* Flying buttresses
Floor levels, 23, 29, 30, 80; pavement restored by Legrand, 21; raised by Cellerier and Debret, 23, 47; between chevet and transept, 23, 95; praise of change in floor level, 29; restored by Viollet-le-Duc, 31. *See also* Pavement; Restoration; Stairs
Flying buttresses, 35, 54, 103, 106, 118–19, 152–53; instability of, 23, 54; restored, 31, 54
Fontaine, Pierre, architect, 29
Foot: royal, 80
Formigé, Jules, architect, 32
Foundations, 34
Freiburg-im-Breisgau, 158

French Revolution, 15, 17
Fulrad, abbot of St-Denis, 3, 9

Gautier de Varinfroy, architect, 119
Glass, stained: removed by Lenoir, 17; installed by Debret, 25; criticism, 29; restored by Viollet-le-Duc, 30
Glazing. *See* Triforium
Gonesse: chevet, 59–61; portal, 75; supports, 84, 91, 147, 159; triforium, 149, 156
Gothic Revival, 15
Gregory X, pope, 136, 137
Grosseteste, Robert, 165
Guilhermy, Roch-François-Ferdinand-Marie-Nolasque, Baron de, 16, 17, 28–29, 30
Guillaume, abbot of St-Denis, 1173–86, 8
Guillaume de Massouris, abbot of St-Denis, 123, 130, 131–33, 137, 174
Guillaume de Nangis, 11, 12, 83, 123, 128, 129, 134

Harmony and concordance, 6, 34, 36, 38, 41, 47, 77, 79–80, 83, 91, 93, 94–95, 97, 98, 104, 106, 161; unity of conception of new church, 33, 161; in measurements and proportions, 80–81
Henri Mallet, abbot of St-Denis, 123, 132, 133–34, 137
Heraldic emblems. *See* Decoration
High Gothic, 4, 41, 59, 138, 139, 140, 143, 161, 162
Hilduin, abbot of St-Denis, 1, 3, 9
Hugh Capet, 9
Hughes Foucault, abbot of St-Denis, 8

Ile-de-France, 139, 147
Imposts. *See* Abaci
Indulgences, 9
Innocent III, 8
Innocent IV, 131–32
Inventories, 127. *See also* Relics

La Chapelle-sur-Crecy, 150
Laon, Cathedral: towers, 36, 152; rose window, 58; nave supports, 144; wall-passages, 147, 148
Larchant, 59
Lassus, J.-B. A., architect, 15, 30
Lebrun, Charles, 16
Legrand, Jacques, architect, 16, 21, 25
Le Mans, Cathedral, 133, 139–40

Lenoir, Alexandre, 17
Les Andelys, St-Sauveur, 144
Linkage, 43, 139, 140–43, 149, 161, 162, 174; absence at Strasbourg and St-Sulpice de Favières, 156, 159
Lisieux, St-Pierre, 143, 144, 149
Liturgical divisions of space at St-Denis, 34, 38. *See also* Choir; Screens
Liturgy, 38, 104, 115, 128, 130, 136
Longpont, 58
Lothair, 9
Louis the Pious, 3, 9
Louis VI, 6, 10
Louis VII, 10
Louis VIII, 11
Louis IX (Saint), 1, 6, 9, 10, 11–12, 107, 131, 134, 136, 137, 162–65; as possible patron of new church, 6, 11–12, 128; devotion to Saint Denis, 9, 12; consulted in reconstruction of St-Denis, 11, 128; crusades, 12, 132, 134, 136–37; affirmation of St-Denis as royal necropolis, 12, 38, 135; reliquary, 38; founds Royaumont, 127; illness, 130; death, 136; canonization, 137; patronage of mendicants, 165
Louis XVIII, 14, 25
Lucian III, pope, 8

Mantes, Collegiate church: rose window, 58; supports, 84, 91, 143, 147, 159; flying buttresses, 153
Marie de Medici: coronation, 16, 32, 41
Martellange, Etienne, 41, *42*
Mass of Saint Giles (painting), 16, *22,* 38, 130
Mathieu de Vendôme, abbot of St-Denis, 4, 55, 123, 133–37
Matthew Paris, 129
Meaux, Cathedral, 162, 163; buttresses, 54, 153; capitals, 66; base profiles, 77; hemicycle monoliths, 84; construction *en sous-oeuvre*, 84, 85; fliers, 119; transept terminal walls, 158
Mello, 150, *151*
Mérimée, Prosper, 30
Monarchy: vassal of St-Denis, 1, 9–10, 12; as patrons, 3, 9, 10–11, 12; consulted in reconstruction, 6, 11–12. *See also* Charles the Bald, Philip Augustus, Louis IX
Monjoie St-Denis, 1
Montalembert, Charles-René Forbes, Count of, 30

Mont-de-Soissons, Templar Chapel, 159
Montiérender, 149, 150
Musée des Monuments Français, 17, 25, 29

Napoleon I, 14, 15, 21, 23, 24, 29
Napoleon III, 14, 30–31
Normandy, 139, 143–47, 149, 157, 163
Noyon, Cathedral, 59, 150; monoliths, 84; piers, 143; wall-passages, 147; trilobed arcading, 150

Oise, 147, 150, 162
Orbais: linkage, 143
Organ, 25, 35, 80, 120. *See also* Restoration
Oriflamme, 1, 10
Ourscamp, 7, 21, 91, *92,* 159

Paris, Cathedral of Notre-Dame, 59, 143, 150, 160, 162, 163; relics of Saint Denis, 8–9; restoration, 14; transept, 55, 58, 59–61, 77, 115, 119, 133, 150, 156, 159, 165, 173; rose window, west facade, 58, 59–61, 106, 158; capital on rebuilt chevet pier, 68, 115, 120; Porte Rouge, 75; base profiles, 77; nave chapels, 88, 133, 160, 174; supports, 115, 144–47; chevet chapels, 120; gallery between towers at west facade, 133, 150, 153, 156, *156,* 162, 170
—Holy Innocents, 150
—St-Germain-des-Prés: Virgin Chapel, 66, 75, 115, 133, 160, 163, 165, 173–74; refectory, 133, 160, 163, 165; abbey church, *114,* 139, 144, 149, 150, *165. See also* Pierre de Montreuil
—St-Julien-le-Pauvre, 143
—St-Martin-des-Champs, refectory, 163
—St-Séverin, 150, 156
—St-Vincent, 10
—Ste-Chapelle, 30, 58, 150, 153, 156, 158, 160, 162, 163, 165; apostles placed at St-Denis, 25; capitals, 62; dado arcade, 157, 159
—Temple Chapel, 163
Passages, 43–45, 47, 55, 58, 110, 159, 161. *See also* Wall-passages
Pavement, 21, 23, 29, 31, 47, 80, 95. *See also* Floor levels; Restoration; Stairs
Pepin the Short, 9, 10
Percier, Charles, architect, 23, 38, *40,* 41, 47
Philip I, 1
Philip Augustus, 8, 11, 128, 130, 163
Philip III, 134, 137

Philip Hurepel, 12, 130

Picardy, 139, 161

Pierre de Montreuil, 75, 132, 133, 160, 173–74. *See also* Architects; Paris, St-Germain-des-Prés

Piers, 4, 43, 45, 62, 95, 107, 143–47, 161, 162; cantonnated, 4, 140, 143, 144, 162; supporting transept towers, 35; compound piers in chevet, transept, and nave, 42–43, 45, 93–95, 97–99, 105; variations in, 94, 97, 120, crossing piers, 98, 100–03, 111; at Strasbourg, 156; influence, 158. *See also* Columns with attached shafts

Pinnacles, 54, 55, 58, 119

Portals, 72–75; Valois, 7, 81, 106; south transept, 31, 62, 72–73, 74, 81, 130, 174; south aisle, 31

Quatrefoils, in triforium design, 156

Rayonnant, 4, 42–43, 54, 59, 61, 138, 150, 151, 161–63, 170

Regalia: stored at St-Denis, 10

Reims, Cathedral, 45, 52, 81, 138, 139, 140, 144, 162; transept towers, 36, 152; sculptural decoration, 59; abaci, 72, 152; base profiles, 75; three-story elevation, 139; piers, *142*, 144; wall-passages, 147–48; triforium, 149; tracery, 152; fliers, 152; transept terminal walls, 157

Reims, St-Nicaise, 150, 162

Reims, St-Remi, 143, 147, 148

Relics, 3, 4, 6, 8, 9, 11, 36, 38, 41, 128, 130

Relieving arch, 52

Restoration: painted ornament, 14–15; imperial mausoleum, 14, 30–31; criticism, 15, 23, 25–30; access to crypt and chevet, 23–38; arcade level plinths and bases, 23, 29, 31; triforium window and roof, 25; stained glass, 25, 29; organ installed, 25, 120; crypt, 25–29; transept roses, 25. *See also* Floor levels; Pavement

Revestiarium. See Treasury

Rieux, 148

Rigord, 8

Riom, 150

Roof: destruction, 17; restoration, 21, 25; aisle roofs restored by Debret, 25, 32, 151; Carolingian, 83; provisional during construction, 105, 135; erected after flying buttresses, 130; aisles, 151

Rose: transept, 25, 36, 52, 58, 80, 106, 111–13, 158

Rouen, Cathedral: work *en sous-oeuvre,* 85; Eudes Clément becomes archbishop, 124, 125, 129; piers, 144; towers, 152

Royaumont, 15, 21, 96, 162, 163, 165, 167, 168; rapidity of construction, 127; burial of princes, 136; triforium design, 149, 150, 151; relation to Troyes Cathedral, 167–68

Sacristy, 16, 124–25. *See also* Treasury; Vestry

St-Benoît-sur-Loire, 152–53

St-Denis, abbey: royal archive, 1; monastic community, 1, 3, 6, 7, 17, 34; Hilduin's extension, 1, 3, 4, 9; crypts, 1, 3, 4, 9; veneration of older buildings, 1, 4; Merovingian church, 3; abbots, 6, 8, 9, 10; reforms, 8, 9, 11; privileges, 8; reforms, 8, 9; conventual buildings, 16–17, 34, 35, 104, 120, 129; *dépôt lapidaire,* 32, 47; bells, 54, 124–27

—Carolingian church, 3, 4, 9, 14, 34, 36, 38, 82, 83, 84, 115, 120–21, 125, 130; crypt, 32, 36; transept, 34, 36; crossing, 36; continuity of site, 36, 38

—thirteenth-century church: spaciousness, 4–6, 41, 43–45, 160; centralizing tendencies in plan, 34, 35, 80; dimensions and proportions, 79–81, 98–99, 105, 139–40, 152; masonry bonding, 88, 98–100, 103, 104–06, 111, 113, 132; disalignment of chevet walls, 94, 98–99, 104, 118; plinth heights, 97, 100, 106; rapidity of construction, 127; influence of, 153–60

—twelfth-century church, 1, 3, 4, 7, 11, 34, 35, 36, 165; western bays and facade, 1, 4, 25, 31, 34, 35, 36, 79, 80, 81, 115, 118, 121, 136, 137, 143; incompletion, 7; continuation of work, 7; restoration, 17, 25, 29, 30; appearance in 1231, 34, *35,* 84; chevet, 34, 36, 45, 52, 54, 79, 80, 82–83, 84, 88, 91, 93, 95, 103, 104–05, 120, 128, 129, 138, 150; transept, 34, 104; condition in thirteenth century, 82–83; monoliths, 84–85; plinths, 91

St-Germain-en-Laye, 12, 58, 59, 72, 107, *109,* 110, 113, 153; rose window, 58, *108,* 113; vaults, 59; abaci, 72; portal, 75; base profiles, 75, 110; architect, 107, 110; wall-

St-Germain-en-Laye (continued)
    passage, 110, 149; tracery, 109, 133, 152,
    153; influence of, 159; in relation to Court
    Style, 163
St-Germer-de-Fly, chapel, 68, 77, 118, 119,
    156, 162
St-Leu-d'Esserent, 150
St-Martin-aux-Bois, 160
Sanctuary, 34, 36, 38–41. See also
    Canterbury
Scaffolding, 123, 134–35
Scamozzi, Vincenzo, 125, 126
Screens, 34, 38–41. See also Choir
Semur-en-Auxois, 158
Senlis, Cathedral, 84, 143
Sens, Cathedral, 52, 143, 160; triforium
    design, 149, 150
Société Française d'archéologie, 15
Soissons, Cathedral, 58, 138, 139, 147, 149
Soissons, St-Leger, 150
Sous-oeuvre, construction, 84–85
Spandrels, 88, 98–99, 107, 121
Stairs: access to chevet, 16, 23, 32, 38–41;
    spiral stairs in transept terminal walls, 55,
    104, 111, 121, 127
Stalls. See Choir, liturgical
Stephen II, pope, 9
Strasbourg, Cathedral, 151, 153–57, 158,
    159, 160
Suger, abbot of St-Denis, 1, 3, 4, 6, 7, 10,
    34, 127, 128, 136, 138

Taxation, 131, 136, 137
Thomas Aquinas, 165
Tombs: royal, 1, 6, 10, 12, 36–38, 135;
    Saint Denis, 3, 4; imperial, 14, 21, 30–31;
    Turenne, 16; removed to the Musée des
    Monuments Français, 17; returned to St-
    Denis, 25–29; restored, 30; Formigé's
    plans for, 32; in transept, 34, 36, 38, 135;
    importance for plan, 36, 135; not identi-
    fied in twelfth century, 36, 38; royal
    necropolis, 36, 135–36, 137, 165; new
    type of tomb in late twelfth and thirteenth
    century, 38; Dagobert, 77; abbots moved
    to south transept arm, 135; royal tombs
    installed in transept, 134–35; relation to
    transept towers, 152
Toul, Cathedral, 148
Toul, St-Gengoult, 158
Tournai, Cathedral, 139–40, 160

Tours, Cathedral, 150, 159
Towers: transept, 35–36, 54–58, 106, 118,
    124–25, 130, 152–53; supporting fliers,
    35, 103; symbolic role, 36; restoration of,
    54; role in construction sequence, 103,
    106, 130; unique arrangement at St-Denis,
    152, 157
—northeast, 54, 103, 106
—northwest, 54, 104, 106, 121
—southeast, 54, 121
—southwest, 54, 125–27, 129–30
Tracery, 45, 52, 59, 80, 140, 149, 152, 160;
    restoration, 23; Strasbourg, 157; Favières,
    159; Troyes, 170; of Pierre de Montreuil,
    173
Transept, 6, 34–36, 41, 52, 135, 165; rose
    windows restored, 25; as space for royal
    burials, 34, 36–38, 135; aisles, 34; transept
    facades, 35–36, 55; transept terminal wall
    design, 52, 55, 58–59, 80, 81, 106, 157–
    58; measurements and proportions, 80–
    81; construction of, 97–99, 103, 104, 105–
    06, 107, 110–11, 120–21. See also Towers
Treasury, 17, 23, 124–25, 130
Trier, Cathedral, 152
Triforium, 4, 21, 43, 45–47, 52, 59, 97–99,
    107, 115–17, 149–51, 167–70; glazing, 4,
    21, 25, 47, 52, 149, 150–51, 159, 165,
    167–68; restoration, 23; capitals, 61–72;
    abaci, 72, 100; plinths, 72, 99–100, 106,
    107, 133; base profiles, 75–77, 120; di-
    mensions, 80, 105; modification in de-
    sign, 99–100, 107–10; glazed openings in
    back wall, 118. See also Capitals
Troyes, Cathedral, 52, 133, 149, 150, 153,
    154, 155, 157, 159, 160, 162, 163, 167–71,
    168, 169
Troyes, St-Urbain, 68, 77, 118, 158

Valois Portal. See Portals
Vaults: completion of, 52, 54, 80, 104–05,
    121, 127, 129, 133–34, 135, 174; damage,
    17; restoration, 21, 31; twelfth-century,
    79, 83, 84, 85, 88; of monks' choir, 122,
    124–27, 130
Vestiarium. See Vestry
Vestry, 16, 25, 124–25. See also Sacristy;
    Treasury
Vexin, 1, 9
Vézelay, 84, 143
Villard de Honnecourt, 150

Viollet-le-Duc, Eugène Emmanuel, architect, 14, 15, 16, 29, 30–31, 32, 47, 54
Vitet, Ludovic, 25, 30

Wall-passages, 43, *46,* 47, 110, 147–48,
  158–59; Strasbourg, 157; St-Sulpice-de-
  Favières, 159

Wall planes, 140–43
Wall-rib: shafts supporting, 140–43, 156
Westminster Abbey, 128
William the Englishman, architect, 41

Yves II, abbot of St-Denis, 8